Communications
in Computer and Information Science   1319

More information about this series at http://www.springer.com/series/7899

Xiaohui Yuan · Mohamed Elhoseny ·
Jianfang Shi (Eds.)

Urban Intelligence and Applications

Second International Conference, ICUIA 2020
Taiyuan, China, August 14–16, 2020
Revised Selected Papers

 Springer

Editors
Xiaohui Yuan 🆔
University of North Texas
Denton, TX, USA

Mohamed Elhoseny 🆔
Mansoura University
Mansoura, Egypt

Jianfang Shi
Taiyuan University of Technology
Taiyuan, China

ISSN 1865-0929   ISSN 1865-0937   (electronic)
Communications in Computer and Information Science
ISBN 978-981-33-4600-0   ISBN 978-981-33-4601-7   (eBook)
https://doi.org/10.1007/978-981-33-4601-7

This Springer imprint is published by the registered company Springer Nature Singapore Pte Ltd.
The registered company address is: 152 Beach Road, #21-01/04 Gateway East, Singapore 189721, Singapore

Preface

The proceedings include papers presented at the International Conference on Urban Intelligence and Applications (ICUIA) held in Taiyuan, China, during August 14–16, 2020. This conference series provided an international forum to present, discuss, and exchange innovative ideas and recent developments in the fields of computer science, computational geography, and management. The proceedings provide new advancements in theories and inspiring applications to scholars, industry leaders, policymakers, and administrators on the current issues and solutions to support the integration of artificial intelligence into modern urban life and to advance the design and implementation of intelligent utilization and management of city assets.

The ICUIA 2020 proceedings include four themes: Technology and Infrastructure for Urban Intelligence, Community and Wellbeing of Smart Cities, Smart Mobility and Transportation, and Security, Safety, and Emergency Management, which are well balanced in content and created an adequate discussion space for trendy topics. Each paper was carefully reviewed by three or more Technical Committee members and the acceptance was based on the revelance to the conference themes, the novelty of the ideas, soundness of the proposed method, and the completeness of the paper. The final acceptance rate is 21%. Unfortunately, due to the COVID-19 pandemic, the conference had to cancel many onsite programs such as industrial exhibits. All presentations were moved online and conducted virtually using Zoom as well as pre-recorded videos considering the large time difference among authors and audiences. There were 26 presentations that brought about a great opportunity to share their recent research findings. Most presentations inspired discussions and the virtual interactions were surprisingly well.

Efforts taken by peer reviewers contributed to improving the quality of papers, which provided constructive critical comments. Comments to the submitted papers are greatly appreciated. We are very grateful to the Organizing Committee members, Technical Committee members, session chairs, volunteers, and colleagues who selflessly contributed to the success of this conference. Also, we thank all the authors who submitted papers, ensuring that the conference turned out to be a success. It was their dedication to science and technology and passion for openly communicating with attendees that truly made this event fruitful and memorable.

October 2020

Xiaohui Yuan
Mohamed Elhoseny
Jianfang Shi

Organization

General Conference Chairs

Sos Agaian   City University of New York, USA
Xiaohui Yuan   University of North Texas, USA
Jinshan Tang   Michigan Technological University, USA

Program Committee Chair

Mohamed Elhoseny   Mansoura University, Egypt

Publication Chairs

Lichuan Gu   Anhui Agricultural University, China
Baofu Fang   Hefei University of Technology, China

Special Session Chairs

Runmei Zhang   Anhui Jianzhu University, China
Xiaojing Yuan   University of Houston, USA
Zhenchun Wei   Hefei University of Technology, China

Publicity Chairs

Qiang Lu   Hefei University of Technology, China
Yu Liang   The University of Tennessee at Chattanooga, USA
T. G. Basavaraju   Government S.K.S.J. Technology Institute, India
Surapong   National Institute of Development Administration,
   Auwatanamongkol   Thailand

Outreach Chair

Tian Chen   Hefei University of Technology, China

Finance Chair

Yuqi Fan   Hefei University of Technology, China

Local Organization Chairs

Jianfang Shi   Taiyuan University of Technology, China
Jianxia Liu   Taiyuan University of Technology, China

Technical Program Committee

Alfredo Cuzzocrea	ICAR-CNR, University of Calabria, Italy
Amit Singh	NIT Patna, India
Angelin Gladston	Anna University, India
Anurag Tiwari	University of Petroleum and Energy Studies, India
Asif Baba	Tuskegee University, USA
Bhushan Patil	Rajiv Gandhi Institute of Technology, India
Bouarara Hadj Ahmed	GeCoDe Laboratory, Algeria
Dana Petcu	West University of Timisoara, Romania
Danda B. Rawat	Howard University, USA
Deze Zeng	University of Aizu, Japan
Farooq Aftab	University of Science and Technology, China
Francesca Lonetti	CNR-ISTI, Italy
Hejun Wu	Sun Yat-sen University, China
Iraklis Varlamis	Harokopio University, Greece
Jianguo Liu	University of North Texas, USA
Jinoh Kim	Texas A&M University, USA
Li Huafeng	Kunming University of Science and Technology, China
Luz Abril Torres-Méndez	Cinvestav-IPN, Mexico
Manisha Vohra	Rajiv Gandhi Institute of Technology, India
Manuel Cardona	Universidad Don Bosco, El Salvador
Massimo Mecella	Sapienza University of Rome, Italy
Mohamed Elhoseny	Mansoura University, Egypt
Narinder Kumar Bhasin	Amity University Noida, India
Peng Zhang	Stony Brook University, USA
Pengcheng Zhang	Hohai University, China
Ponnalagu Nagarajan	Birla Institute of Technology and Science, India
Pradeep Kumar Singh	JayPee University of Information Technology, India
Qiang Chen	Hefei University of Technology, China
Qing Yang	University of North Texas, USA
Seng Loke	La Trobe University, Australia
Shankar K.	Kalasalingam Academy of Research and Education, India
Shigeng Zhang	Central South University, China
Siba K. Udgata	University of Hyderabad, India
Siobhan Clarke	Trinity College Dublin, Ireland
Sundeep Narravula	Electronic Arts, USA
Surapong Auwatanamongkol	National Institute of Development Administration, Thailand
Thippa Reddy Gadekallu	Vellore Institute of Technology, India
Traian Marius	Northern Kentucky University, USA
Xiao Liu	Deakin University, Australia

Contents

Mobility and Transportation

Security, Safety, and Emergency Management

Technology and Infrastructure

Multi-scale Graph Convolutional Neural Network for Object Recognition from Point Cloud Data

Qiang Lu[1,2,3](✉), Chao Chen[2], Jinfeng Teng[2], Chunyuan Zhang[2], Yi Huang[2], and Shanli Xuan[2]

[1] Key Laboratory of Knowledge Engineering with Big Data, Ministry of Education, Hefei University of Technology, Hefei 230009, China
luqiang@hfut.edu.cn
[2] School of Computer and Information, Hefei University of Technology, Hefei 230009, China
[3] Anhui Province Key Laboratory of Industry Safety and Emergency Technology, Hefei 230009, China

Abstract. How to make robots understand the point cloud data which is collected from the 3D sensor and complete the recognition has become a hot research direction in recent years. In this paper, we propose a new approach to improve the critical robotic capability, semantic understanding of the environment (i.e., 3D object recognition). The convolutional neural network (CNN) method has a very good recognition result in the 2D image domain, but it has certain difficulty in applying irregular and unordered 3D point clouds data. The network for point cloud data generally uses the convolution to realize the extraction of point cloud features by finding the neighborhood features on the point set. Due to the different neighborhood scales caused by the irregularity of 3D point cloud data, we propose a CNN structure that combines multi-scale features. By finding multiple neighborhoods of the point set and establishing local graph extraction features, the stable expression of the local neighborhood is obtained. At the same time, the key point calibration method is added, so that the network can dynamically focus on key point features to improve the recognition result. In a series of analytical experiments, we demonstrate competing results that demonstrate the effectiveness of the network structure.

Keywords: 3D recognition · Point clouds · Deep learning

1 Introduction

Smart city has become one of the main application scenarios for Internet of Things. Artificial intelligence technologies, e.g., autonomous robots, have played an important role in smart city. Autonomous robots must be able to sense objects in unknown environments during operation. So 3D object recognition

© Springer Nature Singapore Pte Ltd. 2020
X. Yuan et al. (Eds.): ICUIA 2020, CCIS 1319, pp. 3–17, 2020.
https://doi.org/10.1007/978-981-33-4601-7_1

is an important ability for autonomous robots. Point clouds have become a common choice for input data form because of popularization of 3D point cloud acquisition equipment. However, the ability of semantic understanding of the environment for autonomous robots needs to be further improved.

With the development of deep learning in recent years, more and more deep networks have been applied to process 3D data such as voxels [1, 2, 7, 18, 21, 29, 33], point clouds [3, 5, 11, 13, 14, 16, 20, 22–24, 26–28, 30, 31] and multi-views [17, 25]. The organization of point clouds data is more dense, and it has certain advantages in application scenarios that are more concerned with the surface information of objects. At the same time, the source of point cloud data is more extensive, and the original data form obtained by most commonly used 3D scene scanning devices [32] is point clouds.

Applying CNN to point clouds data for recognition tasks needs to solve the problem of irregularity and unorder of point clouds. The network should be able to extract effective features in irregular points and have some invariance to the input order and rigid transformation. Therefore, we focus on point cloud data and propose a multi-scale Graph Convolutional Neural Network (MGCNN), which uses local graph structure to capture local neighborhood features in point cloud data to complete 3D object recognition task based on point cloud data. Compared with the previous work, we designed a multi-scale feature extraction structure for the irregularity of the point clouds. The network finds multiple neighborhoods at the same point, and effectively combines the neighborhood features to obtain the expression of the structural features around the point, ensuring stable performance for regional networks with different densities. At the same time, considering that the downsampling will cause the loss of information, but keeping the number of points is also easy to make the network difficult to capture effective features. We calculate a set of weights to dynamically calibrate the key points in the point cloud, and guide the network to focus on points that are more responsive to object features, and correspondingly suppresses the redundant feature points to further improve the recognition result. Through comparative experiments on public data sets, our network has achieved better recognition result than existing work, proving the advantages of our network structure.

The key contributions of our work are as follows:

(1) We analyze and summarize the shortcomings of existing networks to extract neighborhood features on irregular point cloud data.

(2) For the irregularity of point clouds, we propose a method for extracting features by combining multi-scale neighborhoods, and design the corresponding network structure to improve the ability of the network to extract neighborhood features.

(3) We use key point calibration methods to dynamically increase or lower features of points in point clouds to guide the network to autonomously capture points with representative information to improve recognition result.

Through experiments, we find the most suitable multi-scale neighborhood combination, and analyze the influence of neighborhood scale on the recognition result, and also prove the effectiveness of our network structure.

The rest of this paper is organized as follows: Sect. 2 reviews related work about deep learning on 3D point clouds and graphs. Section 3 introduces the structure of our model. Section 4 presents the experimental results of our model. Finally, the paper is concluded in Sect. 5.

2   Related Work

The research on 3D object recognition based on point clouds data is roughly divided into two thoughts. One thought is to extract features separately from each independent point in the point clouds. The other thought is to construct the local graph structure in the point clouds and use the spectral graph theory for feature extraction.

In terms of feature extraction of independent points, Qi et al. first proposed PointNet [20] and PointNet++ [22]. They use multi-layer perceptron(MLP) on point clouds to learn a global feature vector describing point clouds for identifying tasks. The key idea is to apply a order-independent symmetric function to 3D coordinates. Although they have achieved great results in point clouds analysis tasks, PointNet handles each point individually, actually learning the mapping from 3D coordinates to potential features without using local geometry structure. In the follow-up work, Qi et al. proposed an improved network Point-Net++, which captures the geometric features of local point sets and aggregates them hierarchically for features learning. Benefit from the local features extraction structure, PointNet++ achieves better results than previous methods in multiple point clouds analysis benchmarks. However, PointNet++ still handles individual points in a local point set independently, regardless of the relationship between points. These two networks are limited by the unordered and irregular features of point clouds, and do not take into account the structural features of objects within a neighborhood.

In addition to symmetry function to ensure the independence between the network output and the input order of the point clouds, building graph structure on the point clouds and using graph convolution to extract point clouds features have gradually become the hot research direction. The neural network on the graph was first proposed by Bruna [3]. It defines the Fourier transform on the graph in the spectral domain, and uses the spectral theory to extract the features of the graph through the Laplacian matrix and feature vectors, thereby defining the convolution operation on the graph. In the spatial domain, Niepert et al. [19] construct a neighborhood subgraph by selecting nodes, normalize the subgraph structure to obtain convolution slices, and then use the convolution structure to operate each slice to extract feature vectors. The appearance of graph convolution makes it possible to apply convolutional neural networks on data of non-matrix structures.

In terms of feature extraction for point clouds construction graph structure, Wang et al.'s DGCNN [27] proposed a new feature extraction operation Edge-Conv, which replaces the common convolution operation in PointNet. EdgeConv not only focuses on the features of the independent point itself, but also captures the local structure by calculating the edge features between the point and its surrounding neighbors. Based on spectral theory, Te et al. proposed RGCNN [24], considering features of points in point clouds as signals on the graph, and using Chebyshev polynomial approximation to define the convolution on the graph to better extract the local graph structure features. RGCNN create global graph on the whole point set to describe overall structure, but compared to the subgraph structure in the local domain, the calculation amount and parameter amount of the global graph are larger, and it is easier to lose local details. Similarly, based on PointNet++, Wang et al. used spectral theory to improve the network and construct a local spectral graph convolutional neural network SpecGCN [26]. The network build local subgraphs and proposes a new pooling strategy, which allows the network to retain multiple separate features in a local graph structure to reduce the loss of effective features caused by max pooling. The design idea of SpecGCN are advanced, but the effect of the new pooling strategy on experimental performance is not outstanding.

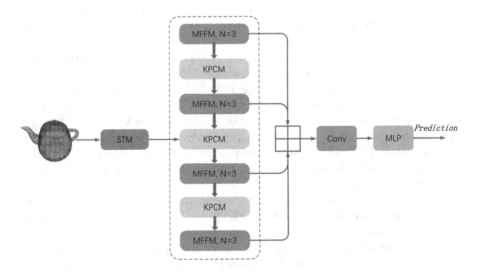

Fig. 1. Structure of MGCNN.

3 The MGCNN

For 3D object recognition of point clouds data, we design and build a convolutional neural network MGCNN using point clouds as input, as shown in Fig. 1. Next, we will elaborate our methods in four aspects.

3.1   The Structure of MGCNN

As mentioned above, point clouds has two features of disorder and irregularity. The network needs to extract order-independent structural features from the point clouds and effectively apply it on irregular data. Based on spectral theory [3, 4, 10], MGCNN uses local graph convolution structure to extract the invariant features from unordered point set. Combined multi-scale domain perception and attention mechanism, so that the network can focus on the representative feature structure and has great recognition result on irregular data. MGCNN draws on the basic structure of PointNet. By constructing multi-scale graph structures in the local neighborhood and calculating features of the signal on the graph by convolution, MGCNN improve the inadequacy that the relationship between the pairs in the neighborhood is not considered in PointNet. In addition, considering that MGCNN does not perform downsampling, the number of points in the point clouds remains unchanged. Therefore, we add a dynamic attention module to highlight points with representative features in the point clouds. It makes network pay more attention to these representative points to further improve the recognition accuracy.

3.2   The Spatial Transformation Module

The idea of network autonomous learning spatial transformation for input was first proposed by Max et al. [9], which is used to rotate the 2D image data to make the network obtain better results. PointNet extends it to 3D point clouds data, using a subnetwork named T-net to learn the 3D transformation matrix for transform alignment of the input point clouds to ensure that the network receives an input at the best angle. The STM in MGCNN is similar to the T-net subnetwork in PointNet. The STM receives the original point clouds input and obtains a feature vector sizeof 256 describing the input through three layers of 1 1 convolutional layer and two layers of fully connected layers. Then, using a matrix sizeof 256 3 3 that can be learned to multiply the feature vector, we can obtain the transformation matrix used for spatial transformation, and apply it to the input point clouds to obtain the converted point clouds.

3.3   The Multi-scale Feature Fusion Module

For the irregular data of the point clouds, the network wants to effectively capture the local structural features. First, it needs to determine the neighborhood of a point, and the local structure can be further extracted after the neighborhood is divided. Commonly used point clouds neighborhood selection methods are k-NN and Ball Query, as shown in Fig.2. Obviously, the former defines the number of points in the domain, and the latter defines the range of the neighborhood. Therefore, the advantage of k-NN is that the number of points in each field is fixed. When using CNN for processing, it is convenient to determine the size of each dimension of the tensor, which is convenient for uniformly processing all neighborhoods. However, the disadvantage is that the irregularity of the point

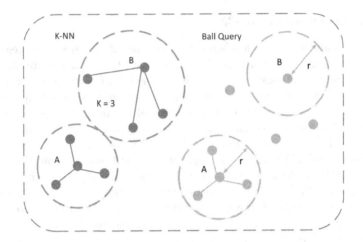

Fig. 2. Examples of two neighborhood point selection methods.

clouds data makes the size of each neighborhood different. Fixing the feature scale of each neighborhood is the advantage of Ball Query, but the irregularity of point clouds causes another problem, that is, there is no guarantee that there will be an ideal number of points under the set radius. Usually, if the number of points in the neighborhood is greater than or equal to n, the number of points in local region used by network, take the first n points, otherwise use the center point to make up. This results in the loss of features in some neighborhoods, while the features in some areas are redundant.

Considering the shortcomings of the existing neighborhood selection methods, MGCNN designed the multi-scale features fusion module (MFFM). The module uses k-NN to select neighborhood points, but the difference is that multiple k values are set in the same layer of network to select different scale neighborhoods, and finally multi-scale features are combined to obtain the optimal representation of a neighborhood, as shown in Fig. 3. The MFFM module designs three branch structures for the input, and the k values set in each branch structure are different, namely k1, k2, and k3, which are used to extract local neighborhood structure features of different scales. MFFM extracts multi-scale neighborhoods through multi-branch design, which effectively compensates for the shortcomings of applying the k-NN method to select neighborhood points on irregular point clouds, and unifies the receptive field of the network at each point. At the same time, the multi-branch design enriches the neighborhood information that the network can perceive, and further integrates the multi-scale features through the average pooling method to help the network capture the effective neighborhood structure features and improve the effect for point clouds recognition.

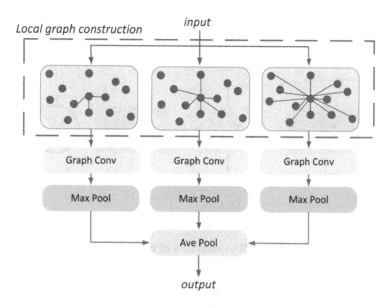

Fig. 3. The structure of MFFM.

3.4   The Key Point Calibration Module

As mentioned above, our network do not perform the downsampling operation, it means that the number of points in the point clouds remains unchanged during the training. On the one hand, downsampling will destroy the topological structure of the point clouds, causing partial loss of point clouds information, which is not conducive to extract local features. On the other hand, the convolution operation has converging effects. After constructing a local graph for neighborhood feature extraction, the generated feature vector represents a neighborhood structure. Continue to construct the graph structure to extract feature, and the range of the original point clouds structure represented by features of each point is gradually expanded. However, not all features of each point in the point clouds have the same effect for recognition result. We hope that the network will focus on the key points that can reflect the overall structure of the point clouds in the process of extracting features. Therefore, the key point calibration module (KPCM) is added to guide the network to focus on the key point features that better reflect the overall structure of the point clouds.

As shown in Fig. 4, The KPCM calibration operation is somewhat similar to the feature recalibration technique [8], but the difference is that KPCM is uniformly weighted for all channels of each point, while the feature recalibration technique is for weighting between multiple feature channels. In simple terms, the calibration of the KPCM acts on the point dimension, while the weighting of the feature recalibration acts on the feature channel dimension. If analogous to a 2D image, the role of KPCM is to highlight representative pixels points. The input point clouds enters KPCM and first performs a Reshape operation for

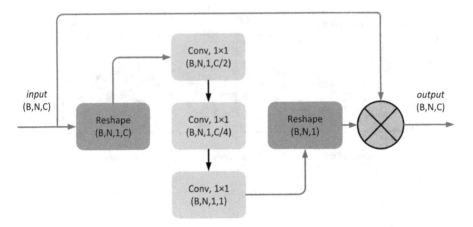

Fig. 4. The structure of KPCM.

subsequent convolution operations. Thereafter, the features of each channel are gradually merged using the 1 1 convolution operation. After convolution, KPCM maps the feature vectors of each point to a value that is used to indicate how important the network considers the feature of the point. Finally, through the element-wise quadrature operation, the weight of each point is applied to the entire feature vector of the point to complete the calibration of the key points.

KPCM enables the network to independently select the set of points of interest without using the downsampling operation to ensure that the information in the point clouds is not lost. KPCM effectively utilizes the multi-scale sensing capability brought by MFFM, highlights the set of points useful for identifying tasks in each layer, and suppresses the point features whose contribution is not obvious, so that the network can obtain better recognition result.

4   Experiments

The experiment uses the same point clouds dataset as PointNet, which is generated by Qi et al. [20] using the ModelNet40 dataset.

4.1   MGCNN Performance Evaluation on ModelNet

For point clouds, we select several representative 3D object recognition networks to compare the recognition result with MGCNN. The comparison results is shown in Table 1.

(1) Compared to voxel-based methods, MGCNN has a 1.5% improvement in accuracy compared to VRN and an increase of 9.8% compared to VoxNet. Compared to the limited-resolution voxel data, point clouds data has a tighter organization structure, so that the network does not need to pay

Table 1. Recognition accuracy of each network model on ModelNet40.

Model	Input	Data augmentation	Accuracy (%)
MGCNN	Point clouds, 1K	single angle	**92.8**
PointNet [20]	Point clouds, 1K	single angle	89.2
PointNet++ [22]	Point clouds, 1K	single angle	90.7
SpiderCNN [30]	Point clouds, 1K+Normal	single angle	92.4
A-CNN [12]	Point clouds, 1K	single angle	92.6
DGCNN [27]	Point clouds, 1K	single angle	92.2
PointConv [28]	Point clouds, 1K	single angle	91.5
SRN-PointNet++ [5]	Point clouds, 1K	single angle	92.5
RGCNN [24]	Point clouds, 1K	single angle	90.5
PAT [31]	Point clouds, 1K	single angle	91.7
DPAM [16]	Point clouds, 1K	single angle	91.9
FPConv [15]	Point clouds, 1K	single angle	92.5
AdvectiveNet [6]	Point clouds, 1K	single angle	**92.8**
Point2Sequence [16]	Point clouds, 2K	single angle	92.6
PAT [31]	Point clouds, 1K	single angle	91.7
SpecGCN [26]	Point clouds, 1K+Normal	single angle	91.8
VoxNet [18]	Voxel, 32^3	vertical, 12 angle	83.0
VRN [2]	Voxel, 32^3	vertical, 24 angle	91.3
MVCNN [21]	Multi-view	80 angle	90.1

attention to redundant spatial units, so as to better capture useful information in the data. At the same time, due to the structural design for disorder and irregularity of point clouds, MGCNN has input invariance to the original data, so it can achieve great recognition result without multi-angle data augmentation.

(2) MGCNN improves recognition accuracy by 2.7% compared to MVCNN with multiview. MVCNN uses a 2D image convolution network to synthesize multi-angle views of the same object into one feature descriptor to complete 3D recognition, which not only has high requirements of input, but also does not capture the 3D structure of the object. The MGCNN uses point clouds data with 3D information to effectively capture the structural features of the object without additional augmentation, thereby better accomplishing the task of 3D object recognition.

(3) Compared with the point clouds based method, MGCNN achieved the best recognition result under the premise of 1K points as input. Benefit by the use of graph structure in local neighborhoods to represent local features, MGCNN has obvious advantages among PointNet, PointNet++ and SpiderCNN with independent extraction point features, and the accuracy rates are respectively increased by 3.6%, 2.1% and 0.6%. There is not much improvement compared to SpiderCNN because SpiderCNN additionally uses normal information to extract the trend of the point clouds surface,

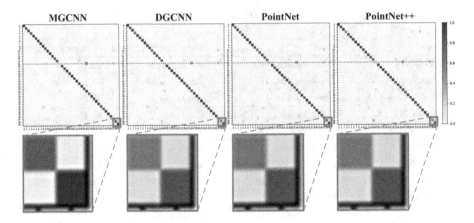

Fig. 5. Confusion matrix of recognition result by four networks.

while MGCNN focuses on extracting structural features, so normal information is not used. Compared with other networks that use graph structures, MGCNN also has certain advantages. Benefit by the role of MFFM and KPCM, MGCNN has a 0.6% advantage over DGCNN. Based on the Point-Net++ structure, SpecGCN proposes a new pooling strategy. The idea of retaining multiple valid features in a neighborhood is very attractive, but in practice how to determine the validity of the feature and sort the multiple features is still room for improvement. In contrast, MGCNN's recognition accuracy increased by 1%.

Fig. 6. Partial model example of wardrobe and Xbox in ModelNet40. The upper part is wardrobe category, and the lower part is Xbox category.

Figure 5 shows the confusion matrix for several network recognition result on the ModelNet40, where the vertical axis represents the real label category and the horizontal axis represents the network prediction label category. It can be seen that the four networks can correctly identify most objects, but in comparison, the MGCNN confusion matrix has a darker color on the diagonal, and the color of the position other than the diagonal is more uniform, which proves that MGCNN has the best recognition result. At the same time, it is observed in the experimental results that the last two categories are easily confused by the network. The corresponding categories in ModelNet40 are Xbox and wardrobe, and the model representation is shown in Fig. 6. It can be seen that the models of these two categories are mostly cuboids with high similarity. The difference is mainly due to the small structure of the surface, such as the handle of the wardrobe and the surface opening of the Xbox. Figure 5 shows the corresponding position in the confusion matrix. It can be clearly seen that MGCNN has the best recognition result in the last two categories compared to the other three networks, which proves that MGCNN can effectively capture and distinguish the small structural differences of point clouds.

We iterated 100 times during the training process and plotted the curve of the recognition accuracy of the four networks, as shown in Fig. 7. It can be seen that at the beginning of the training, the recognition accuracy of MGCNN rises steadily at the fastest speed, and the oscillation amplitude is the smallest compared with the other three networks. Then, as the learning rate decreases, the accuracy of each network slows down the speed of improvement. Among them, MGCNN always maintains the minimum amplitude oscillation and the best recognition result, which proves that MGCNN is stable and effective in extracting features of point clouds. After the training, MGCNN achieved the best recognition accuracy, which fully proved that MGCNN has good recognition performance for disordered and irregular point clouds data.

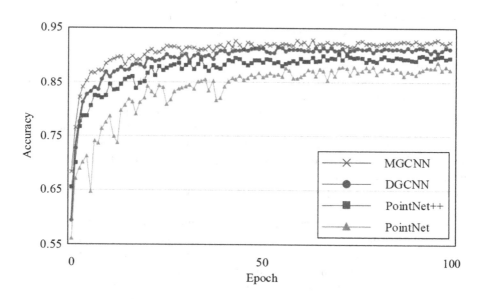

Fig. 7. Recognition accuracy curve of four networks.

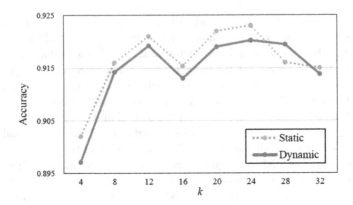

Fig. 8. The network performance curve with k of different ways to build graph.

4.2   The Structure Assessment of MGCNN

Furthermore, in order to determine the best multi-scale combination, we compare the recognition performance of networks with multiple neighborhood scales k, and draw two curves under static and dynamic construction of local graph, as shown in Fig. 8. The static construction method means that the neighborhood of each point is determined according to the distance between the pairs of points in the original point cloud, and will not change along with the change of the point features. The dynamic construction method updates the distance between the points along with the change of point features, thereby dynamically calculating the new neighborhood points. MGCNN uses static method to build local graphs, as can be seen from Fig. 8, the static method at multiple neighborhood scales k has certain advantages over the dynamic method, and the network recognition accuracy is higher, indicating that the way of static construction is better on the recognition task. At the same time, it can be noted that the recognition result of the network is not linear growth with the increase of the k value. There are two maximum points, which are obtained at k = 12 and k = 24. When the value of k is small, there are too little neighborhood information for the network to calculate, and it is difficult to capture effective local structurt features. When k is large, the network loses more information due to the maximum pooling strategy, and it is difficult to represent excessive neighborhood information. Under the maximum pooling strategy, the existence of the maximum value can guarantee the size of network's receptive field and the expression ability of features vector is suitable.

When the neighborhood scale k = 4, the recognition accuracy of the network is not high, because the receptive field is too small, but it is worth noting that the nearest neighbor point may have a greater impact on local features, and through multi-scale fusion we can effectively avoid the problem of limited of receptive field. Figure 9 shows the recognition result of the network under the combination of multiple scale neighborhoods. It can be seen that the multi-scale neighborhood feature fusion has obvious advantages over the single scale, which

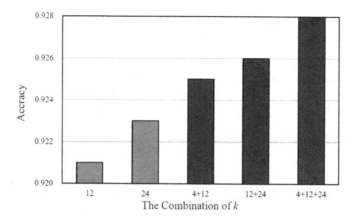

Fig. 9. Recognition accuracy of networks with different combinations of k.

proves the validity of the MFFM we proposed. According to the experimental results, we select three neighborhood scales that k = 4, 12, 24 to extract and fuse multi-scale neighborhood features.

5   Conclusion

MGCNN applies a multi-branch structure for extracting neighborhood graph structure features of different scales to compensate for the shortcomings of commonly used neighborhood selection methods. At the same time, the network captures multi-domain information in each feature dimension, and further enriches the structural features represented by each point in the point clouds through effective fusion means. In addition, the network produces the attention structure of the point clouds data, and completes the calibration of the key points in the point clouds through self-learning. The experimental results show that compared with the existing methods, MGCNN can effectively capture the tiny structural information in the point clouds, and has obvious advantages in feature extraction.

Acknowledgements. This work was supported in part by the National Natural Science Foundation of China under Grant 61972130 and 61906061, partly supported by the Science and Technology Program of Huangshan of China under Grant 2019KN-05 and partly supported by the Key Research and Development Plan of Anhui Province under Grant 1704d0802177.

References

1. Arvind, V., Costa, A., Badgeley, M., Cho, S., Oermann, E.: Wide and deep volumetric residual networks for volumetric image classification. arXiv preprint arXiv:1710.01217 (2017)

2. Brock, A., Lim, T., Ritchie, J.M., Weston, N.: Generative and discriminative voxel modeling with convolutional neural networks. arXiv preprint arXiv:1608.04236 (2016)
3. Bruna, J., Zaremba, W., Szlam, A., LeCun, Y.: Spectral networks and locally connected networks on graphs. arXiv preprint arXiv:1312.6203 (2013)
4. Defferrard, M., Bresson, X., Vandergheynst, P.: Convolutional neural networks on graphs with fast localized spectral filtering. In: Advances in Neural Information Processing Systems, pp. 3844–3852 (2016)
5. Duan, Y., Zheng, Y., Lu, J., Zhou, J., Tian, Q.: Structural relational reasoning of point clouds. In: Proceedings of the IEEE Conference on Computer Vision and Pattern Recognition, pp. 949–958 (2019)
6. He, X., Cao, H.L., Zhu, B.: Advectivenet: An Eulerian-Lagrangian fluidic reservoir for point cloud processing. arXiv preprint arXiv:2002.00118 (2020)
7. Hegde, V., Zadeh, R.: Fusionnet: 3D object classification using multiple data representations. arXiv preprint arXiv:1607.05695 (2016)
8. Hu, J., Shen, L., Sun, G.: Squeeze-and-excitation networks. In: Proceedings of the IEEE Conference on Computer Vision and Pattern Recognition, pp. 7132–7141 (2018)
9. Jaderberg, M., Simonyan, K., Zisserman, A., et al.: Spatial transformer networks. In: Advances in Neural Information Processing Systems, pp. 2017–2025 (2015)
10. Kipf, T.N., Welling, M.: Semi-supervised classification with graph convolutional networks. arXiv preprint arXiv:1609.02907 (2016)
11. Klokov, R., Lempitsky, V.: Escape from cells: deep Kd-networks for the recognition of 3D point cloud models. In: Proceedings of the IEEE International Conference on Computer Vision, pp. 863–872 (2017)
12. Komarichev, A., Zhong, Z., Hua, J.: A-CNN: annularly convolutional neural networks on point clouds. In: Proceedings of the IEEE Conference on Computer Vision and Pattern Recognition, pp. 7421–7430 (2019)
13. Li, J., Chen, B.M., Hee Lee, G.: So-net: self-organizing network for point cloud analysis. In: Proceedings of the IEEE Conference on Computer Vision and Pattern Recognition, pp. 9397–9406 (2018)
14. Li, Y., Bu, R., Sun, M., Wu, W., Di, X., Chen, B.: PointCNN: Convolution on X-transformed points. In: Advances in Neural Information Processing Systems, pp. 820–830 (2018)
15. Lin, Y., et al.: Fpconv: Learning local flattening for point convolution. arXiv preprint arXiv:2002.10701 (2020)
16. Liu, X., Han, Z., Liu, Y.S., Zwicker, M.: Point2sequence: learning the shape representation of 3d point clouds with an attention-based sequence to sequence network. In: Proceedings of the AAAI Conference on Artificial Intelligence, vol. 33, pp. 8778–8785 (2019)
17. Ma, Y., Zheng, B., Guo, Y., Lei, Y., Zhang, J.: Boosting multi-view convolutional neural networks for 3D object recognition via view saliency. In: Wang, Y., et al. (eds.) IGTA 2017. CCIS, vol. 757, pp. 199–209. Springer, Singapore (2018). https://doi.org/10.1007/978-981-10-7389-2_20
18. Maturana, D., Scherer, S.: Voxnet: a 3D convolutional neural network for real-time object recognition. In: 2015 IEEE/RSJ International Conference on Intelligent Robots and Systems (IROS), pp. 922–928. IEEE (2015)
19. Niepert, M., Ahmed, M., Kutzkov, K.: Learning convolutional neural networks for graphs. In: International Conference on Machine Learning, pp. 2014–2023 (2016)

20. Qi, C.R., Su, H., Mo, K., Guibas, L.J.: Pointnet: deep learning on point sets for 3D classification and segmentation. In: Proceedings of the IEEE Conference on Computer Vision and Pattern Recognition, pp. 652–660 (2017)
21. Qi, C.R., Su, H., Nießner, M., Dai, A., Yan, M., Guibas, L.J.: Volumetric and multi-view cnns for object classification on 3D data. In: Proceedings of the IEEE Conference on Computer Vision and Pattern Recognition, pp. 5648–5656 (2016)
22. Qi, C.R., Yi, L., Su, H., Guibas, L.J.: Pointnet++: deep hierarchical feature learning on point sets in a metric space. In: Advances in Neural Information Processing Systems, pp. 5099–5108 (2017)
23. Shen, Y., Feng, C., Yang, Y., Tian, D.: Mining point cloud local structures by kernel correlation and graph pooling. In: Proceedings of the IEEE Conference on Computer Vision and Pattern Recognition, pp. 4548–4557 (2018)
24. Te, G., Hu, W., Zheng, A., Guo, Z.: RGCNN: Regularized graph CNN for point cloud segmentation. In: Proceedings of the 26th ACM International Conference on Multimedia, pp. 746–754 (2018)
25. Wang, C., Pelillo, M., Siddiqi, K.: Dominant set clustering and pooling for multi-view 3D object recognition. arXiv preprint arXiv:1906.01592 (2019)
26. Wang, C., Samari, B., Siddiqi, K.: Local spectral graph convolution for point set feature learning. In: Ferrari, V., Hebert, M., Sminchisescu, C., Weiss, Y. (eds.) ECCV 2018. LNCS, vol. 11208, pp. 56–71. Springer, Cham (2018). https://doi.org/10.1007/978-3-030-01225-0_4
27. Wang, Y., Sun, Y., Liu, Z., Sarma, S.E., Bronstein, M.M., Solomon, J.M.: Dynamic graph CNN for learning on point clouds. ACM Trans. Graph. (TOG) **38**(5), 1–12 (2019)
28. Wu, W., Qi, Z., Fuxin, L.: Pointconv: deep convolutional networks on 3D point clouds. In: Proceedings of the IEEE Conference on Computer Vision and Pattern Recognition, pp. 9621–9630 (2019)
29. Wu, Z., et al.: 3D shapenets: a deep representation for volumetric shapes. In: Proceedings of the IEEE Conference on Computer Vision and Pattern Recognition, pp. 1912–1920 (2015)
30. Xu, Y., Fan, T., Xu, M., Zeng, L., Qiao, Yu.: SpiderCNN: deep learning on point sets with parameterized convolutional filters. In: Ferrari, V., Hebert, M., Sminchisescu, C., Weiss, Y. (eds.) ECCV 2018. LNCS, vol. 11212, pp. 90–105. Springer, Cham (2018). https://doi.org/10.1007/978-3-030-01237-3_6
31. Yang, J., et al.: Modeling point clouds with self-attention and gumbel subset sampling. In: Proceedings of the IEEE Conference on Computer Vision and Pattern Recognition, pp. 3323–3332 (2019)
32. Zhang, Z.: Microsoft kinect sensor and its effect. IEEE Multimedia **19**(2), 4–10 (2012)
33. Zhi, S., Liu, Y., Li, X., Guo, Y.: Lightnet: a lightweight 3D convolutional neural network for real-time 3D object recognition. In: 3DOR (2017)

Semi-global Alignment of Range Videos

Jiancheng Li, Xuan Guo$^{(\boxtimes)}$, and Xiaohui Yuan

Department of Computer Science and Engineering, University of North Texas,
Denton, TX 76203, USA
{xuan.guo,xiaohui.yuan}@unt.edu

Abstract. Temporal alignment of videos is an important requirement of
tasks such as video comparison, slicing, synchronization, and classification. Most of the approaches proposed to date for video alignment treat
videos equivalent and leverage dynamic programming algorithms whose
parameters are manually tuned. In this paper, we develop a semi-global
alignment algorithm for aligning depth videos and use human movement
tracking as an application. The key idea is to integrate the temporal
constraints to select a template for each input depth frame such that
the overall similarity of aligned templates and all input frames are max-
imized. By registering resampled videos of a single person, our method
improves the accuracy by more than 12.4%. This accuracy improvement
is also confirmed by our experiments of registering videos of different
persons. It is hence evident that our proposed method finds the pattern
of movement of people and correctly aligns the frames between the input
video and template video.

Keywords: Dynamic programming · Video alignment · Temporal
alignment

1 Introduction

When dealing with sequential data, one of the urgent problems is to align multiple sequences to allow a meaningful comparison. This problem, known as
sequence alignment or warping, concerns many fields such as bioinformatics,
finance, climate analysis and meteorology, and multimedia signal processing at
large. The problem is often framed as the alignment of two sequences, with the
first being used as the reference and the second being aligned, or "warped",
against the first. In the case of video clips, sequence alignment finds the most
similar frames under the temporal constraint in two videos for further analysis
such as comparison, slicing, synchronization, and, possibly, classification.

A range video consists of a sequence of temporally ordered point sets, which
has been widely employed in tracking human movements [6,7,17] and creating a
three dimension structure of the field [15]. Each point set is analogous to a frame
in a video [16,20]. In this paper, we propose a semi-global alignment for aligning
frames of range videos. Our goal is to ensure each input frame is assigned with a
template that depicts the closest pose under the temporal constraint. To show the

© Springer Nature Singapore Pte Ltd. 2020
X. Yuan et al. (Eds.): ICUIA 2020, CCIS 1319, pp. 18–26, 2020.
https://doi.org/10.1007/978-981-33-4601-7_2

quality of select templates, we estimate body joint from a point set throughout movements by registering the point sets to a template (i.e., a point set showing a similar pose that contains annotated key points). Hence, the annotated key points in the template are inherited by the input point set. To minimize the pose-induced registration error, a proper template is usually demanded. The experimental results from four video movement datasets show that provided with a sequence of templates of the same action, a temporal alignment of the template sequence and the input sequence reveals the best template for precise, consistent point set registration.

The remainder of this paper is organized as follows. Section 2 reviews the related work. Section 3 presents the proposed method for video similarity measurement and movement evaluation. Section 4 discusses the experimental results. We conclude this paper in Sect. 5 with a summary.

2   Related Work

A well-known sequence alignment technique is dynamic time warping (DTW). Its main idea is to scan both sequences while looking for local correspondences of minimum cost, where the cost is a function that reflects both the similarity between the frames and their indices [3]. The outputs of DTW are a path, i.e., a set of index correspondences in the two sequences, and a total cost, which can be interpreted as an overall dissimilarity between the sequences. DTW is an instance of dynamic programming algorithms and, as such, the returned path is guaranteed to be globally optimal.

While DTW was originally proposed for the alignment of time series, it has later found use in a number of applications including data mining [11], speech processing [1], and classification of genome signals [13]. Over the years, many extensions have been proposed for video alignment in particular. Rao et al. [10] proposed a view-invariant dynamic time wrapping method to align the trajectories of manually marked points in two videos. Junejo et al. [5] computed pairwise distances between landmark points along their trajectories under the assumption that the self-similarity of action remains unchanged under different view angles. Zhou and De la Torre [18] developed Canonical Time Warping (CTW) that combines Canonical Correlation Analysis (CCA) [2] and DTW for spatiotemporal alignment of motion sequences between two human subjects. Gong and Medioni [4] extended the CTW method for aligning videos by integrating manifold learning using manually annotated training data sets. Nicolaou et al. [8] proposed a probabilistic extension of CTW for fusing multiple continuous expert annotations in tasks related to affective behavior. Zhou and De la Torre [19] presented a generalized canonical time warping (GCTW) method that extends the DTW by using a linear combination of monotonic functions to represent the warping path. Trigeorgis et al. [14] present a Deep Canonical Time Warping (DCTW) that learns non-linear representations of time-series that are correlated in a shared, temporally aligned subspace. Padua et al. [9] applied a linear transformation model to solve the spatio-temporal alignment of video sequences.

Shariat and Pavlovic [12] enforced the monotonicity to CCA to achieve arbitrary permutations of time indexes for video synchronization.

3 Method

To find the best match from a sequence of templates, we devise an algorithm based on dynamic programming, which is inspired by pairwise sequence alignment methods that have been widely used in the context of biological data analysis. In the following sections, we first introduce a similarity measurement, called normalized cross-correlation, which is employed for comparing two depth frames, and then describe the semi-global alignment algorithm with the normalized cross-correlation.

3.1 Normalized Cross-Correlation

The normalized cross-correlation, denoted with s, is used for evaluating the similarity between two depth frames:

$$s(f,g) = \frac{\sum_{x,y}(f(x,y) - f_\mu)(g(x,y) - g_\mu)}{\sqrt{\sum_{x,y}(f(x,y) - f_\mu)^2(g(x,y) - g_\mu)^2}}, \tag{1}$$

where $f(x,y)$ and $g(x,y)$ are the value of two frames at coordinates (x,y) and $x \in (0,1,\ldots,m-1)$, $y \in (0,1,\ldots,n-1)$ and f_μ and g_μ are the means of the depth value of each frame. In Eq. (1), depth frames are formatted as two dimensional $m \times n$ matrices. The range of s is from 1 to -1. When s is close to 1, the two frames are similar to each other.

3.2 Semi-global Video Alignment

In aligning two video sequences, a score is assigned to a pair of frames from these two videos. The highest similarity score gives the best matches of templates to the input frames. In our method, a score matrix and a trace matrix are used to find the alignment. The score matrix, as shown in Table 1, stores the accumulated s calculated using Eq. (1), and the matrix is filled with the recurrence expressed using Eqs. (2) and (3). The given template video is $\{T_0, T_1, \ldots, T_{N-1}\}$ with length N. The input video is $\{Q_0, Q_1, \ldots, Q_{M-1}\}$ with length M. $S_{i,j}$ is the value in cell (i,j) in score matrix. $s(Q_i, T_j)$ is the normalized cross-correlation between the template T_j and the input Q_i.

$$S_{0,j} = s(0,j) \tag{2}$$

$$S_{i,j} = \max(S_{i-1,0}, S_{i-1,1}, \ldots, S_{i-1,k}, \ldots S_{i-1,j}) + s_{i,j} \tag{3}$$

The trace matrix as shown in Table 2 is used to save the choice we make in Eq. (3) for calculating each cell value in the score matrix (Eq. (4)). The trace matrix help construct the best semi-global alignment.

Table 1. Score matrix

	T_0	T_1	...	T_j	...	T_{N-1}
Q_0	$S_{0,0}$	$S_{0,1}$	...	$S_{0,j}$	...	$S_{0,N-1}$
Q_1	$S_{1,0}$	$S_{1,1}$	...	$S_{1,j}$	...	$S_{1,N-1}$
...	...	...	...	...	...	
Q_i	$S_{i,0}$	$S_{i,1}$	...	$S_{i,j}$	...	$S_{i,N-1}$
...	...	...	...	...	...	
Q_{M-1}	$S_{M-1,0}$	$S_{M-1,1}$	...	$S_{M-1,j}$	...	$S_{M-1,N-1}$

Table 2. Trace matrix

	T_0	T_1	...	T_j	...	T_{N-1}
Q_0	$TB_{0,0}$	$TB_{0,1}$	...	$TB_{0,j}$	...	$TB_{0,N-1}$
Q_1	$TB_{1,0}$	$TB_{1,1}$	...	$TB_{1,j}$	...	$TB_{1,N-1}$
...	...	...	...	...	...	
Q_i	$TB_{i,0}$	$TB_{i,1}$	...	$TB_{i,j}$	...	$TB_{i,N-1}$
...	...	...	...	...	...	
Q_{M-1}	$TB_{M-1,0}$	$TB_{M-1,1}$	...	$TB_{M-1,j}$	...	$TB_{M-1,N-1}$

$$TB_{i,j} = \arg \max_{k} \left(S_{i-1,0}, \ldots, S_{i-1,k}, \ldots, S_{i-1,j} \right) \qquad (4)$$

For example, when $S_{i,j}$ is filled in score matrix, the Eq. (3) is used. $S_{i,j} = \max(S_{i-1,0}, S_{i-1,1}, ..., S_{i-1,k}, ...S_{i-1,j}) + s_{i,j}$. If the $S_{i-1,j-1}$ make the $S_{i,j}$ maximum, The $TB_{i,j}$ will be filled by $j-1$ in trace matrix. After all of score matrix and trace matrix are filled, the maximum score is found from the least line of score matrix. If the maximum score is $S_{M-1,j}$, T_j is aligned to Q_{M-1}. Then the trace matrix will be checked from bottom to top. If $TB_{M-1,j}$ is $j-1$, we can go to the $TB_{M-2,j-1}$ cell, and T_{j-1} is aligned to Q_{M-2}. This process will be repeated until i reaches to 0, where i is the index of Q_i. The final alignment will be achieved. The detailed description of our proposed video alignment method is presented in Algorithm 1.

4 Experimental Results

4.1 Data and Experimental Settings

To evaluate the performance of our proposed method, we acquired four depth videos with participants performing the same actions. These depth videos were recorded by Microsoft Kinect. Each participant squatted down and stood up with their hands in the air all the time and repeated this action three times, as shown in Fig. 1. The participants contain one female and three males with

---

Algorithm 1. Semi-global video alignment algorithm.

---

template sequence T, where length is N
query sequence Q, where length is M
score matrix S, where size is $M \times N$
trace matrix TB, where size is $M \times N$
normalized cross-correlation s
for $j \leftarrow 0$ to $N - 1$ **do**
  $S_{0,j} \leftarrow s_{0,j}$
end for
for $i \leftarrow 1$ to $M - 1$ **do**
  for $j \leftarrow 0$ to $N - 1$ **do**
    $max \leftarrow -INF$
    for $k \leftarrow 0$ to j **do**
      if $S_{i-1,k} >= max$ **then**
        $max \leftarrow S_{i-1,k}$
        $TB_{i,j} \leftarrow k$
      end if
    end for
    $S_{i,j} \leftarrow max + s_{i,j}$
  end for
end for
for $j \leftarrow 0$ to $N - 1$ **do**
  find max $S_{M-1,j}$ and store the location L which is max $S_{M-1,j}$
end for
$l \leftarrow L$
for $i \leftarrow M - 1$ to 0 **do**
  find pair of Q_i and T_l from trace matrix
  $l \leftarrow TB_{i,l}$
end for

---

different heights, widths, and body shapes. We label these four videos as V_1, V_2, V_3, and V_4 based on the number of frames, which are 101, 98, 89, and 86, respectively. Note that V_2 is of a female subject.

The subjects in the input and template may not be necessary for the same environment. To eliminate the effect of non-pose related information, we apply an easy and effective procedure to remove the background. Both input and template videos need to contain a few frames with background only. A composite background frame is generated by averaging from those background frames and used to subtract from the frames of interest. We assume that the subjects are closer to the depth camera than the background in a continuous region. With this operation, the point corresponding to the background will have a depth value set to zero. A sample depth frame without background is shown in Fig. 1.

To reduce the impact from the physical appearance of subjects, all frames in input and template videos are normalized, respectively, such that the height and the width of a subject range from 0 to 1. The frame with the largest height and width is set as the baseline, and all the other frames are scaled according to that frame.

Fig. 1. An example of depth frames of various poses of different people after background removal.

To evaluate the performance of the proposed semi-global alignment method, we conducted experiments against the baseline method, DTW [3] over our four videos. We designed two experiments (single person alignment and inter-person alignment) to investigate the accuracy and robustness with respect to movement agility, pose variation, and body shape disparity.

4.2 Alignment of Videos of the Same Person

For the single person alignment dataset, we generated and applied alignment pair-wisely on a set of new depth videos by down-sampling the original video. For the shared frames between any two down-sampled videos, the best alignment is matching them with themselves no matter they are inputs or templates. For those unique frames that only present in input not in the template, the frames in the template closest to the input frame are considered as the right template frames. We used V_4 to generated four down-sampled videos. Totally, four temporally down-sampled videos $\{V'_{50}, V'_{40}, V'_{30}, V'_{20}\}$ are created with 50, 40, 30, and 20 percents of frames removed randomly.

We applied our semi-global alignment and DTW on the aforementioned four down-sampled videos and the original video V_4. The downsampled videos represent the scenarios of random temporal gaps, which are analogous to different movement speeds. Seven alignments were created by each method, as shown in Table 3. In each column, the alignment accuracy is reported for a pair of videos. For the seven video pairs, our method consistently achieved 100% of accuracy, whereas the DTW method yielded an inferior performance and the best performance by DTW is 89%. In contrast to the DTW method, our proposed method improves accuracy by more than 12.4%. It is hence evident that our semi-global alignment identifies the correct templates regardless of the magnitude of the temporal gaps.

Table 3. Alignment accuracy of single person experiment. SG denotes our proposed semi-global alignment.

Input Video	V'_{50}	V'_{40}	V'_{30}	V'_{20}	V'_{50}	V'_{20}	V_4
Template Video	V_4	V_4	V_4	V_4	V'_{20}	V'_{50}	V'_{50}
SG	100%	100%	100%	100%	100%	100%	100%
DTW	63%	75%	75%	89%	81%	69%	77%

4.3 Alignment of Videos of Different Subjects

For the inter-person alignment dataset, we intend to do the pairwise alignment for all four depth videos, each of which is used as a template and input once. Since the matching pairs of frames between different participants are unknown, we visually checked the similarity between any two videos and annotated paired frames with the consideration of temporal consistency. The accuracy is calculated as the faction of the input frames that match with the ground-truth templates.

To evaluate the performance of our method in the close-to-practice scenarios, we performed pairwise alignments of the four depth videos. The alignment results are presented in Table 4. Most of the alignments by our proposed method achieved an accuracy above 90% and the average accuracy is 91%. In contrast, the average accuracy of DTW is 81%. This represents a 12.3% improvement by our method, which is consistent with our previous results.

We carefully checked the two alignments by our semi-global alignment with an accuracy below 90% and found that the accuracy drops when the input video is longer than the template video. The cause of such lower performance is that two or more input frames are mapped to the same frame in the template and some of these input frames may not contain identical poses as in the template. In general, the semi-global alignment method can find the pattern of movement of people. It can align most of the frames between the input video and template video.

Table 4. Alignment accuracy for inter-person alignment experiment. SG denotes our proposed semi-global alignment.

Input video	V_2	V_3	V_4	V_3	V_4	V_4	V_1	V_2
Template video	V_1	V_1	V_1	V_2	V_2	V_3	V_4	V_3
SG	91%	92%	96%	88%	91%	95%	94%	81%
DTW	81%	83%	88%	87%	83%	72%	75%	79%

5   Conclusion

In this paper, we propose a novel approach for range video alignment. The proposed semi-global alignment integrates temporal constrains and uses 2D cross-correlation to measure the similarity between two depth frames. The proposed method has been evaluated with four depth videos and a comparison study against the baseline algorithm (DTW) is conducted. By registering resampled videos of a single person, our method improves the accuracy by more than 12.4%. This accuracy improvement is also confirmed by our experiments of registering videos of different persons. It is hence evident that our semi-global alignment identifies the correct templates regardless of the magnitude of the temporal gaps. Overall, our proposed method finds the pattern of movement of people and correctly aligns the frames between the input video and template video. The experimental results can be regarded as very encouraging since the proposed method has outperformed the compared algorithm by a large margin in all experiments. In the future, we plan to assess the ability of the proposed method to act as a generalized distance measurement between action videos.

References

1. Abdulla, W.H., Chow, D., Sin, G.: Cross-words reference template for DTW-based speech recognition systems. In: TENCON 2003. Conference on Convergent Technologies for Asia-Pacific Region, vol. 4, pp. 1576–1579. IEEE (2003)
2. Bach, F.R., Jordan, M.I.: Kernel independent component analysis. J. Mach. Learn. Res. **3**(Jul), 1–48 (2002)
3. Berndt, D.J., Clifford, J.: Using dynamic time warping to find patterns in time series. In: KDD Workshop, vol. 10, pp. 359–370. Seattle, WA (1994)
4. Gong, D., Medioni, G.: Dynamic manifold warping for view invariant action recognition. In: 2011 International Conference on Computer Vision, pp. 571–578. IEEE (2011)
5. Junejo, I.N., Dexter, E., Laptev, I., Perez, P.: View-independent action recognition from temporal self-similarities. IEEE Trans. Pattern Anal. Mach. Intell. **33**(1), 172–185 (2010)
6. Kong, L., Yuan, X., Maharjan, A.M.: A hybrid framework for automatic joint detection of human poses in depth frames. Pattern Recogn. **77**, 216–225 (2018)
7. Lu, Q., Xiao, M., Lu, Y., Yuan, X., Yu, Y.: Attention-based dense point cloud reconstruction from a single image. IEEE Access **7**, 137420–137431 (2019)
8. Nicolaou, M.A., Pavlovic, V., Pantic, M.: Dynamic probabilistic CCA for analysis of affective behavior and fusion of continuous annotations. IEEE Trans. Pattern Anal. Mach. Intell. **36**(7), 1299–1311 (2014)
9. Padua, F., Carceroni, R., Santos, G., Kutulakos, K.: Linear sequence-to-sequence alignment. IEEE Trans. Pattern Anal. Mach. Intell. **32**(2), 304–320 (2008)
10. Rao, C., Gritai, A., Shah, M., Syeda-Mahmood, T.: View-invariant alignment and matching of video sequences. In: Null, p. 939. IEEE (2003)
11. Ratanamahatana, C.A., Keogh, E.: Three myths about dynamic time warping data mining. In: Proceedings of the 2005 SIAM International Conference on Data Mining, pp. 506–510. SIAM (2005)
12. Shariat, S., Pavlovic, V.: Isotonic CCA for sequence alignment and activity recognition. In: 2011 International Conference on Computer Vision, pp. 2572–2578. IEEE (2011)
13. Skutkova, H., Vitek, M., Babula, P., Kizek, R., Provaznik, I.: Classification of genomic signals using dynamic time warping. BMC Bioinform. **14**(10), S1 (2013)

14. Trigeorgis, G., Nicolaou, M.A., Schuller, B.W., Zafeiriou, S.: Deep canonical time warping for simultaneous alignment and representation learning of sequences. IEEE Trans. Pattern Anal. Mach. Intell. **40**(5), 1128–1138 (2017)
15. Wang, H., Liu, X., Yuan, X., Liang, D.: Multi-perspective terrestrial lidar point cloud registration using planar primitives. In: 2016 IEEE International Geoscience and Remote Sensing Symposium (IGARSS), pp. 6722–6725. IEEE (2016)
16. Xu, C., Cheng, L.: Efficient hand pose estimation from a single depth image. In: Proceedings of the IEEE International Conference on Computer Vision, pp. 3456–3462 (2013)
17. Yuan, X., Kong, L., Feng, D., Wei, Z.: Automatic feature point detection and tracking of human actions in time-of-flight videos. IEEE/CAA J. Automatica Sinica **4**(4), 677–685 (2017)
18. Zhou, F., Torre, F.: Canonical time warping for alignment of human behavior. In: Advances in Neural Information Processing Systems, pp. 2286–2294 (2009)
19. Zhou, F., De la Torre, F.: Generalized canonical time warping. IEEE Trans. Pattern Anal. Mach. Intell. **38**(2), 279–294 (2015)
20. Zhu, Y., Dariush, B., Fujimura, K.: Controlled human pose estimation from depth image streams. In: 2008 IEEE Computer Society Conference on Computer Vision and Pattern Recognition Workshops, pp. 1–8. IEEE (2008)

Label Distribution Learning-Based Semantic Retrieval Model on Knowledge Graph

Chao Wang[1,2], Ning Sun[1,2], Jiajun Zhang[1,2], Yingchun Xia[1,2], and Lichuan Gu[1,2(✉)]

[1] Anhui Agricultural University, Hefei, China
{wangchao_ICLE,glc}@ahau.edu.cn
[2] Key Laboratory of Agricultural Electronic Commerce of the Ministry of Agriculture, Hefei, China

Abstract. The traditional retrieval technology is difficult to grip users' intention accurately and apace in massive and fragmented data. To organize fragmented knowledge in reason and retrieve useful knowledge to recommend for users in a big data environment, this paper proposes a label distribution learning-based semantic retrieval model on the knowledge graph. The model firstly constructs the knowledge graph based on the topic map model. And then it clusters knowledge by using K-means label distribution learning (KM-LDL) and reduces retrieval scope. To address the problem that the space vector converted from the input text is sparse, this paper improves K-means label distribution learning according to the idea of probability and constructs a semantic retrieval model on a knowledge graph based on Bayes-K-means label distribution learning (Bayes-KM-LDL). The experimental results show that the proposed model can organize fragmented knowledge more reasonably than the traditional retrieval approach and its accuracy and recall rate have good performance.

Keywords: Semantic retrieval · Label distribution learning · Knowledge graph · Topic map

1 Introduction

The information retrieval tool is an important way for the user to obtain knowledge from massive information. However, the extensive use of computers and networks leads to information overload. Users always consume a lot of time to find their answers in massive fragmented information, and even can not find the right answers. It is the research focus to organize domain knowledge and accurately grip the user's intention in various domains.

Most of the data in the different domain knowledge bases are high-dimensional and lacks hierarchy and logical structure [11,14]. Retrieval based on

© Springer Nature Singapore Pte Ltd. 2020
X. Yuan et al. (Eds.): ICUIA 2020, CCIS 1319, pp. 27–38, 2020.
https://doi.org/10.1007/978-981-33-4601-7_3

classification and keyword are not universal and need to manually label knowledge base [16]. Facing to the massive and fragmented knowledge, it is meaningful to organize these data and use semantic retrieval technology to provide resources for users. In the filed of semantic retrieval, Tserng [12] proposed a knowledge graph model to share and reuse knowledge. Lee and Segev [8] developed a method that can use text mining and other techniques to automatically generate a domain knowledge graph. However, these approaches are suitable for the scenes that knowledge has clear classification and hierarchy. The other scenes usually use string-based retrieval approaches and need the participation of domain experts. However, the string-based retrieval can not meet user's need with the increasing of information. Gao et al. [4] proposed a semantic similarity model with constraint and a feedback correction mechanism based on knowledge graph and semantic calculation. Its accuracy can reach to 85%. Zhu et al. [17] proposed an approach of semantic retrieval and clustering analysis for geology big data. The results are more accurate than other traditional methods. The above approaches improved retrieval efficiency in different filed by using semantic retrieval techniques. However, these approaches are still needed to be improved to achieve more efficient retrieval.

To achieve this purpose, this paper organizes fragmented knowledge by constructing a knowledge graph based on the topic map. Label distribution learning based on K-Means (LDL-KM) is applied in the semantic retrieval model to cluster knowledge and reduce the scope of retrieval. In addition, to address the limitation of long text, this paper also proposes a semantic retrieval model on a knowledge graph based on Bayes-K-means label distribution learning (Bayes-KM-LDL).

The rest of this paper is organized as follows: Sect. 2 reviews the related work on methods for risk assessment. Section 3 presents our proposed method in details. Section 4 discusses our experimental results. Section 5 concludes this paper with a summary.

2   Related Work

The mainstream semantic retrieval models have three directions, including the ontology-based model, data mining-based model, and knowledge graph-based model. The ontology-based semantic retrieval model mainly makes semantic reasoning according to the pre-established domain knowledge ontology and then mines semantic relations. For example, Guo [6] proposed a semantic retrieval and recommendation system framework based on the agricultural product ontology. Bhattacharjee [2] solved semantic heterogeneous problems by using ontology. Semantic expansion is not only achieved by using domain ontology, but also achieved by using an open-source dictionary. Moldovan [10] applied open-source dictionary WordNet in the AltaVista system to extend query terms by defining synonyms. Gao and Yan [3] proposed a word disambiguation approach based on the Jaccard coefficient to divide the ambiguous words into the questions. The accuracy improved by 10%.

Data mining-based semantic retrieval model explores automatically the relationship among the objects by using data mining technologies, which is highly operable and objective [15]. On the basis of the extraction of Solar-Earth space discipline meta information, Liu [9] proposed a semantic retrieval model to analyze data by using potential semantic indexing technology. The recall rate of the model is much better than traditional approaches. Janowicz [7] mined semantic labels to support data discovery services by using data mining methods. Christidis [1] classified large-scale data collections to improve the performance of information retrieval systems by using clustering.

The knowledge graph is a knowledge system that is widely used in agriculture, medical care, commerce, and other fields. Xiao [18] constructed a Chinese medicine health knowledge graph and semantic retrieval model for the Chinese medicine health management based on the entity recognition algorithm and the word vector stitching. The model can understand the user's retrieval intention better. Zhao [19] classified and located texts by using Convolutional Neural Networks (CNN) based on an entrepreneurship knowledge graph. The results had a good performance in accuracy and recall rate.

The ontology-based semantic retrieval model has a clear hierarchy, but its accuracy relies on the construction of ontology. The construction of an excellent domain ontology needs to spend much time and manpower. Although the data mining-based semantic retrieval model is operable, it will be very difficult in document vectorization and dimension reduction when the retrieval collection is large-scale. The knowledge graph-based retrieval model can easily cope with complex correlations and obtain better results according to the relationship among entities. Moreover, the model understands the potential meaning of input questions more deeply and accurately from a semantic perspective.

3   Semantic Retrieval Model Based on Label Distribution Learning

The common clustering algorithms can be classified into the density-based method, hierarchical clustering method, partition-based method [5]. To reduce the retrieval scope and address the problem of sparse space vector of short input text, the paper proposes a semantic retrieval model based on K-means label distribution learning (KM-LDL) and label distribution learning approach Bayes-KM-LDL, respectively.

3.1   Label Distribution Learning

LDL provides a general framework for label learning. Single-label learning and multiple-label learning are special cases in LDL. At present, LDL has three directions, including problem transformation, algorithm adaptation, and specialization. LDL marks the corresponding instance x using a general approach and gives a corresponding value d_x^y for the label y that is related to x. Variable d_x^y represents the degree of which label y describes instance x. To complete the integrity of the description, assume d_x^y is between 0 and 1. The full description for x must use d_x^y of all labels. For a given instance, the process that the description degree becomes similar to the probability distribution is called LDL. The description degree is formed by all labels in collection for the instance.

Following the idea of problem transformation, this paper applies K-means to the construction of semantic retrieval model on the knowledge graph. Problem transformation is to transform the problem of label distribution into an existing learning paradigm. It converts the training set of label distribution learning into a single-label training set by using weighted sampling. Classifications can be trained by using traditional machine learning algorithms on the single-label training set.

3.2   KM-LDL-Based Semantic Retrieval Model on Knowledge Graph

3.2.1 Label Distribution Learning Based on K-means

The different k value in K-means has a great influence on the cluster results. This paper exploits the elbow approach to determine the k value [13]. After determining the k value, K-means is used to determine the average vectors of actual label distribution that is corresponding with each cluster. According to divided clusters, label distributions that are corresponding to samples are divided into clusters. The distance matrix of the sample in the test set to the mean vector of each cluster can be obtained by the common method of seeking distance, including Euclidean distance, Manhattan distance, etc. In this paper, we use Euclidean distance:

$$d(x,y) = \sqrt{\sum_i^n (x_i - y_i)^2} \tag{1}$$

The weight matrix of predictive label distribution can be converted from the central vectors of the sample's actual label distribution by taking the countdown and normalizing for all values in cluster T. The calculation formula is shown as formula (2). n represents the total number of the samples in the test set. W is the weight matrix that is used for the final predictive label distribution.

$$W_a = \frac{\exp(T_{ab})}{\sum_{b=1}^k \exp(T_{ab})} \tag{2}$$

where P, which is the final predictive label distribution, is obtained by multiplying W and matrix U, $P = W \times U$.

3.2.2 KM-LDL-Based Semantic Retrieval Model on Knowledge Graph

Although the knowledge graph-based retrieval model can easily cope with complex correlations, user input is needed to match all entities that spend much time. The KM-LDL algorithm has a good result in reducing the retrieval scope of entities and improving retrieval efficiency. Figure 1 shows the retrieval process of the proposed semantic retrieval model. The details are as follows:

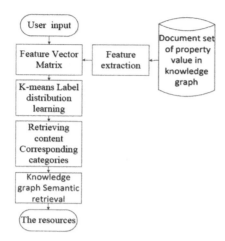

Fig. 1. KM-LDL-based semantic retrieval model.

Step 1: Paradigm of KM-LDL is used to convert the texts of the entity property value in knowledge base into the space vectors. The cluster labels and the mean vector of the cluster are obtained.

Step 2: User input is converted into a space vector. The classification label distribution of user input is obtained by using the Euclidean distance and softmax function.

Step 3: The corresponding resources are obtained by using the semantic retrieval model.

The KM-LDL algorithm improves retrieval efficiency. However, if user input is mostly short texts, the dimension of the space vector will be high. It has a bad influence on calculating the vector distance and lowering retrieval efficiency.

3.3   Bayes-KM-LDL-Based Semantic Retrieval Model on Knowledge Graph

To address the problem of the sparse space vector, this paper proposes Bayes-KM-LDL. According to the idea of probability statistics, the proposed method is more accurate in select the appropriate clusters. Compared to KM-LDL, its recall rate and accuracy are obviously improved. Generally speaking, a document is composed of many words and sentences. Some of them can be used as keywords to describe the document. The proposed approach uses K-means to cluster the texts and forms topic words cluster by extracting topic words from the entity properties document. The cluster of retrieval keyword is composed of word segmentation results of the input sentence. According to the thesis of Bayes statistical classification, label distribution based on Bayes-KM is obtained. The final retrieval results are obtained by using a semantic retrieval model based on the knowledge graph. As shown in Fig. 2, The process of the proposed model is as follows.

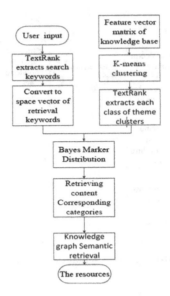

Fig. 2. Bayes-KM-LDL-based semantic retrieval model.

Step 1: K-means is used to cluster the text set $\{T, T1, T2, \lambda, Tm\}$, and the number of clusters is k.

Step 2: The topic words of texts in each cluster are extracted and deduplicated by using Text-Rank.

Step 3: The retrieval keywords $\{D, D1, D2, \lambda, Dm\}$ in input sentence are extracted by using Text-Rank. All the keywords are regarded as features and converted to space vector.

Step 4: According to the keyword cluster, the space vectors are constructed by the topic word clusters of each cluster. If the value of similarity between the keyword cluster and topic word cluster is higher than 0.9, the feature value is 1. Otherwise, the feature value is 0.

Step 5: The label distribution of input is obtained by using Bayesian and full probability formula.

Step 6: According to the results of the label distribution, the final answer is obtained by matching the retrieval keyword cluster D with the entities in the cluster.

4   Experiments

4.1   Dataset

Due to the lack of knowledge graph in the agricultural field, this paper supplements the crop pest database and the other database published by the Chinese Academy of Agricultural Sciences based on the Chinese general encyclopedia knowledge graph (CN-DBpedia). The dataset format is "entity-properties-property values". After extracting agricultural knowledge, the entity set contains more than 77,000 entities and their properties and property values. To avoid missing some relationship, the paper extends CN-Dbpedia-A by extracting entities among which exist relationships. The final knowledge graph is named CN-Dbpedia-AFLE, which contains more than 74,000 entities.

4.2 Knowledge Graph-Based Semantic Retrieval

In this experiment, we select eight retrieval keywords ("wheat", "corn", "Wheat spike malformation and black", "Wheat root decay", "Haplothrips tritici", "Pantatomidae", "rose cultivars", "Cuttage methods of rose") to verify the performance and calculate their accuracy and recall rate.

Figure 3 shows the comparison of the accuracy and recall rate for the eight retrieval keywords which are retrieved in CN-Dbpedia-A and CN-Dbpedia-AFLE by using two retrieval modes. The two retrieval modes are the original retrieval and extended retrieval.

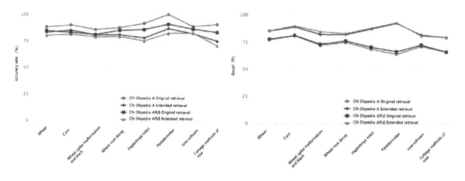

Fig. 3. Comparison of accuracy and recall.

As shown in the results, the accuracy of the retrieval in CN-Dbpedia-A is higher, but the recall rate is lower than the retrieval in CN-Dbpedia-AFLE. For entities that lack description, the accuracy and recall rates are basically the same. From different retrieval methods, whether CN-Dbpedia-A or CN-Dbpedia-AFLE, the recall rate of the extended query is always higher than the original query, while the accuracy of the extended query is lower than the original one. It is in line with the reverse relationship between recall rate and accuracy. In summary, the extended query mode can improve the recall rate of queries to some extent, but the two modes have a common drawback that user input needs to match all entities. It leads to a high time complexity and low retrieval efficiency.

4.3 Knowledge Graph Semantic Retrieval Based on K-Means Label Distribution Learning

According to the results in the last experiment, CN-Dbpedia-A is selected as the knowledge base for the next experiment. This experiment uses TF-IDF to transform the text which is composed of the entity property values into space vector. K-means is used to cluster space vector. The number of clusters is 10. Figure 4 shows the cluster results. The output of the algorithm includes clusters information, the clusters to which all texts belong, the label name of each cluster, and the corresponding text clusters.

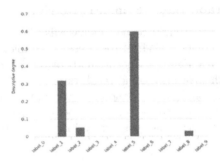

Fig. 4. Cluster results.

```
410.41691892578956
[[ 2.05998413e-18 -4.60785923e-19  0.00000000e+00 ... -1.69406589e-21
   1.10114283e-20 -1.27054942e-20]
 [ 1.94058969e-04  1.41683926e-04 -7.15928687e-18 ... -2.78673840e-19
   2.61733181e-19  4.67562187e-19]
 [ 3.11219779e-04  2.85815306e-04 -3.38813179e-19 ...  1.53312963e-19
  -1.51618896e-19 -3.21872520e-20]
 ...
 [ 3.99340628e-04  1.08555743e-17  3.71627037e-04 ... -3.49824607e-19
   5.04831637e-19  5.37018889e-19]
 [-4.01154804e-18  4.74338450e-19  2.71050543e-19 ...  2.96461532e-20
  -5.25160427e-20 -2.71050543e-20]
 [ 1.86482774e-17 -2.69695290e-18  1.27393755e-18 ...  1.36372305e-19
  -1.38066370e-19 -3.13402190e-20]]
[5 5 5 ... 1 1 6]
label_0:[' 中国数字植物园 ', ' 听湖丙勤村 ', ' 周坚 (南京林业大学教授) ', ' 咖啡属 ', ' 哈密尔顿 (加
label_1:[' somnus ', ' 两优5845 ', ' [竹+桐] 竹生氟点壳 ', ' [ 6乾杭] 子桔属 ', ' × 迷迭香火坝草 (杂种
label_2:[' cc-65天 ', ' N118S ', ' Nelumbonucifera 'ApricotBlossom' ', ' NO4583-5-2-4A ', ' RH1122
label_3:[' 启明星优结土清洁者 ', ' 美季辉 ', ' 周玉19号 ', ' 周莱28 ', ' 叮伦贝尔天桥宾官 ', ' 呼单10号
label_4:[' banksia ', ' g-香毛盛花葱 ', ' kayak (非佛制的品种) ', ' PQ穿根 ', ' Psylla ', ' P型雪糕
label_5:[' aconite ', ' adidas茉莉香水 ', ' alfalfa ', ' aphis ', ' arbuscular ', ' aster (植物名称) '
label_6:[' 吴幼胶 ', ' 吴茱萸叶五加 ', ' 吴莱萸果 ', ' 吴莱萸 (原变种) ', ' 吴莱叶五加 ', ' 吸油烟 ', ' e
label_7:[' ell优315 ', ' ell优316 ', ' ell优317 ', ' eK优10号 ', ' eK优11号 ', ' eK优18 ', ' e优27 ', ' e·
label_8:[' bra化杆 ', ' eK优21 ', ' hn国肥 ', ' npk ', ' Ptt土壤活化酶 ', ' S181 ', ' SD12830 ', ' SD13806
label_9:[' 京z柳 ', ' 光果要 ', ' 卿枝莱 (原变种) ', ' 北堂谷 ', ' 赵叶杜鹃 ', ' 单叶星陀藤 ', ' 吊无童草
```

Fig. 5. K-means label distribution for input text.

The text "the plant growth and development is poor. It occurred pests and diseases and defoliated seriously in growth period" is transformed into space vector. The results in Fig. 5 are obtained by using the paradigm of KM-LDL. The clusters, of which the description degree is higher than 0.1, are selected as the clusters which are corresponding to the text. The result indicates the cluster "label_1", cluster "label_5" have highly descriptive for input text.

Following the experiment approaches, we computed the accuracy and recall rate of each retrieval word group. The experiment results are shown in Table 1.

Table 1. Results of knowledge graph retrieval based on KM-LDL.

Query words	Number of relevant documents retrieved	Number of documents retrieved	Number of relevant documents in the system
Wheat	418	497	720
Corn	123	143	197
Wheat spike malformation and black	28	33	50
Wheat root decay	32	38	56
Haplothrips tritici	10	11	16
Pantatomidae	8	8	14
Rose cultivars	41	48	67
Cuttage methods of rose	9	11	15

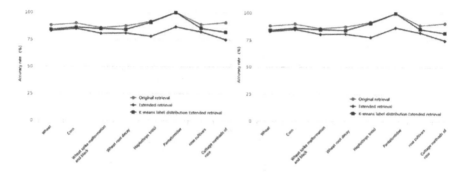

Fig. 6. Comparison of accuracy and recall.

Figure 6 shows the accuracy and the recall rate of the improved model, the extended retrieval model, and the original retrieval model. It can be seen that the accuracy of the retrieval model based on KM-LDL is slightly higher than the extended semantic retrieval model. However, the recall rate of the retrieval model based on KM-LDL is significantly lower. The main reason is that users input mostly short texts of which the space vector dimension is high. It has a bad effect on the distance calculation of the space vector.

4.4   Knowledge Graph Semantic Retrieval Based on Bayes-K-means

This experiment firstly clusters documents of entity property value. And then topic words are extracted from the documents which have clustered. Figure 8 shows the results of the topic word extraction. The text "the plant growth and development is poor. It occurred pests and diseases and defoliated seriously in growth period" is transformed into space vector. The label distribution results are obtained by using the Bayes-KM-LDL algorithm. The clusters which describe the text better are regarded as the final clusters for input text. As shown in Fig. 7, the cluster "label_1", the cluster "label_2" and the cluster "label_5" describe the input text better and selected to describe input text.

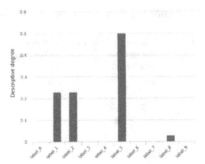

Fig. 7. Cluster results.

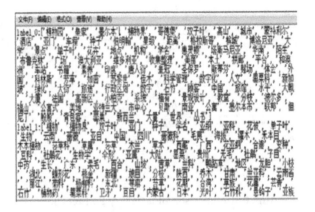

Fig. 8. K-means label distribution for input text.

Figure 9 shows the accuracy and the recall rate of the Bayes-KM-LDL-based extended retrieval model, the KM-LDL-based extended retrieval model, the extended retrieval model, and the original retrieval model. It can be seen that

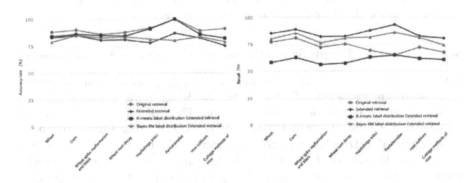

Fig. 9. Comparison of accuracy and recall.

the accuracy of the Bayes-KM-LDL-based extended retrieval model is slightly lower than that of the KM-LDL-based extended retrieval model, but the recall rate is significantly improved. Compared with the original retrieval model, the accuracy is still lower, but the recall rate is higher. In summary, the knowledge graph semantic retrieval model based on Bayes-KM-LDL can effectively reduce retrieval scope while keeping a higher accuracy and recall rate.

5 Conclusion

This paper studies the knowledge graph based on the topic map model according to the similarity of data structure between topic map and knowledge graph. The fragmented knowledge is organized by using the knowledge graph with the topic map and stored in the graph database. To address the shortcomings of KM-LDL in knowledge graph retrieval, this paper proposed the Bayes-KM-LDL. The proposed method solves the problem that the space vector converted from input text is sparse by using probability statistics. It improves the efficiency of knowledge graph retrieval. However, the approach that knowledge base resources are organized by clustering, does not have dynamic adaptability. In the next research, some simple information organization model can be applied to the knowledge graph to achieve a certain generality.

Acknowledgements. This work is partially supported by the Natural Science Foundation of China under Grant (31771679, 31671589), the Anhui Foundation for Science and Technology Major Project, China, under Grants 18030901034, 201904e01020006, 201903 a06020009, the Key Laboratory of Agricultural Electronic, Commerce, Ministry of Agriculture of China under Grant AEC2018003, AEC2018006, the 2019 Anhui University collaborative innovation project sn:GXXT-2019-013, the Hefei Major Research Project of Key Technology J2018G14.

References

1. Christidis, K., Mentzas, G., Apostolou, D.: Using latent topics to enhance search and recommendation in Enterprise Social Software. Expert Syst. Appl. **39**(10), 9297–9307 (2012)
2. Bhattacharjee, S., Ghosh, S.K.: Automatic resolution of semantic heterogeneity in GIS: an ontology based approach. In: Kumar Kundu, M., Mohapatra, D.P., Konar, A., Chakraborty, A. (eds.) Advanced Computing, Networking and Informatics-Volume 1. SIST, vol. 27, pp. 585–591. Springer, Cham (2014). https://doi.org/10.1007/978-3-319-07353-8_67
3. Gao, X., Yan, S.: Semantic Search Research based on WordNet word meaning to dispel differences. Xiangtan Univ. J. Nat. Sci. **39**(02), 118–121 (2017)
4. Gao, L., Zhang, H., Yang, L.: Research on intelligent information search technology based on knowledge map and semantic computing. Intell. Theory Practice **41**(7), 42–47 (2018)
5. Gu, L., Han, Y., Wang, C., Chen, W., Jiao, J., Yuan, X.: Module overlapping structure detection in PPI using an improved link similarity-based Markov clustering algorithm. Neural Comput. Appl. **31**(5), 1481–1490 (2018). https://doi.org/10.1007/s00521-018-3508-z

6. Guo, W.: Framework of semantic retrieval recommendation system based on agricultural body. Comput. Knowl. Technol. **15**(17), 191–193 (2019)
7. Janowicz, K.: Observation-driven geo-ontology engineering. Trans. GIS **16**(3), 351–374 (2012)
8. Lee, J.H., Segev, A.: Knowledge maps for e-learning. Comput. Educ. **59**(2), 353–364 (2012)
9. Liu, C., Zhai, Z., Zhai, J.: Semantic retrieval model of scientific data in the field of sun-earth space based on LSI. J. Univ. Chinese Acad. Sci. **33**(5), 711–719 (2016)
10. Moldovan, D.I., Mihalcea, R.: Using WordNet and lexical operators to improve Internet searches. IEEE Internet Comput. **4**(1), 34–43 (2000)
11. Rao, H., et al.: Feature selection based on artificial bee colony and gradient boosting decision tree. Appl. Soft Comput. J. **74**(1), 634–642 (2019)
12. Tserng, H.P., Yin, S.Y.L., Lee, M.H.: The use of knowledge map model in construction industry. J. Civil Eng. Manag. **16**(3), 332–344 (2010)
13. Wang, J., Ma, X., Duan, G.: Improved K-means cluster k-value selection algorithm. Comput. Eng. Appl. **2019**(8), 27–33 (2019)
14. Xia, Y., Wang, X., Gu, L., Gao, Q., Jiao, J., Wang, C.: A collective entity linking algorithm with parallel computing on large-scale knowledge base. J. Supercomputing **76**(2), 948–963 (2019). https://doi.org/10.1007/s11227-019-03046-7
15. Yuan, X., Buckles, B.P., Yuan, Z., Zhang, J.: Mining negative association rules. In: Proceedings. ISCC 2002 Seventh International Symposium on Computers and Communications, pp. 623–628 (2002)
16. Yuan, X., Xie, L., Abouelenien, M.: A regularized ensemble framework of deep learning for cancer detection from multi-class, imbalanced training data. Pattern Recogn. **77**, 160–172 (2018)
17. Zhu, Y., Tan, Y., Wu, Y., Zhang, L., Li, Y., Zhao, Y.: Semantic Retrieval Model study of big geological data. China Mining **26**(12), 143–149 (2017)
18. Xiao, M.: Research on the construction and application of knowledge map in the field of health for Chinese medicine certificate. Jilin University (2019)
19. Zhao, L.: Research on the construction and application of literature knowledge map in the field of entrepreneurship. Jilin University (2019)

An Improved Local Binary Descriptor Based Polar Gridding for Rotation Change

Jinqin Zhong[1]([✉]), Yingying Li[2], Qianqian Wang[1], Liang Zhang[1], and Yan Hu[1]

[1] School of Electronics and Information Engineering, Anhui University, Hefei 230039, China
`00571@ahu.edu.cn`
[2] School of Electronics and Information Engineering, Anhui Jianzhu University, Hefei 230601, China

Abstract. Rotation change is widespread in many computer vision applications. Robustness in rotation is an important evaluation for local descriptor. This paper proposes a fast and rotation-robust local binary descriptor using polar location, called rotation-invariant local difference binary descriptor (RLDB). RLDB computes binary test of average intensity and gradient in radial and tangent directions of grid cells partitioned by multiple log-polar grids. The proposed local descriptors need no extra work to deal with rotation specially. Integral image in polar coordinate and lookup table mapping between discretized polar coordinates and image pixel locations are proposed and applied to speed up the computation in the presented descriptors' construction. The proposed descriptor is compared with some of state-of-the-art local descriptors. The experimental results indicate that the proposed descriptor has a better performance in large rotation change and viewpoint change. The proposed descriptor has comparable distinctive performance and construction speed owing to fast computing in polar coordinate.

Keywords: Local binary pattern (LBP) · Local difference binary (LDB) · Log-polar gridding · Image matching · Rotation

1 Introduction

Image local features have been successfully employed in many computer vision tasks such as image classification [1], object recognition [2], image representation [3], registration [4] and 3D modeling and scene reconstruction [5, 6]. Many different image local descriptors are presented according to the demands of abundant vision tasks. Distinctiveness, robustness, and fast construction and matching are always ideal target in designing local descriptor. However, any local descriptor cannot perform well in all the aspects.

In computer vision tasks, viewpoint altering and rotation change can drastically change the description of local feature, resulting in low matching between the corresponding pairs. The existing solutions to deal with rotation for local descriptor are commonly as follows: RIFT [7], uses concentric circle grid for partitioning the region; SIFT [8], SURF, EF-VGG [9] normalize the detected region referring to dominant orientation

© Springer Nature Singapore Pte Ltd. 2020
X. Yuan et al. (Eds.): ICUIA 2020, CCIS 1319, pp. 39–46, 2020.
https://doi.org/10.1007/978-981-33-4601-7_4

estimated or trained by Convolutional Neural Network. These solutions undoubtedly weaken the discriminative ability at the expense of losing important spatial information. MRRID and MROGH [10] apply intensity order pooling scheme avoiding renormalizing the region or losing spatial information. However, the two solutions face the burden of expensive computation, normalizing the region or intensity order pooling both need extra complex works. For this reason, many local binary descriptors ORB [9], BRISK [12], Freak [13] only rotate discretized corresponding points instead of completely detected region to keep descriptor rotation-robust.

In recent years, owing to the demand of the application in low-power devices or real-time systems, the existing local binary descriptors are either too computationally expensive to achieve rotation invariance, or not sufficiently robust to rotation transformations. It is still a challenge to balance between the distinctiveness and robustness and light computational burden in construction of local descriptor. This paper presents a novel rotation-invariant local binary descriptor using polar location, which offers higher robustness in rotation change, and keeps the comparable distinctiveness and construction speed. The presented descriptor is obtained by binary test of cell information on polar location, named Rotation-robust Local Difference Binary Descriptor (RLDB). Main contributions are as follows: This paper proposes multiple log-polar location grids instead of Cartesian location grid and cell description in polar coordinate to achieve rotation invariance. Lookup table of location mapping and integral image polar coordinates are proposed to speed up the construction.

The rest of this paper is organized as follows: Sect. 2 reviews the related work. In Sect. 3 our proposed method is explained. In Sect. 4 the results of our experiments are presented. Finally, conclusions are remarked in Sect. 5.

2   Related Work

The local binary descriptors compare a pixel's intensity with the intensities of its neighborhood pixels to create the binary codes. Many local binary descriptors are widely used in low-power devices or real-time systems due to low memory and fast matching. One of the well-known descriptor is the LBP. Inspired by the simplicity of its idea, several LBP versions were proposed in the literature. For example, LBP is the local intensity order pattern, which encodes both the local intensity ordinal information of each pixel and the overall intensity ordinal information by dividing a local patch into sub-regions. BRIEF is the binary robust independent elementary feature, which encodes the local intensities of random pairs to get the fast calculations, but it is not considering rotation change. ORB is proposed to improve BRIEF method by steering test sample pairs to the orientation estimated by intensity centroid. BRISK uses a similar steering method to deal with rotation change by utilizing a circular sampling pattern instead of the random sampling pattern of BRIEF [11]. FREAK [13] improves BRISK's performance by using a retinal sampling pattern. These local descriptors are fast but lower discriminate compared with the famous gradient distribution-based local descriptors SIFT and SURF. To overcome the limitation, LDB use simple intensity and gradient difference tests on pairwise grid cells within the patch to achieve more discrimination. However, LDB using a salient bit-selection method to capture the distinct patterns of the patch at different spatial granularities need more consuming.

In this study, Inspired by the properties of log-polar location, a modified LDB method (PLDB) is proposed using multiple log-polar location grids instead of Cartesian location grid and cell description in polar coordinate to achieve rotation invariance. Experimental results show that compared to the existing state-of-the-art binary descriptors, our method achieves a greater accuracy and faster speed for image matching.

3 Proposed Method

In this section, the robust local binary descriptor (PLDB) in rotation is introduced in detail. The proposed descriptor utilizes multiple log-polar gridding to divide the detected region. Then, calculates average intensity, radial gradient and tangent gradient of each log-polar grid cells, and compares them corresponding between any pair of grid cells to produce binary strings. Finally, generates local binary descriptor of a given length by AdaBoost algorithm.

In order to overcome rotation change limitation, the presented descriptor partitions the interesting patch into $n \times m + 1$ non-overlapping sub-regions by multiple log-polar gridding from coarse to fine, shown in Fig. 1. The grid is composed of n concentric circles and m radial lines with the quantitative angle orientations as the detected key point. The log-polar orientation is set as dominant orientation of the patch. Thus, grid cell does not change in rotation.

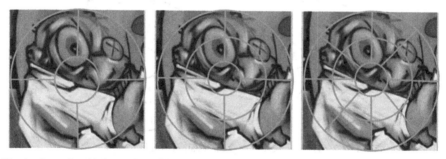

Fig. 1. A patch with log-polar gridding. (n = 1, m = 4 in the left panel; n = 2, m = 4 in the middle panel; n = 2, m = 8 in the right panel)

The average intensity I(S), average radial gradient $d_r(S)$ and average tangent gradient $d_t(S)$ of a grid cell S are defined as follows:

$$I(S) = \frac{\sum\limits_{p \in S} I(p)}{N_S} \tag{1}$$

$$d_r(S) = \frac{\sum\limits_{p \in S} d_r(p)}{N_S} \tag{2}$$

$$d_t(S) = \frac{\sum\limits_{p \in S} d_t(p)}{N_S} \tag{3}$$

where p is a point in cell S, N_s is the number of points in a cell, $I(p)$ is the intensity of point p; $d_r(p)$ is the radial gradient of point p, $d_t(p)$ is the tangent gradient of point p.

Binary triple $B_{i,j}$ obtained by comparing any two cells at any given log-polar grid can be constructed using the following equation:

$$B_{ij} = (F_{i,j}^1, F_{i,j}^2, F_{i,j}^3)$$
$$F_{i,j}^1 = \begin{cases} 1 & I(S_i) > I(S_j) \quad and \quad i \neq j \\ 0 & otherwise \end{cases}$$
$$F_{i,j}^2 = \begin{cases} 1 & dr(S_i) > dr(S_j) \quad and \quad i \neq j \\ 0 & otherwise \end{cases} \qquad (4)$$
$$F_{i,j}^3 = \begin{cases} 1 & dt(S_i) > dt(S_j) \quad and \quad i \neq j \\ 0 & otherwise \end{cases}$$

where, i and j are the number of cell in the scanning order of clockwise circumference first, radial direction second. All the $B_{i,j}$ are ordered from coarse grids to fine grids, which are then ordered by the cell number to obtain binary string. Multiple gridding cells are coded incrementally according the cell location clockwise spirally from inside to outside with regard of dominant orientation of region, as shown in Fig. 2.

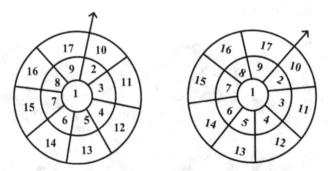

Fig. 2. The numbering of polar location grid in rotation

We compare between every pairs of the sub-regions in the order of the number of two sub-regions to generate the binary string, and then utilize selected distinctive bits by AdaBoost method to construct the robust descriptor in rotation, shown in Fig. 3.

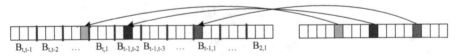

$B_{t,t-1}$ $B_{t,t-2}$ ... $B_{t,1}$ $B_{t-1,t-2}$ $B_{t-1,t-3}$ ... $B_{t-1,1}$ ... $B_{2,1}$

Fig. 3. The data structure for original binary descriptor and the final descriptor in selecting

4 Experiments

The proposed descriptor is evaluated using Oxford Data Set [14] and is compared with some closely related existing local descriptors with the same length. In the experiments, each sequence contains six images, the first is original image, the others are ordered by increasing distortions degree to the original image. A few example images are shown in Fig. 4. We select 32-byte to construct the descriptors on many image sequences.

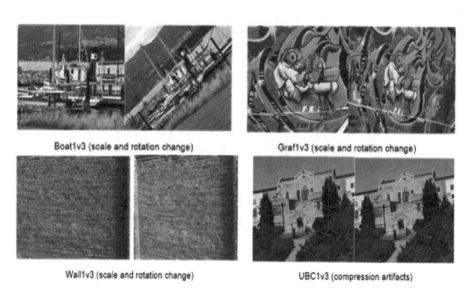

Boat1v3 (scale and rotation change)   Graf1v3 (scale and rotation change)

Wall1v3 (scale and rotation change)   UBC1v3 (compression artifacts)

Fig. 4. Image pairs from Oxford data set

Figure 5 shows our descriptor has better recognition rate than the other three local binary descriptors in 1v5, 1v6, which comprise images with viewpoint change and rotation change dramatically. This advantage is attributed to the fact that the polar coordinate and log-polar grid are better at dealing with rotation change than Cartesian coordinate and Cartesian grid.

To meet the needs of the real-time applications, we recorded and analyzed the construction and matching times of the tested descriptors during the previous experiments. All the descriptors were implemented on platform consisting of 2.93 GHZ Inter(R) Core(TM) CPU, 4G memory. The average times for constructing descriptor and matching are shown in Table 1. In construction, our descriptor is faster than ORB, BRISK and LDB with same length. However, our descriptor is the same speed as ORB, BRISK and LDB in matching. They all match faster than SURF due to binary string. Nevertheless, our descriptor time consumption is acceptable for most real-time application, and it is highly robust to rotation challenge.

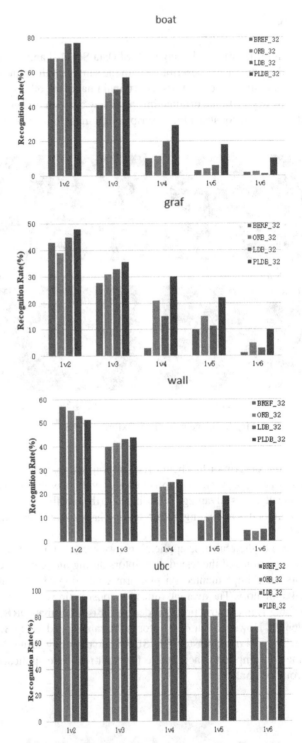

Fig. 5. Recognition rate for 32 bytes descriptors matching

Table 1. The average times of local descriptors during constructing and matching

Method	ORB-32	LDB-32	PLDB-32
Time of construction (ms)	0.062	0.082	0.076
Time of matching (ms)	0.013	0.013	0.013

5 Conclusion

In this study, a robust local binary descriptor in rotation is proposed. It was compared to several state-of-art local binary descriptors and in all criteria, our proposed descriptor outperformed the competitors. The main success of the proposed descriptor is to conjunct log-polar partition and cell feature description in polar coordinate. Average intensity, radial gradient and tangent gradient information of each log-polar grid cells are extracted, and information corresponding between any pair of grid cells is compared to produce binary strings, and then using an AdaBoost method reduces to given length. Our descriptor is highly robust to rotation challenge than lastly local binary descriptors and time consumption is acceptable for most real-time application.

Acknowledgments. This work was supported in part by the 2019 Anhui University collaborative innovation project(SN: GXXT-2019-013), the Key Laboratory of Agricultural Electronic Commerce, Ministry of Agriculture of China under Grant (AEC2018006), the Anhui Major Scientific and Technological Special Project (18030901034), the Hefei Major Research Project of Key Technology (J2018G14), Natural Science Research Project of Educational Commission of Anhui Province of China under Grant (KJ2018A0521) and the Visiting Scholar Researcher Program at North Texas University through Young Talents Foreign Visiting and Training Program of Educational Commission of Anhui Province of China under Grant (gxgwfx2018047).

References

1. Hu, P., Peng, D., Guo, J., Zhen, L.: Local feature based multi-view discriminant analysis. Knowl.-Based Syst. 1(149), 34–46 (2018)
2. Zhang, C., Sang, J., Zhu, G., Tian, Q.: Bundled local features for image representation. IEEE Trans. Circuits Syst. Video Technol. **28**(8), 1719–1726 (2018)
3. Brendel, W., Bethge, M.: Approximating CNNs with Bag-of-local-Features models works surprisingly well on ImageNet. arXiv preprint arXiv:1904.00760. Accessed 20 Mar 2019
4. Yuan, X.J., Zhang, J., Yuan, X., Buckles, B.: Multi-scale feature identification using evolution strategies. Image Vis. Comput. **23**(6), 555–563 (2005)
5. Yuan, X., Kong, L., Feng, D., Wei, Z.: Automatic feature point detection and tracking of human action in time-of-flight videos. IEEE/CAA J. Automatica Sinica **4**(4), 677–685 (2017)
6. Ojala, T., Pietikäinen, M., Harwood, D.: A comparative study of texture measures with classification based on featured distributions. Pattern Recogn. **29**(1), 51–59 (1996)
7. Guo, Z., Zhang, D.: A completed modeling of local binary pattern operator for texture classification. IEEE Trans. Image Process. **19**(6), 1657–1663 (2010)
8. Liu, L., Zhao, L., Long, Y., Kuang, G., Fieguth, P.: Extended local binary patterns for texture classification. Image Vis. Comput. **30**(2), 86–99 (2012)

9. Bay, H., Ess, A., Tuytelaars, T., Van Gool, L.: Speeded-up robust features (SURF). Comput. Vis. Image Understand. **110**(3), 346–359 (2008)
10. Rublee, E., Rabaud, V., Konolige, K., Bradski, G.R.: ORB: an efficient alternative to SIFT or SURF. In: ICCV 2011 (2011)
11. Calonder, M., Lepetit, V., Strecha, C., Fua, P.: BRIEF: binary robust independent elementary features. In: Daniilidis, K., Maragos, P., Paragios, N. (eds.) ECCV 2010. LNCS, vol. 6314, pp. 778–792. Springer, Heidelberg (2010). https://doi.org/10.1007/978-3-642-15561-1_56
12. Leutenegger, S., Chli, M., Siegwart, R.: BRISK: binary robust invariant scalable keypoints. In: ICCV 2011, pp. 2548–2555 (2012)
13. Alahi, A., Ortiz, R., Vandergheynst, P.: FREAK: fast retina key-point. In: Proceedings of IEEE Conference Computer Vision Pattern Recognition, vol. 157, no. 10, pp. 510–517 (2012)
14. http://www.robots.ox.ac.uk/~vgg/research/affine/

A Task-Aware Network for Multi-task Learning

Abolfazl Meyarian[1(✉)], Xiaohui Yuan[1(✉)], Borna Rahnamay Farnod[2],
Jianfang Shi[3], and Jianxia Liu[3]

[1] University of North Texas, Denton, TX 76207, USA
`AbolfazlMeyarian@my.unt.edu, xiaohui.yuan@unt.edu`
[2] Azad University Central Tehran Branch, Tehran, Iran
`brfarnood@gmail.com`
[3] Taiyuan University of Technology, Taiyuan 030024, China
`shijianfang66@163.com, tyljx@163.com`

Abstract. Creating a model capable of learning new tasks without deteriorating its performance on the previously learned tasks has been a
challenge of multi-task learning. Fine-tuning a pre-trained network for
another task could change the network in a way that degrades the performance on its original task. In this paper, we proposed a novel deep
network for learning multiple tasks based on extendable Dynamic Convolutional Blocks. Using the dynamic residual connections between layers,
our method adjusts the network depth to enable adaptability. The activation function selection strategy accommodates a variety of choices in the
training of the network for a specific task. We evaluated our method
using a publicly available dataset ALFW and conduct a comparison
study against the state-of-the-art methods. It was demonstrated that
our multi-task network outperforms the existing single and multi-task
methods by reducing the average error by as much as 25%. Our method
also exhibits a greater consistency for different tasks. By training variations of our proposed MTN, we observed that MTN-3 achieved the best
performance with a cumulative error rate of 1.87% and 5.7% reduction
in average error.

Keywords: Multi-task learning · Parameter sharing · Task-aware
network

1 Introduction

Multi-Task Learning, by obviating the need for training different networks for
multiple tasks, allows a single-network to perform many tasks while conserving
memory for storing models [1]. Creating a model capable of learning new tasks
without deteriorating its performance on the previously learned tasks has been
a challenge of multi-task learning. The main problem is that when a model,
e.g., a neural network, is trained for a task its parameters are optimized for
the target problem [6,14]. Fine-tuning a pre-trained network for another task

© Springer Nature Singapore Pte Ltd. 2020
X. Yuan et al. (Eds.): ICUIA 2020, CCIS 1319, pp. 47–58, 2020.
https://doi.org/10.1007/978-981-33-4601-7_5

could change the network in a way that degrades the performance on its original task [11,13]. While these tasks come from a shared feature space, improper feature sharing brings about the problem of *Destructive Interference* [15]. Convectional applications that can benefit from multi-task learning include natural language processing, surveillance, medical image analysis, etc. [8]

Many multi-task learning methods share a backbone for the whole model. The common features among all tasks are extracted and used in task-specific layers to handle the desired target tasks. This strategy is called hard parameter sharing. Kokkinos [4] introduced a multi-task model that consists of three main streams working with three different scales of the input image. The output is achieved by fusing the features in the three scales. Ranjan et al. [9] proposed a model based on hard parameter sharing for pose estimation, gender classification, visibility estimation, landmark estimation, and face detection. The face detection task was done by adopting an R-CNN approach, but for the rest of the tasks AlexNet [5] was used as the backbone, and the features from both deep and shallow layers are aggregated, used by the task-specific fully-connected layers at the end of the model.

Alternatively, soft parameter sharing has been explored, in which a replica of a base model is created, each of which is trained for a specific task. Mallya et al. [7] designed a method for activating and deactivating neurons in each convolutional block to pass the related features to the next layers based on the requirements of each task. The method uses a set of binary masks to control the structure of the feature passing through in a base model. PiggyBack [7] applies binary masks on the base model and has a distinct model specifically designed for the task at hand. However, the backbone remains the same and is shared among tasks. Ruder et al. [10] presented a model with hard parameter sharing and cross-stitch networks as the baselines on related tasks. Matrix regularization techniques were used to determine the shared layers between deep recurrent networks. Tissera et al. [12] proposed a multi-task learning method that changes the data flow in the network based on context based on the activation signal. When the task is changed, the units are turned off or on to extract useful features for the task.

In this paper, we propose a method that extends Context-Aware Multi-Path Networks [12] for feature and parameter sharing. The proposed method leverages Dynamic Convolutional Blocks (DCBs) to generalize a model to perform multiple tasks. A DCB consists of a sequence of convolution layers to allow the network to choose any units for a given task. Using dynamic residual connections between layers, our method adjusts the network depth to enable adaptability. The activation function selection strategy accommodates a variety of choices in the training of the network for a specific task. To evaluate our method, we study the effects of training samples and architectural differences with respect to three tasks: pose estimation, landmark localization, and visibility estimation.

The organization of the rest of this paper is as follows: Sect. 2 presents our multi-task network architecture that benefits from adaptive activation functions and dynamic feature routing mechanism. Section 3 discusses the experimental results based on the ALFW dataset for pose estimation, landmark localization, and visibility estimation. Section 4 concludes this paper with a summary and future work.

2   Proposed Method

2.1   Dynamic Convolutional Blocks (DCBs)

Inspired by context-aware multi-path networks [12], we propose a novel Dynamic Convolutional Blocks and a Dynamic Activation Function Selection method to extract features according to the needs of tasks. Figure 1 illustrates the architecture of our proposed network that consists of a set of Dynamic Convolutional Blocks (DCBs). In our network, Res represents a residual connection and their functionality will be discussed later on in this section. The outputs of residual connection and DCB are combined using an element-wise addition operation, which is fed into the next level of the network. Four network units are used in our illustration. The outputs from the last unit are processed with a fully connected (FC) layer for decision making.

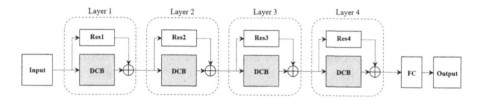

Fig. 1. Network architecture of our MTN-4.

To accommodate learning for different tasks, our method leverages network path selection strategy. By setting the weight of an input connection to zero, the contribution of this input is greatly suppressed to the decision; whereas a non-zero weight allows the input to moderate the final decision. In contrast to context-aware, multi-path networks [12], the path selection weight of our method allows decimal values in the range of [0–1]. The weights are represented in form of a vector, known as *Activation Signal*, which indicates the importance of the output of each block.

To choose the right path among all the available paths based on the requirements of the context of the given task, we propose Dynamic Convolutional Blocks (DCBs) which provide the network with a variety of options for feature extraction using the same shared backbone network for different tasks. We designed two types of DCBs. In one type of DCB, namely DCB-a as shown in Fig. 2(a), we apply convolutions with 1×1, 3×3, and 5×5 kernel. The outputs of the convolutions are added together followed by a max pooling to reduce the dimensionality. The result of the max pooling is processed with atrous convolutions at

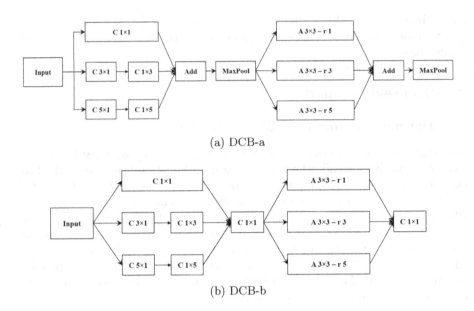

(a) DCB-a

(b) DCB-b

Fig. 2. Structure of the dynamic convolutional blocks

rates of 1, 3, and 5. The output of atrous convolutions are also added together and fed to a max pooling block as well. In the other type of DCB, DCB-b, depicted in Fig. 2(b), we replaced the summation and max pooling operations with a 1 × 1 convolution for dimensionality reduction. In our implementation, we used 3 × 1, 1 × 3 to achieve a 3 × 3 convolution that reduces the number of parameters. Such a strategy is also applied to the 5 × 5 operation. The data flow in all DCBs is controlled by means of the signals described before, in a way that when a convolution in a DCB is performed its output (all the values in the output feature map) are multiplied with the corresponding weight for that convolutional unit. The network, by manipulating the strength of each signal, changes the importance of each unit in the procedure of producing the final output.

2.2 Depth Adaptation

Our model is also equipped with a depth adaption mechanism. In each layer, the network is provided with two choices, one is to choose a path with more convolutional blocks (DCB) or the one with a Res (residual unit, which is a 3 × 3 convolution unit). The mechanism for controlling the strength of each connection is the same as what was done inside DCBs. There are again activation signals assigned to the output feature maps coming from the Res and the DCB in a layer. These weights are indicators of importance for each feature map and are multiplied to all the features in the feature map. After the multiplication, the results are added together and passed to the next layer. To get the final out of each layer, we combine the outputs as follows:

$$O_i = s_{i_1} R_i + s_{i_2} D_i, \qquad (1)$$

where s_{i_1} and s_{i_2} are activation signals and R_i and D_i are the outputs of the residual unit and DCB unit in the ith layer, respectively. Since the values for the signals are not binary, the network is able to use both of the feature maps in a network layer, which enables our model to have the same structure as a residual network.

2.3   Dynamic Activation Function Selection

Assume that there are N fully connected layers with M neurons in each, and we have T activation functions. The total number of possible network configurations with these activation functions is $T^{N \times M}$. By making them constantly assigned to an unit, only one configuration is chosen, even for multiple tasks. Hence, we allow a network to choose which activation function or combination of them is better for the task at hand. Assuming that $\{f_1, f_2, \ldots, f_n\}$ are the functions, the final output of each unit is calculated as follows:

$$A(x, S) = \sum_{i=1}^{T} s_i f_i(x), \qquad (2)$$

where S is the activation signal vector with i^{th} element of s_i chosen in the range of $[0\ 1]$. A convolutional unit inside a DCB benefits from the dynamic activation function selection mechanism, which allows the most suitable output produced for the task at hand. In-depth adaptation the same mechanism is used to weigh the outputs of a DCB and a Res.

2.4   Network Objective Function

Training of a multi-task network bears a close resemblance to the so-called *Multi-Objective Optimization*. Each task has its specific cost function that needs to be minimized. These functions can often be combined using a weighted sum to form a unified cost function [9]. Given the position of landmarks, the visibility factors, and the face poses provided in the form of continuous numerical values in the ALFW dataset, the optimization is modeled as a multi-regression problem. In this work, we use Mean Squared Error (MSE) as the cost function for all the tasks. Other error metrics could also be used.

Our cost function for training the multi-task networks consists of four terms as follows:

$$C = \lambda_l C_l + \lambda_v C_v + \lambda_p C_p + C_r \qquad (3)$$

where C_l, C_v, C_p, C_r denote the landmark localization cost, visibility estimation error, pose estimation error, and regularization term, and λ_l, λ_v, and λ_p are the weights assigned to each term. Each term is computed as follows:

$$C_l(L, \hat{L}, V) = \sum_{i=1}^{N} \sum_{j=1}^{21} [(v_{ij}\hat{l}_{ij_x} - l_{ij_x})^2 + (v_{ij}\hat{l}_{ij_y} - l_{ij_y})^2] \tag{4}$$

The landmark localization cost C_l computes the sum of the squared error between the original landmark coordinates L and the generated corresponding points by the network $\hat{L}$. In this formula, N is the number of samples in the batch. The cost of visibility is also computed based on the sum of the squared error as follows:

$$C_v(V, \hat{V}) = \sum_{i=1}^{N} \sum_{j=1}^{Q} (v_{ij} - \hat{v}_{ij})^2 \tag{5}$$

where Q is the number of landmarks. In the ALFW dataset, there are a maximum of 21 landmarks in a face image. Hence, we have $Q = 21$. Each of landmark is represented with a x, y tuple. l_{ij_x} denotes the x coordinate of the jth landmark for i^{th} sample in the batch. Landmark positions are defined in a 2D plane, for which the values of x-coordinate and y-coordinate are given, represented by l_{ij_x} and l_{ij_y} correspondingly, where l_{ij_x} refers to x coordinate of the jth landmark for i^{th} sample in the batch. The number of visible landmarks depends on face pose. The network predicts the coordinates for the visible landmarks represented with a visibility indicator vector V, which consists of binary element of 0 or 1 indicating the visibility of landmarks.

$$C_p(P, \hat{P}) = \sum_{i=1}^{N} \sum_{j=1}^{R} (p_{ij} - \hat{p}_{ij})^2 \tag{6}$$

where P is a pose vector that consists of roll, pitch, and yaw angles. R is the number of freedoms. Here, because we have the above three freedoms, R is 3. p_{ij} denotes the jth angular component (roll, pitch, or yaw) of a face pose for the ith sample in the batch.

$$C_r(\Theta) = \lambda \Theta \cdot \Theta \tag{7}$$

where λ is the regularization coefficient and Θ is the vector of network parameters. The dot product gives the sum of the magnitude of the parameter vectors.

3   Experimental Results

In our experiments, we used the Annotated Facial Landmarks in the Wild (AFLW) [3] dataset to train and test our models. AFLW contains 25k annotated face images (RGB and grayscale) collected from Flicker, 59% of the subjects are female and 41% are labeled as male. In each image, there are at most 21 landmarks with x, y coordinates for each if all are visible. In addition, for each subject in the image (there can be multiple faces in a picture), encompassing bounding box, gender, pose attributes (roll, pitch, yaw), and visibility factor of each landmark is provided. As we wanted to focus only on the tasks related to a single face we cropped the faces using the bounding box coordinated which were originally provided. We used 20% of the face images as the test set and the rest of 80% as the training set.

We trained eight networks, three single-task networks (STN), five multi-task networks (MTN-2, MTN-3, and MTN-4, MTN-5, MTN-8) based on DCB-a block. Each single-task network has one convolutional block in each layer similar to DCBs without activation signals. STNs have five layers followed by a fully-connected layer at the end. In STNs The depth of output feature maps for the layers are 32, 64, 128, 256, 512. As candidate activation functions, we have chosen ReLU, Leaky-ReLU, ELU [2], and the networks choose a combination of them as the final activation function. Worth mentioning that all the networks are implemented using the Tensorflow framework in Python.

To train the networks all the convolutional kernels are randomly initialized with a mean of 0 and standard deviation set to 0.01. Adam optimizer has been used as the optimizer with beta1 of 0.9 and beta2 of 0.999. We trained our model with a learning rate of 0.0001 initially and then decreased it to 0.00001 after 40k iterations. The models were trained batch size of 12 for the single-task networks and 5 for the multi-task network. In order to find the best value for the regularization coefficient λ, we trained an MTN-3 with λ in the range of 0.1 to 0.00001. Table 1 provides the total error rate of the MTN-3 trained with its corresponding regularization term. According to the results of our experiments, choosing larger values for λ restricts the range of weights in MTN-3 and leads to poor performance in all three tasks. To tune the values of λ_l, λ_v, and λ_p, we first trained a network with the same weight for all terms of the cost function, then we selected $\lambda_l = 2$, $\lambda_v = 5$, and $\lambda_p = 1$ based on the contribution of each error term in the cost function. We trained all variations of our MTNs on a GeForce RTX 2080 Ti. The training time for the MTNs is 7 hours, and almost 1 hour for HyperFace. Our MTN-3 network has a real-time performance and runs at 51 frames per second.

Table 1. The cumulative error rate of MTN-3 for pose estimation, landmark localization, and landmark visibility estimation with respect to the value of regularization term λ.

λ	10^{-1}	10^{-2}	10^{-3}	10^{-4}	10^{-5}
Cumulative error	2.28	2.10	1.91	1.87	**1.87**

3.1   Network Performance and Memory Efficiency

Table 6 compares the performance of our proposed model (MTN-3) against three single-task and multi-task models on the ALFW dataset for pose estimation, landmark localization, and landmark visibility estimation. We used Mean-Squared-Error (MSE) for evaluating models' performance. The best results are

Table 2. Comparison of MTN-3 and HyperFace on pose estimation, landmark localization, landmark visibility estimation when the subject wears glasses.

Glasses	Task	MTN-3	HyperFace
w	Pose estimation	**0.06**	0.07
	Landmark localization	**0.61**	0.84
	Landmark visibility estimation	**1.07**	1.47
w/o	Pose estimation	**0.08**	0.10
	Landmark localization	**0.97**	1.27
	Landmark visibility estimation	**1.87**	2.50

Table 3. Comparison of MTN-3 and HyperFace on pose estimation, landmark localization, landmark visibility estimation with respect to the gender of the subject.

Gender	Task	MTN-3	HyperFace
Female	Pose estimation	**0.06**	0.07
	Landmark localization	**0.62**	0.85
	Landmark visibility estimation	**1.11**	1.53
Male	Pose estimation	**0.05**	0.06
	Landmark localization	**0.70**	0.94
	Landmark visibility estimation	**1.21**	1.64

highlighted in boldface font and the second best results are underlined. In our experiments, we trained a VGG-16 and STN for every single task with 18k samples and tested with 4k samples. The average error of five repetitions, using the same training configuration, and the standard deviation (in parenthesis) for each model are reported. The last row of this table reports the cumulative average error rate on all tasks for each model.

Table 4. Comparison of MTN-3 and HyperFace in terms of average error rate on pose estimation, landmark localization, landmark visibility estimation with respect to occlusion of the face.

Occlusion	Task	MTN-3	HyperFace
w	Pose estimation	**0.06**	0.07
	Landmark localization	**0.62**	0.85
	Landmark visibility estimation	**1.10**	1.50
w/o	Pose estimation	**0.08**	0.09
	Landmark localization	**1.34**	1.75
	Landmark visibility estimation	**2.28**	3.06

The cumulative error rate of all tasks of our proposed method MTN-3 is 1.87, which is superior to all of the compared methods. In contrast to the second best method (HyperFace), the error reduction rate is 15.8%. Among the three tasks, landmark visibility estimation was the most difficult one. For each of the three tasks, MTN-3 also achieved the lowest error rates. Compared to the second best performer of each task, the error reduction rates are 25%, 15%, and 10% for pose estimation, landmark localization, and landmark visibility estimation, respectively.

By comparing the standard deviation, it is evident that our method exhibited better consistency among all methods. The standard deviations of MTN-3 for the three tasks are 0.28, 0.66, and 1.45, which are less than that of the other methods. A smaller standard deviation suggests that the predictions are more consistent with respect to the variety of the inputs.

Table 5 reports the amount of disk space used to store the trained network and the number of parameters of each network. For the single-task networks STN and VGG-16, both the memory and number of parameters are reported for handling three tasks as well as for handling a single task (in parenthesis).

Table 5. Memory required for storing the weights of the models after training.

Model	Single-task network		Multi-task network	
	STN	VGG-16	MTN-3	HyperFace
Memory size (GB)	0.66 (0.22)	5.04 (1.68)	0.48	0.34
# of parameters (10^6)	56.1 (18.7)	453 (151)	41	29

Among all methods, HyperFace used the least amount of memory and less number of parameters. MTN-3, STN, and HyperFace are on a very similar scale. VGG-16 required about ten times of memory space compared to the other three methods. Table 4 presents a comparison of MTN-3 and HyperFace in the absence and presence of occlusion in the test samples. According to the results, occlusion decreases the cumulative error rate 50% for both methods, furthermore, among all of the tasks, landmark visibility estimation and landmark localization are the most highly affected tasks. In all of the cases of this experiment, MTN-3 has shown better performance compared to HyperFace. In addition to occlusion, there are many test cases in which the subject wears glasses, that have an effect of visibility of the landmarks. Based on the results shown in Table 2, the error rate is decreased by 40% and 38% when the subject wears glasses, because when the landmarks are invisible the network is not responsible for localizing them or estimating the amount of their visibility. However, our MTN-3 achieved the best results for all of the tasks in both cases. Additionally, Table 3 reports the results of comparing the performance of MTN-3 to HyperFace with respect to the gender of the subject. Based on the results, the error rates in all of the tasks are less for female test cases compared to the males. MTN-3 has also achieved better results in this experiment compared to HyperFace.

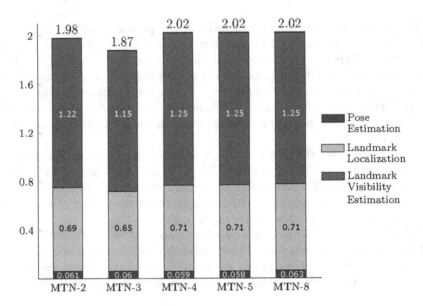

Fig. 3. Illustration of the effect of network size on its performance

3.2   Effect of Network Layers

Figure 3 illustrates the cumulative average error rate of MTNs with respect to the different number of network layers (DCB blocks). The colored sections depict the average error of the three tasks, and the numbers are shown in the middle of the section. The number on top of each bar is the cumulative error rate of the corresponding MTN architecture on all tasks. We trained each MTN with 18 thousand examples and tested it with four thousand examples. The experiments were repeated five times for each model to get the average error rate.

Among all MTN variants, MTN-3 exhibits the least cumulative average error rate, which is 1.87, and its performance in landmark localization and landmark visibility estimation are 0.65 and 1.15, respectively. MTN-3 achieved a reduction of 5.7% compared to the second best method MTN-2. The cumulative average error for MTN-4, MTN-5, and MTN-8 are almost the same, which also represents the worst performance of the proposed method. Yet, compared to the second best reported in Table 6, there is an improvement of 9%. Among all three tasks, landmark visibility estimation appeared to be the most difficult one, which resulted in 61% of the cumulative error on average. The error rates of pose estimation are more consistent among the variants of MTNs and are in a close range around 0.06.

Table 7 presents the storage space and number of parameters of MTNs. The storage space reported in this table is in GB and the number of network parameters is in million. It is clear that as the number of DCB layers increases the storage space and the number of parameters increase. The rate of increment, however, is non-linear. The increment of storage space and the increment of the

Table 6. MSE of the compared methods using the ALFW dataset. STN: single task network. MTN-3: multi-task network with three layers. The best performance is highlighted with bold-face font; the second bast performance is highlighted with underscore.

Task	STN	VGG-16	MTN-3	HyperFace [9]
Pose estimation	0.24 (0.43)	0.26 (0.45)	**0.06** (0.28)	<u>0.08</u> (0.34)
Landmark localization	1.14 (0.88)	0.97 (0.87)	**0.66** (0.70)	<u>0.78</u> (0.78)
Visibility estimation	2.68 (1.53)	<u>1.30</u> (1.68)	**1.15** (1.45)	1.36(1.59)
Cumulative	4.06	2.53	**1.87**	<u>2.22</u>

number of parameters are about 0.08 GB and 4 million, respectively, for one additional DCB block. This is due to the difference in the size of feature maps reaching the fully-connected layers. As shown in Fig. 2(a), two feature aggregation operations are used to reduce the dimensionality of the feature maps: one for the first three convolutions and another for atrous convolutions. Depending on the number of DCB blocks in each network and the stride step in each block, the feature map size could be different, which affects the size of weight matrices for the terminal layers.

Table 7. Memory and number of parameters required for storing the weights of the models after training.

Model	MTN-2	MTN-3	MTN-4	MTN-5	MTN-8
Memory size (GB)	0.36	0.48	0.41	0.49	0.71
# of parameters (10^6)	31	41	35	42	61

4   Conclusion

In this paper, we proposed a novel deep network for learning multiple tasks at the same time. The key component of our proposed method includes extendable Dynamic Convolutional Blocks and the depth adaptation mechanism provides the network with the ability to change the data flow and its size based on the needs of the task at hand.

We evaluated our method with a publicly available dataset for three tasks: face pose estimation, landmark localization, and landmark visibility estimation. Our multi-task network outperforms all the single and multi-task methods. Specifically, MTN-3 reduced the average error rate by 25%, 15%, and 10% for pose estimation, landmark localization, and landmark visibility estimation, respectively, in contrast to the second-best method on each task. Our method also exhibits a greater consistency suggested by the smaller standard deviations in the average error rate. By training variations of our proposed MTN, we observed that MTN-3 achieved the best performance with a cumulative error rate of 1.87 and 5.7% reduction in error rate compared to the second-best. Among all the three tasks, landmark visibility was the most difficult one with 61% contribution to the cumulative error rate; whereas a greater consistency was observed in the pose estimation task.

References

1. Caruana, R.: Multitask learning. Mach. Learn. **28**(1), 41–75 (1997)
2. Clevert, D., Unterthiner, T., Hochreiter, S.: Fast and accurate deep network learning by exponential linear units (ELUs). arXiv preprint arXiv:1511.07289 (2015)
3. Koestinger, M., Wohlhart, P., Roth, P.M., Bischof, H.: Annotated facial landmarks in the wild: a large-scale, real-world database for facial landmark localization. In: 2011 IEEE International Conference on Computer Vision Workshops (ICCV workshops), pp. 2144–2151. IEEE (2011)
4. Kokkinos, I.: UberNet: training a universal convolutional neural network for low-, mid-, and high-level vision using diverse datasets and limited memory. In: Proceedings of the IEEE Conference on Computer Vision and Pattern Recognition, pp. 6129–6138 (2017)
5. Krizhevsky, A., Sutskever, I., Hinton, G.E.: ImageNet classification with deep convolutional neural networks. In: Advances in Neural Information Processing Systems, pp. 1097–1105 (2012)
6. Lu, Q., Liu, Y., Huang, J., Yuan, X., Hu, Q.: License plate detection and recognition using hierarchical feature layers from CNN. Multimed. Tools Appl. **78**(11), 15665–15680 (2019)
7. Mallya, A., Davis, D., Lazebnik, S.: Piggyback: adapting a single network to multiple tasks by learning to mask weights. In: Proceedings of the European Conference on Computer Vision (ECCV), pp. 67–82 (2018)
8. Qin, F., Fang, S., Wang, L., Yuan, X., Elhoseny, M., Yuan, X.: Kernel learning for blind image recovery from motion blur. Multimed. Tools Appl. 21873–21887 (2020). https://doi.org/10.1007/s11042-020-09012-3
9. Ranjan, R., Patel, V.M., Chellappa, R.: A deep multi-task learning framework for face detection, landmark localization, pose estimation, and gender recognition. IEEE Trans. Pattern Anal. Mach. Intell. **41**(1), 121–135 (2017)
10. Ruder, S., Bingel, J., Augenstein, I., Søgaard, A.: Latent multi-task architecture learning. In: Proceedings of the AAAI Conference on Artificial Intelligence, vol. 33, pp. 4822–4829 (2019)
11. Shi, J., Yuan, X., Elhoseny, M., Yuan, X.: Weakly supervised deep learning for objects detection from images. In: Yuan, X., Elhoseny, M. (eds.) Urban Intelligence and Applications. SDI, pp. 231–242. Springer, Cham (2020). https://doi.org/10.1007/978-3-030-45099-1_18
12. Tissera, D., Kahatapitiya, K., Wijesinghe, R., Fernando, S., Rodrigo, R.: Context-aware multipath networks. arXiv preprint arXiv:1907.11519 (2019)
13. Yuan, X., Kong, L., Feng, D., Wei, Z.: Automatic feature point detection and tracking of human actions in time-of-flight videos. IEEE/CAA J. Autom. Sinica **4**(4), 677–685 (2017)
14. Yuan, X., Xie, L., Abouelenien, M.: A regularized ensemble framework of deep learning for cancer detection from multi-class, imbalanced training data. Pattern Recogn. **77**, 160–172 (2018)
15. Zhao, X., Li, H., Shen, X., Liang, X., Wu, Y.: A modulation module for multi-task learning with applications in image retrieval. In: Proceedings of the European Conference on Computer Vision (ECCV), pp. 401–416 (2018)

Data Mining Technology in Detection and Identification of Bad Data in Power System

Honghai Wang[(✉)]

Anhui Sanlian College, Hefei 230601, Anhui, China
2858093479@qq.com

Abstract. Traditional bad data detection methods are estimated algorithms that require repeated state estimations. A large number of calculations may also cause "residual flooding" or "residual pollution" phenomena, which is the ideal state. The bad data can be detected and identified before the estimation, and the bad data detection and identification method based on association rule mining studied in this paper can solve these problems to a certain extent. This paper first analyzes the traditional bad data detection and identification methods and then leads to data mining technology. Second, it delves into the classic algorithm Apriori and improvement in association rules and studies the basic algorithm and improvement of periodic association rule mining. Application of improved algorithm. The current, active, and reactive power data of a certain line collected in the SCADA system of a dispatching center from May to September and five months were selected as sample data to finally verify the feasibility and effectiveness of the method.

Keywords: Data mining · Power system · Bad data · Detection and identification

1 Introduction

In order to meet the needs of the national economy, the scale of China's power grid is constantly expanding, and its structure and operation mode is becoming more and more complicated than before [1]. As the data acquisition and victory control system, the SCADA system has been widely used in power networks, the system may fail to measure or transmit data due to various force majeure factors during the process of measuring data or transmitting data. Abnormal, that is, bad data [2]. In order to improve the reliability of power system state estimation, and select and eliminate a small amount of bad data that occasionally appears in the SCADA system measurement sampling, many scholars at home and abroad have conducted in-depth research on bad data mining techniques. But looking at all kinds of methods, the accuracy, fastness, and comprehensiveness of the detection and identification of bad data are still big problems that plague electric power workers [3, 4].

At this stage, the protection and control system of the power grid has achieved a high degree of automation, which places higher requirements on the accuracy of the system data [5]. Obviously, once the data received by a substation automation system or dispatch

© Springer Nature Singapore Pte Ltd. 2020
X. Yuan et al. (Eds.): ICUIA 2020, CCIS 1319, pp. 59–64, 2020.
https://doi.org/10.1007/978-981-33-4601-7_6

automation system is bad data, the impact of these error messages will interfere with the dispatcher's judgment and may cause the dispatcher to make wrong control decisions and even cause protection and control. The device malfunctioned, which seriously affected the safety of the power grid [6].

The focus of this paper is to obtain the association rules by mining historical data samples collected by the SCADA system when the topology and operating status of the power system network are unclear, to conduct research on the detection and identification of bad data before state estimation. It will provide a certain theoretical and practical basis for related fields, and contribute to the improvement of China's power system security.

2 Method

2.1 Data Mining

Data mining is not a random application of some existing or known analysis techniques to specific situations to solve specific problems [7, 8], but a way to solve problems and analyze problems. The whole process of data mining is shown in Fig. 1.

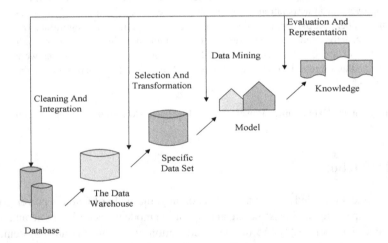

Fig. 1. Data mining process

2.2 Improvement of Association Rule Algorithm

This paper reduces the number of data subsets that need to be counted for the periodic support and proposes the CARM2 algorithm., Reducing the time complexity of the algorithm, the specific improvement steps are as follows:

Assume that the number of data subsets contained in period (l, o) is $|db (l, o)|$,

$$|db(l, o)| = |(n - o)/l| \tag{1}$$

The minimum periodic support is minCycle. If $|db\ (l,\ o)|$ is divided into two parts of the data subset, they are:

$$|db(l, o)| \times (1 - \min Cycle) \qquad (2)$$

$$|db(l, o)| \times \min Cycle - 1 \qquad (3)$$

Then only the periodic support number of the association rules of the first part of the data subset can be counted, because the association rules of the second part of the data subset periodically do not meet the minimum periodicity support condition, so it cannot become periodic Association rules. On the other hand, assuming that the first m data subsets of $|db\ (l,\ o)|$ have been calculated, if the periodic support number of an association rule in these m data subsets is less than:

$$m - |db(l, o)| \times (1 - \min Cycle) \qquad (4)$$

Then this rule cannot become a periodic association rule.

Proof: Because the number of data subsets contained in period $(l,\ o)$ is $|db(l,\ o)|$, assuming that the minimum periodic support specified by the user is $minCycle$, an association rule must become a periodic association rule. The number of periodic support must be at least $|db(l,\ o)| \times \min Cycle$. The first m data subsets of $|db(l,\ o)|$ have been calculated, and $|db\ (l,\ o)|\text{-}m$ data subsets remain, then in the first m data subsets that have been calculated This association rule appears at least:

$$|db(l, o)| \times \min Cycle - (|db(l, o)| - m) = m - |db(l, o)| \times (1 - \min Cycle) \qquad (5)$$

Only then can this association rule become a periodic association rule and an improved CARM2 algorithm.

3 Experiment

3.1 Data

In this paper, the current, active, and reactive power data of a line collected in the SCADA system of a dispatch center from May to September and five months are used as sample data. Each daily active power, reactive power, and current data curve has 96 curves. Sampling point, the sampling interval is 15 min/time. It is known that the sample data used in this article has been trapped and cleaned up, and all are good data, and there is no missing in the middle.

3.2 Association Rule Mining

Because the selected historical data includes five months (150 days) of current and power distribution, the sampling interval is 15 min, and the time attribute is 96 timestamps per day, and the five months are divided into five periods of I-V according to the month, A total of 480 time units, the original database storage unit is shown in Table 1. Set the minimum support degree to 0.05, and perform periodic association rule mining on the data subset of each period to obtain the periodic frequent itemsets at each moment, and then to summarize the current and power distribution rules at that moment.

Table 1. Raw database storage unit

Sampling point on September 1st	Active	Reactive	Current
1	556.13	−32.47	653.93
2	548.02	−26.39	643.38
3	542.94	−26.39	648.07
4	549.03	−26.39	645.72
5	529.75	−31.46	623.46
6	503.36	−31.46	595.33
7	500.32	−30.45	592.99
8	505.39	−32.47	595.33
9	481.04	−35.52	569.55
10	489.15	−32.47	580.1

4   Discussion

4.1   Detection and Identification of Single Bad Data

Sample data of No. 2 is randomly selected, and the active power data of No. 10 sampling point is set as bad data. The active power data is increased by 10% based on the original

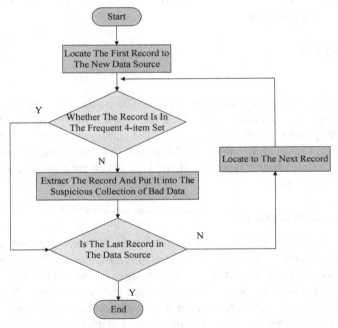

Fig. 2. Bad data detection process

normal data. It is known that the original data of this sampling point are: active power 489.15 MW, reactive power −32.47 MW, current 580.1A. The form after discretization is: T10, P7, Q6, 17. The point in active power increased by 10% to 538.06 MW, and the level changed from P7 to P3. All the modified sample data of No. 2 are discretized and stored as a new data source. The bad data detection process is shown in Fig. 2.

The test results are shown in Table 2. The results show that the data record (T10, P3, Q6, 17) was extracted into the suspicious collection of bad data. The record has a timestamp T10. It is obvious that the record can be identified. There is bad data in the 10th sampling record. The corresponding association rules obtained from the sample data mining in the previous section are as follows: T10 → P7, Q6, 17 (Sup = 0.17, Conf = 0.68), T10 → P7, Q6, 16 (Sup = 0.08, Conf = 0.32). It can be seen that there are only two cases of normal data at the 10th sampling point, so it can be determined that the active power of the record is bad data.

Table 2. Single bad data detection result

Suspect bad data set	Corresponding association rule
T10, P3, Q6, 17	T10 → P7, Q6, 17 (Sup = 0.17, Conf = 0.68)
	T10 ↛ P7, Q6, 16 (Sup = 0.08, Conf = 0.32)

4.2 Detection and Identification of Multiple Bad Data

Sample data No. 18 was randomly selected, and the active power data at the 35th sampling point and the reactive power data at the 65th sampling point were set as bad data. One reduced the active power by 10% and the other reduced the reactive power by 20%. It is known that the original data of the 35th sampling point are: active power 527.72 MW, reactive power −52.77 MW, current 623.46A. After discretization: T35, P4, Q8, 14. Now reduce the active power by 10% to 474.95 MW, the grade becomes P8. The original data of sampling point 65 is known as: active power 553.09 MW, reactive power −33.49 MW, current 655.1A. After discretization: T65, P2, Q6, 12. Reduce the reactive power by 20% to −26.54 MW, and the grade becomes Q3. The test results are shown in Table 3. According to the table, the data records (T35, P8, Q8, 14) and (T65, P2, Q3, 12) were extracted into the suspicious set of bad data, and the 35th Bad data were present in the and 65th sampling records [9, 10].

Table 3. Multiple bad data detection result

Bad data set	Corresponding association rule
T35, P4, Q8, 14	T35 → P4, Q8, 14 (Sup = 0.25, Conf = 1)
T65, P2, Q3, 12	T65 → P2, Q6, 12 (Sup = 0.115, Conf = 0.46)
	T65 → P2, Q7, 12 (Sup = 0.135, Conf = 0.54)

5   Conclusion

In this paper, the association rules in data mining and the detection and identification of bad data in power systems are studied in-depth, and the association rules are introduced into the detection and identification of bad data. Detect and identify models to derive information with practical application value. The information obtained from the historical data of the power system using association rules helps to obtain the measured and predicted amount at each moment so that the decision has a scientific basis.

Acknowledgments. The Academic Funding Project for Outstanding Talents of Universities and Colleges (Professional) in Anhui Province in 2018 (Project Number: gxbjZD57).

References

1. Khan, Z., Razali, R.B., Daud, H.: Bad data detection in power system state estimation based on generalized likelihood ratio test. Int. J. Energy Stat. **04**(4), 1650016 (2016)
2. Deng, S., Zhou, A., Yue, D.: Distributed intrusion detection based on hybrid gene expression programming and cloud computing in cyber physical power system. IET Control Theory Appl. **11**(11), 1822–1829 (2017)
3. Jiang, X., Sheng, G.: Research and application of big data analysis of power equipment condition. High Volt. Eng. **44**(4), 1041–1050 (2018)
4. Zhou, W.: Research and application of data mining algorithm based on fuzzy neural network for nonlinear problems in large data environment. J. Comput. Theor. Nanosci. **13**(7), 4735–4738 (2016)
5. Falkenthal, M., Barzen, J., Breitenbücher, U.: Pattern research in the digital humanities: how data mining techniques support the identification of costume patterns. Comput. Sci. – Res. Dev. **32**(3–4), 1–11 (2016)
6. Fan, S.-K.S., Lin, S.-C., Tsai, P.-F.: Wafer fault detection and key step identification for semiconductor manufacturing using principal component analysis, AdaBoost and decision tree. J. Chin. Inst. Ind. Eng. **33**(3), 151–168 (2016)
7. Fatima, B., Ramzan, H., Asghar, S.: Session identification techniques used in web usage mining: a systematic mapping of scholarly literature. Online Inf. Rev. **40**(7), 1033–1053 (2016)
8. Yu, H., Du, Y., Ma, C.: Survey of compressed sensing technology for signal and data of power system. Yi Qi Yi Biao Xue Bao/Chin. J. Sci. Instr. **38**(8), 1943–1953 (2017)
9. Zhu, Y., Xing, N., Ji, Y.: Fault location algorithm of integrated data network for power system based on interactive active detection. Autom. Electr. Power Syst. **41**(4), 35–40 (2017)
10. Fernandes, E.R., Ghiocel, S.G., Chow, J.H.: Application of a phasor-only state estimator to a large power system using real PMU data. IEEE Trans. Power Syst. **32**(1), 1 (2016)

Community and Wellbeing

An EEMD-IVA Approach to Removing Muscle Artifacts from the Electroencephalogram

Qiang Chen[1](✉)(iD) and Yingying Li[2](iD)

[1] Department of Biomedical Engineering, Hefei University of Technology,
Hefei 230009, China
chenqiang@hfut.edu.cn
[2] School of Electronics and Information Engineering, Anhui Jianzhu University,
Hefei 230601, China

Abstract. Electroencephalogram (EEG) is often contaminated by massive muscle artifacts. In this article, a new approach to removing muscle artifacts is proposed, which is based on ensemble empirical mode decomposition (EEMD) and independent vector analysis (IVA). Each channel of EEG is decomposed into intrinsic mode functions (IMFs) with EEMD to achieve an extended data set that contains more channels than the original data set. The potential artifact components are decomposed by IVA for further isolation. Quantitative results are obtained on semi-simulated and real-life EEG data sets. These results show that the proposed EEMD-IVA approach outperforms independent component analysis (ICA), IVA, and EEMD-ICA.

Keywords: Independent vector analysis · Ensemble empirical mode decomposition · Electroencephalogram

1 Introduction

Among artifacts in EEG, muscle artifacts are particularly difficult to remove because they can overlap all EEG rhythms [1]. ICA, a widely used blind source separation (BSS) algorithm, makes use of higher order statistics (HOS) to decompose EEG data set to independent components (ICs) [2]. The ICs, which resemble muscle artifacts, are discarded during reconstruction, leaving clean data. However, ICA is good at eliminating the artifacts with invariable topographical distribution, while muscle artifacts possess a variable topography since they are often induced by the movement of muscle groups. Most ICs may contain both cerebral and noncerebral components [1]. Due to the broad frequency spectrum, muscle artifacts usually have a lower autocorrelation value than brain activities. Independent vector analysis (IVA) [3] is an extension of ICA to multiple data sets. Independent sources are estimated from each data set, and meanwhile, each source is dependent on corresponding sources from other data set. IVA emphasizes both HOS and second order statistics (SOS) and solves the muscle artifact

© Springer Nature Singapore Pte Ltd. 2020
X. Yuan et al. (Eds.): ICUIA 2020, CCIS 1319, pp. 67–73, 2020.
https://doi.org/10.1007/978-981-33-4601-7_7

removal problem better [4,5]. However, in many real-world applications [6–8], wireless and wearable EEG headsets are often employed. Under this situation, IVA faces challenges in separating muscle artifacts from EEG effectively since the number of cerebral and muscle sources may be more than the number of electrodes. If each channel of raw EEG data is decomposed into several components, the extended data set containing more channels would satisfy the condition of IVA. Inspired by [9], EEMD is chosen since it is a mature tool for nonlinear and nonstationary signal analysis [10]. The proposed EEMD-IVA approach is tested against the ICA, IVA and EEMD-ICA [9] approaches and is shown to produce improved results.

2   Background

2.1   ICA

ICA approach works based on the assumption that muscle artifacts and EEG come from independent sources, and the artifact-like ICs are removed to achieve clean EEG. It should be noted that this study is not to investigate ICA algorithms, therefore the widely used FastICA is adopted in this work [2].

2.2   IVA

IVA can be formulated in a unified joint BSS framework [5] to ensure that the derived components are mutually independent within each data set and have maximal dependence across multiple data sets [3]. The IVA approach uses two data sets. The first one is the raw EEG data and the second one is its time-delayed version. Considering the importance of HOS and SOS, the IVA decomposes the EEG data set into mutually independent and self-correlated sources, which can exploit both the temporal and spatial structure of muscle artifacts. Muscle artifacts are concentrated into several independent sources with the least autocorrelation values, then the clean EEG data can be recovered [4].

2.3   EEMD

EEMD [10] decomposes a one-dimensional signal into a series of IMFs without prior knowledge. Each IMF has its own frequency range. The muscle artifacts usually contain a wider frequency range than neural activities, that is, the muscle artifact related information may be concentrated in the high-frequency IMFs. However, EEMD cannot reject all muscle artifacts since the spectrum of muscle artifacts and EEG may overlap each other.

3   Ensemble Empirical Mode Decomposition and Independent Vector Analysis (EEMD-IVA)

Our proposed EEMD-IVA approach includes the following stages: 1) EEG decomposition with EEMD, 2) selection of IMFs that contain artifacts, 3) identification of artifacts from the selected IMFs with IVA, 4) artifact elimination, and 5) restoration of the "clean" EEG.

For the first stage, each channel of EEG is decomposed with EEMD into a series of IMFs. An extended data set is constructed from all of the IMFs of every channel. The new data set comprises more channels than the original data set to meet the condition of IVA.

For the second stage, regarding the computational complexity of IVA, not all IMFs but the ones containing artifacts will be selected for further processing. Since the muscle artifacts generally behave like white noise and have a broad frequency spectrum, they commonly have lower autocorrelation value. The threshold is empirically set up to 0.95. The IMFs with autocorrelation value less than the threshold are reorganized into a new data set, denoted as $\mathbf{Y}$. For all control approaches, the same method and criteria are used to detect muscle artifact components.

For the third stage, IVA uses two data sets. The first one is $\mathbf{Y}$ and the second one is an instantly delayed version of $\mathbf{Y}$. IVA derives two groups of sources, denoted as $\mathbf{S}_1$ and $\mathbf{S}_2$. The sources in $\mathbf{S}_1$ or $\mathbf{S}_2$ are mutually independent, and the corresponding sources of $\mathbf{S}_1$ and $\mathbf{S}_2$ are dependent while the sources are sorted in descending order by their autocorrelation values. In this case, muscle artifacts should be concentrated into the last independent sources [4].

As for the fourth stage, the artifact sources are automatically identified in the same way as described in the second stage. The sources with autocorrelation value less than the threshold are treated as muscle artifacts and suppressed to zero. The cleaned $\mathbf{S}$ is denoted as $\mathbf{S}_{\text{clean}}$. Finally, the "clean" EEG data set is reconstructed in the reverse procedure of the third stage and the first stage.

4   Data Description

To illustrate the performance of the EEMD-IVA and other comparison approaches quantitatively, semi-simulated EEG data sets are used which are composite of real clean EEG, and real electromyogram (EMG). The details of the data sets are described below.

Pure EEG data were recorded from 20 healthy subjects. The EEG was recorded from an EEG Quick-Cap and a NuAmps amplifier (Compumedics Neuroscan, El Paso, TX). The sampling rate was 500 Hz with a bandpass filter in the range of 1 and 70 Hz on 19 channels. A 10 seconds muscle artifact-free EEG epoch was selected from each subject through visual inspection by an independent neurophysiologist. Thus, there are 20 clean EEG data sets for subsequent data simulation, denoted as $\mathbf{X}_{\text{EEG}}^{(i)}$ ($i = 1, 2, ..., 20$).

It is difficult to acquire pure muscle activity from contaminated EEG, thus pure EMG signals are used in this work. EMG data were collected from 23 healthy volunteers by placing four electrodes on forearms with a Trigno wireless surface EMG system (DELSYS INC., Natick, MA). To simulate realistic situations, we generated not only continuous muscle artifacts but also transient ones by controlling the contraction intervals. To simulate massive muscle artifacts, A 19-channel muscle artifacts data matrix, denoted as $\mathbf{X}_{\text{EMG}}^{(i)}$, can be generated with a random mixing matrix and a 19-channel EMG source matrix [11], which is randomly chosen from the EMG data set.

A contaminated EEG matrix can be obtained according the following equation: $\mathbf{X}^{(i)} = \mathbf{X}^{(i)}_{EEG} + \lambda \cdot \mathbf{X}^{(i)}_{EMG}$. By adjusting the parameter λ, the signal-to-noise ratio (SNR) can be changed from 0.5 to 4.5 by a step size of 0.5.

5   Evaluation Metric

The performance of our proposed approach is evaluated by two measures.

The first measure, relative root-mean-squared error (RRMSE), is defined as

$$RRMSE = \frac{RMS\left(\mathbf{X}_{EEG} - \widetilde{\mathbf{X}}_{EEG}\right)}{RMS\left(\mathbf{X}_{EEG}\right)} \tag{1}$$

Where $\widetilde{\mathbf{X}}_{EEG}$ is the EEG signal after muscle artifact removal, and the root mean squared (RMS) value is defined as

$$RMS\left(\mathbf{X}\right) = \sqrt{\frac{1}{CT}\sum_{c=1}^{C}\sum_{t=1}^{T}\mathbf{X}^2\left(c,t\right)} \tag{2}$$

Where C is the number of EEG channel and T is the number of time samples.

The correlation coefficient (CC) between the raw EEG and its reconstructed counterpart is calculated for each channel. The second evaluation measure is the average CC (ACC) between two data sets which could be obtained by averaging the CC values across multiple channels.

6   Results

6.1   Results of Simulated Data

We compared the muscle artifact removal performance of our proposed method EEMD-IVA with state-of-the-art methods, including ICA, IVA, EEMD-ICA [9], through semi-simulated 19-channel EEG data sets. The comparisons were conducted with data sets of different SNR. At each SNR value, each approach was repeated independently on the 20 mixed data sets. The overall performance in terms of the average RRMSE and ACC is shown in Fig. 1.

As mentioned above, 19 EMG sources were projected to each 19-channel EEG data set, that is, the number of cerebral and non-cerebral sources must be more than the number of electrodes. As shown in Fig. 1, both ICA and IVA performed poorly in separating muscle artifacts from EEG. EEMD-ICA and EEMD-IVA consistently yielded better performance than IVA and ICA in terms of RRMSE at different SNR values in Fig. 1a, and ACC in Fig. 1b. It can be seen that EEMD-IVA outperformed EEMD-ICA when the SNR values are less than 3. This demonstrates that IVA, exploiting both HOS and SOS, can better adapt to the characters of muscle artifacts. EEMD-IVA achieved better muscle artifact source separation in contrast to EEMD-ICA.

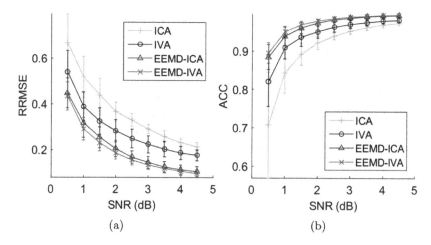

Fig. 1. The performance comparison in terms of (a) RRMSE and (b) ACC at various SNR values.

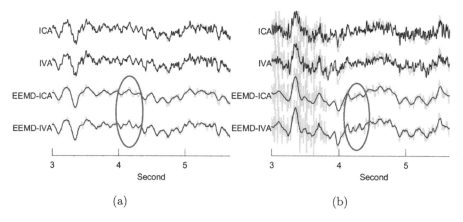

Fig. 2. The cleaned EEG signals (black) of (a) Fz, (b) T5 after using ICA, IVA, EEMD-ICA and EEMD-IVA approach in contrast to the original EEG (green). (Color figure online)

6.2 Results Using Real Data

A real-life EEG data set is also employed to evaluate the performance of the approaches. The ictal EEG data set is a 21-channel 10-second scalp EEG recording from a long-term epilepsy monitoring unit (http://www.esat.kuleuven.be/sista/member/biomedng/biosource.htm). Due to the limited space, we only show the waveforms and denoised results of two representative channels Fz and T5 in Fig. 2. The EEMD-ICA and EEMD-IVA results appeared cleaner than the ICA and IVA results. However, the EEMD-ICA results seem unduly smooth (circled in Fig. 2). Although there is no ground truth, qualitative analysis can be described in the frequency domain.

As shown in Fig. 3, the original power spectrums of EEG extend to the high-frequency band due to severe muscle artifacts. ICA and IVA do not deal with those abnormal components sufficiently since there still exist abnormal high-frequency components, while the EEMD-ICA and EEMD-IVA do well. But the EEMD-ICA heavily restrain all the components over 10 Hz which overlap the spectrum of EEG, while the EEMD-IVA result presents a smooth transition from around 10 Hz to higher frequencies instead. That indicates that EEMD-IVA eliminates muscle artifacts and keeps the underlying EEG activities.

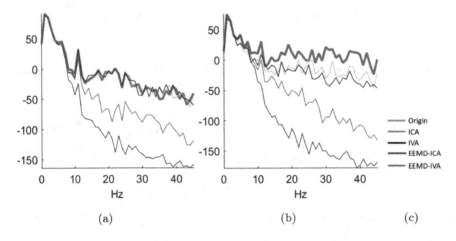

Fig. 3. Power spectrum density comparision of the results of ICA, IVA, EEMD-ICA and EEMD-IVA. (a) Fz. (b) T5.

7   Conclusion

An effective EEMD-IVA approach for muscle artifact removal from the EEG signal is proposed. In the approach, each channel of the contaminated EEG is decomposed separately by EEMD to several IMFs, and the raw EEG data set is extended to more channels to fulfill the condition of the following IVA procedure. IVA exploits both HOS and SOS to isolate muscular artifacts. The performance of EEMD-IVA is compared with the results of other approaches. It can be seen from the semi-simulation and real-life results that the proposed approach yielded the best performance and is capable of removing muscle artifacts with little distortion to the EEG components.

References

1. Nam, H., Yim, T.-G., Han, S.K., Oh, J.-B., Lee, S.K.: Independent component analysis of ictal EEG in medial temporal lobe epilepsy. Epilepsia **43**(2), 160–164 (2002)
2. Albera, L., et al.: ICA-based EEG denoising: a comparative analysis of fifteen methods. Bull. Pol. Acad.: Tech. **60**(3), 407–418 (2012)
3. Adali, T., Anderson, M., Fu, G.-S.: Joint blind source separation with multivariate Gaussian model: algorithms and performance analysis. IEEE Trans. Signal Process. **60**(4), 1672–1683 (2012)
4. Chen, X., Peng, H., Yu, F., Wang, K.: Independent vector analysis applied to remove muscle artifacts in EEG data. IEEE Trans. Instrum. Meas. **66**(7), 1770–1779 (2017)
5. Chen, X., Wang, Z.J., McKeown, M.J.: Joint blind source separation for neurophysiological data analysis. IEEE Signal Process. Mag. **33**(3), 86–107 (2016)
6. Garcia, L., Benitez, C., Macizo, P., Bajo, T.: Using neurofeedback for English phonetics learning: potentiality of MMN. Electron. Lett. **51**(22), 1750–1752 (2015)
7. Govindan, S.M., Duraisamy, P., Yuan, X.: Adaptive wavelet shrinkage for noise robust speaker recognition. Digit. Signal Proc. **33**, 180–190 (2014)
8. Wang, H., Bezerianos, A.: Brain-controlled wheelchair controlled by sustained and brief motor imagery BCIs. Electron. Lett. **53**(17), 1178–1180 (2017)
9. Zeng, K., Chen, D., Ouyang, G., Wang, L., Liu, X., Li, X.: An EEMD-ICA approach to enhancing artifacts rejection for noisy multivariate neural data. IEEE Trans. Neural Syst. Rehabil. Eng. **24**(6), 630–638 (2016)
10. Wu, Z., Huang, N.E.: Ensemble empirical mode decomposition: a noise-assisted data analysis method. Adv. Adapt. Data Anal. **1**(1), 1–41 (2009)
11. Chen, X., et al.: Removing muscle artifacts from eeg data: multichannel or single-channel techniques? IEEE Sens. J. **16**(7), 1986–1997 (2016)

Recommendation Based on Attention Degree and Entropy

Fei Li[1,2], Mengyao Wang[1,2], Caifeng Ye[1,2], Hui Wang[1,2], Chao Wang[1,2], Jun Jiao[1,2], Nengfeng Zou[1,2], Aiwen Chen[1,2], and Lichuan Gu[1,2(✉)]

[1] Anhui Agricultural University, Hefei, China
970241175@qq.com, glc@ahau.edu.cn
[2] Key Laboratory of Agricultural Electronic Commerce
of the Ministry of Agriculture, Hefei, China

Abstract. With the development of the Internet, the problem of information overload becomes more and more serious. The personalized recommendation technology can establish user profiles through the user's behavior and other information, and automatically recommend the items that best match the user's preferences, thus effectively reducing the information overload problem. Although scholars from all over the world have proposed many solutions to the personalized news recommendation system, there are still problems such as computing redundancy, incomplete data, and the inability to make a personalized recommendation to users. Based on the problem, this paper will focus on selected IHUMCF algorithm in computing the user similarity neighbor reason is inadequate to some extent, and the attention degree impact factor is put forward, and then puts forward the L-HUMCF algorithm, and then this paper based on L-HUMCF recommended to improve, as a result, joined the user of information entropy, EL-HUMCF algorithm is proposed, and experimental verification algorithm is effective. Experimental results show that the proposed algorithm is better than other personalized recommendation algorithms.

Keywords: Entropy · Personalized recommendation · Attention

1 Introduction

With the rapid development of information technology, users cannot get a useful message. As an important approach to information filtering, a recommendation system is able to address the present problem of information overload [10,14]. To improve efficiency and quality while processing big data [4,15], many studies have been conducted. In the traditional recommendation models, the association between the user and the project is weak, which results in low recommendation accuracy. The traditional collaborative filtering algorithms use the user-item scoring matrix to construct user interest models with the following problems: (1) the size of the matrix is huge due to a large number of users, which will

© Springer Nature Singapore Pte Ltd. 2020
X. Yuan et al. (Eds.): ICUIA 2020, CCIS 1319, pp. 74–85, 2020.
https://doi.org/10.1007/978-981-33-4601-7_8

make the calculation expensive. (2) incomplete data cause sparse data matrices, making it impossible to personalize recommendations to users [9]; (3) different users have different scoring habits, resulting in differences in scoring; (4) there are insufficient reasons for recommending results to users [3,8].

In practical applications, whether it is a content-based recommendation or collaborative filtering or other recommendation technologies, it is not perfect, and various problems will inevitably be encountered. Therefore, some researchers have begun to try combining the advantages of each method to learn from each other's strengths and improve the recommendation effect, and have proposed a hybrid recommendation algorithm [1,2].

To overcome the problems of computational redundancy, insufficient data volume, and inability to complete personalized recommendations, so as to make the recommendation results more reasonable and achieve the goal of improving the quality of recommendations, this paper proposes a novel recommendation method. On the premise of analyzing the Attention Degree of the project [7], the Attention Degree factor of the project was introduced into the recommendation model, and the user similarity calculation method was optimized. The user's similarity problem with other users was eliminated because the Attention Degree of the project was high. Make the recommendation result more convincing and the recommendation reason more sufficient; at the same time, calculate the user's information entropy based on the history of user rating [6,11]. By using user information entropy when predicting a user's rating of an item, the predicted item's rating will be more reliable, thereby improving the quality of recommendations [12].

The rest of this paper is organized as follows: Sect. 2 provides a background of the research problem. Section 3 presents our proposed method in details. Section 4 discusses our experimental results. Section 5 concludes this paper with a summary.

2   Background

This article uses a hybrid user model. From a combination perspective, hybrid recommendation techniques usually use weighting and layering methods [5]. The mixed user model used in this paper combines population statistical data and item types. First, the user's preference matrix for the item type is obtained by analyzing the user's scoring matrix, and then the user-specific attribute-item type attribute matrix is obtained by combining the user's characteristic attributes. This model is used to calculate the similarity between users. Considering the differences in user ratings and the popularity of the project itself, the rationality factor and hotspot factors of user ratings are introduced. Therefore, when calculating the similarity between users, add these two based on these factors, we obtain the Top-N neighbor user set and then start scoring prediction of the items. In the prediction process, considering the stability of the user itself, the user information entropy is introduced to obtain the final recommended item list.

(1) user-project score and project type record Table 1 presents part of the data from the integrated MovieLens dataset, showing the ratings of 12 movies by six users and the records of the types of the 12 movies. In the MovieLens dataset, there are 19 types of movies, e.g., Action, Adventure, Animation, Children, Comedy, and Western, in table S1, S2, S3, S4, ..., S19. The MovieID in the table records the ID Numbers of the 12 movies. S19 records the types of these 12 movies. If the movie belongs to the type, it is 1; otherwise, it is 0. The column User6 records the specific rating of the 12 movies by 6 users. Here, the rating range is 1 through 5, and the value is 0 for the movie without a rating. As shown in the table, User3, User4, and User5 have no rating for the movie with movie 1.

Table 1. User-project score and project type re-score.

MovieID	S1	S2	S3	S4	S5	...	User1	User2	User3	User4	User5	User6
1	0	0	1	1	1	...	5	4	0	1	0	4
2	1	1	0	0	0	...	3	0	0	0	0	0
3	0	0	0	0	0	...	4	0	0	0	0	0
4	1	0	0	0	1	...	3	0	0	0	0	0
5	0	0	0	0	0	...	3	0	0	0	0	0
6	0	0	0	0	0	...	0	0	0	0	0	0
7	0	0	0	0	0	...	4	0	0	0	0	2
8	0	0	0	1	1	...	1	0	0	0	0	4
9	0	0	0	0	0	...	5	0	0	0	0	4
10	0	0	0	0	0	...	0	2	0	0	0	0
11	0	0	0	0	0	...	2	0	0	4	0	0
12	0	0	0	0	0	...	0	0	0	0	0	4

(2) users' interest in the movie genre Regarding a user's interest in the movie, types determine the user's preference for movie types. In this article, the following terms are used to calculate the final user's interest in movie types:

Definition 1: user-item set, $T_i = \{j | R_{ij} > 1\}$, represents the set of user i for the rated item.

Definition 2: User-effective item set, $E_i = \{j | R_{ij} > V/2\}$, where V represents the maximum possible rating of user i.

Definition 3: User-item type effective rating set, $R(i, a) = \{R_{ij} | R_{ij} > V/2\}$, which represents user i's effective set of item (movie) ratings of type a. Table 2 summarizes the total number of projects overrated by the 6 users and total score of the over-rated items by users.

Table 2. Use ratings.

UserID	$|T_i|$	$TR(i)$
1	135	497
2	40	152
3	28	84
4	14	61
5	59	188
6	61	213

Definition 4: The relative attribute (item type) score, $RAR(i,a) = \frac{AR(i,a)}{TR(i)}$, givesuser i's total effective score for item of type a among user i's total scores.

Definition 5: The relative attribute (item type) frequency, $RAF(i,a) = \frac{|Aa|}{|T_i|}$, which gives user i's effective rating times for items of type a accounted for the number of times that user i has rated the items.

Definition 6: The revised relative attribute (item type) frequency $MRAF(i,a)$ $= \frac{\sum_{j \in A_a} W_r}{|T_i|}$, where $W_r = (R_{ij} - V/2 + 1)(V/2 + 1)$ is the wright of user i for item j.

Definition 7: Type (attribute) interest measure, $AIM(i,a) = \frac{RAR(i,a)MRAF(i,a)}{RAR(i,a)+MRAF(i,a)}$. It indicates the degree of interest of user i in an item of type a. Table 3 shows the degree of interest of these 19 types of 6 users using different calculation methods.

Definition 8: User score reasonable factor, $\delta_i = \frac{\sqrt{\sum_{j \in T_i} (R_{ij} - \overline{(R)}_i)^2}}{\sqrt{|T_i|}}$, where $\overline{(R)}_i)$ is the average score of the user i on rating items.

Definition 9: Hotspot impact factor, $\mu_j = \frac{1}{\log |N_j|}$, where $|N_j|$ denotes the number of users who rated item j over a period of time.

Definition 10: User information entropy, $H(k) = -p_k \log p_k$ and $p_k = \frac{N_k}{N}$, where N_k and N denotes the counts of items rated by user k and the total items, respectively.

Table 3. User interest

	UserID	S1	S2	S3	S4	S5		S19
RAR	1	0.16	0.06	0.05	0.04	0.31	...	0.01
	2	0.11	0.03	0.03	0.05	0.21	...	0
	3	0.17	0.12	0	0	0.17	...	0
	4	0.33	0.11	0	0	0.16	...	0
	5	0.44	0.3	0.12	0.09	0.46	...	0
	6	0.18	0.1	0.06	0.11	0.31	...	0.03
RAF	1	0.14	0.05	0.04	0.04	0.28	...	0.01
	2	0.1	0.03	0.03	0.05	0.2	...	0
	3	0.14	0.11	0	0	0.11	...	0
	4	0.36	0.14	0	0	0.14	...	0
	5	0.36	0.24	0.08	0.08	0.37	...	0
	6	0.16	0.08	0.05	0.1	0.28	...	0.03
MRAF	1	0.3	0.11	0.09	0.08	0.57	...	0.01
	2	0.21	0.05	0.05	0.1	0.4	...	0
	3	0.26	0.19	0	0	0.24	...	0
	4	0.71	0.26	0	0	0.34	...	0
	5	0.71	0.47	0.18	0.14	0.74	...	0
	6	0.31	0.17	0.1	0.19	0.54	...	0.06
AIM	1	0.1	0.04	0.03	0.03	0.2	...	0.01
	2	0.07	0.02	0.02	0.03	0.14	...	0
	3	0.1	0.07	0	0	0.1	...	0
	4	0.23	0.08	0	0	0.11	...	0
	5	0.27	0.18	0.07	0.05	0.28	...	0
	6	0.11	0.06	0.04	0.07	0.2	...	0.02

3   Method

3.1   User Interest Model

The technology of Collaborative Filtering can be divided into two categories, namely project-based and user-based collaborative filtering. Traditional collaborative filtering algorithms only rely on user-item scoring data to build user models. Although this shows users' interest measure to some extent, it does not take into account users' characteristics such as age, gender, occupation, etc. To some extent, these attributes of the user can reflect the relationship between the project and the user. When user scoring data are sparse, just use the traditional collaborative filtering algorithm effect often is not ideal. Xu [12] extended the collaborative filtering algorithm and used the user-scoring matrix to calculate the user's interest measure in the project type, AIM, constant quantified for the user's characteristics, to build the user interest model.

The steps to build the user interest model are as follows:

1. the user-project type interest measure is shown by the user-project score and project type;
2. the user characteristic attribute value is quantified by the user information table;
3. the user model is obtained by combining the user characteristic attribute value and user-item type interest measure.

As shown in Table 4, is the user model table built, where A1, A2, ..., An is the user characteristic property, S1, S2, ..., Sm is the project type;

Table 4. User interest model.

UserID	A1	A2	...	An	S1	S2	...	Sm
1	A11	A12	...	A1n	S11	S12	...	S1m
2	A21	A22	...	A2n	S21	S22	...	S2m
3	A31	A32	...	A3n	S31	S32	...	S3m
4	A41	A42	...	A4n	S41	S42	...	S4m
...	...	...	...	...	...	...	...	...
i	Ai1	Ai2		Ain	Si1	Si2	...	Sim
...	...	...	...	...	...	...	...	...

After building the user interest model based on the document, we join user scoring reasonable factor to calculate the similarity between users, although this method is compared with the traditional collaborative filtering algorithm, is a great improvement on the recommendation results, but when calculating the similarity between user get the result of the reason is not very enough, so when calculating the similarity between users, this paper puts forward the similarity algorithm based on the hot spot (L-HUMCF), the algorithm of user interest model [12] introduces the user scoring reasonable factor and adds the project's popular factor.

3.2   Prediction Score

After obtaining the top-N neighbor set of user i, select some items from the neighbor set scoring items to recommend to user i, and the selection of recommended items ensure that these items are preferred by the neighbor set and these items are the items that the target user i has not performed (that is, the items that the target user i has not scored). The score is computed as follows:

$$P'(i,j) = \bar{R}_i + \frac{\sum_{k \in U} \text{sim}(i,k)(R_{kj} - \bar{R}_k)}{\sum_{k \in U} \text{sim}(i,k)} \tag{1}$$

where $\bar{R}_i$ denotes the average score of the target user on all the scoring items, U denotes the neighbor set of the target user, k is the neighbor of the target user. $\text{sim}(i, k)$ computes the similarity between users i and k, R_{kj} represents the true score of user k on item j, $\bar{R}_k$ represents the average score of user k on all the scored items.

The user's scoring of the project is subjective, but the user's information entropy is objective. It is also a reference for whether the user's rating of a certain item is reliable and meaningful. When the user performs project prediction and scoring, he introduces the user's information entropy and proposes a recommendation algorithm based on attention degree and entropy (EL-HUMCF).

$$P(i, j) = \bar{R}_i + \frac{\sum_{k \in U} \text{sim}(i, k)(R_{kj} - \bar{R}_k)H(k)}{\sum_{k \in U} \text{sim}(i,k)} \qquad (2)$$

The predicted scores $P'(i, j)$ and $P(i, j)$ of the target user i for item j can be calculated, and then the predicted scores are sorted from large to small, and the top n (top-n) recommended target users i are selected.

3.3 L-HUMCF Algorithm

Among the collaborative filtering algorithms, the more common algorithms for calculating similarity include cosine similarity, modified cosine similarity, Euclidean distance similarity, and Pearson correlation similarity. Related experiments have shown that the Pearson correlation similarity algorithm performs better than the other three algorithms [13], because the average value of user scoring is used in the calculation of Pearson correlation similarity so that the problem of user scoring bias is alleviated to some extent; this paper uses the L-HUMCF algorithm to calculate the similarity between users. This algorithm is based on the calculation of Pearson's correlation similarity algorithm. The similarity of the L-HUMCF algorithm is computed as follows:

$$\text{sim}(i, j) = \frac{1}{2}\left(1 + \sum_{m \in R} \mu_m\right) \frac{\sum_{k=1}^{n} |\dot{S}| + \sum_{k=n+1}^{n+p} |\delta_i \delta_j \dot{S}|}{(\sum_{k=1}^{n} \dot{S}^2 \sum_{k=n+1}^{n+p} \delta_i \delta_j \dot{S}^2)^{\frac{1}{2}}} \qquad (3)$$

where

$$\dot{S} = (S_{ik} - \bar{S}_i)(S_{jk} - \bar{S}_j)$$

and μ_m represents the hotspot impact factor of item m, and R represents the set of effective scoring items jointly performed by user i and user j, $\sum_{m \in R} \mu_m$ represents one of the hotspot impact factors of effective scoring items jointly by user i and user j. The similarity is calculated in descending order, and the first N (most similar) users are selected as the neighbor set of the target a and user i.

The recommendation process mainly uses the user scoring data and the user's attribute data to obtain a user-type interest degree matrix and a user-attribute feature matrix and then constructs users from these matrices. Model, and then use the L-HUMCF algorithm to calculate the similarity between users according to the user interest model. When calculating the similarity between users, the L-HUMCF algorithm introduces the attention degree factor of the project to make the target user's user neighbor set more accurate and improve Recommended results. The L-HUMCF algorithm method is presented in Algorithm 1.

Algorithm 1. L-HUMCF algorithm.

1: **Input**: user-item scoring data, user-attribute feature data, item-type feature data
2: **Output**: recommendation set
3: The user-item-item type table is obtained from the input user-item scoring data and item-type characteristic data, and the user-item-item type table is used to calculate the user's interest measure AIM from the item type.
4: User-attribute feature data and user-item scoring data are used to calculate the user's own attribute to the item preference value Attr based on population statistical data.
5: Calculate the user scoring a reasonable factor δ from the user-item scoring data.
6: Calculate the attention degree impact factor μ from the user-item scoring data.
7: Construct a user hybrid model.
8: The user model constructed in (5), adding the user scoring reasonable factor δ and attention degree impact factor μ in (3) and (4) to improve the Pearson algorithm, that is, the average absolute error to calculate the similarity between the target user and other users $\text{sim}(i, j)$.
9: Sort the similarity from large to small, and select the top N (Top-N) users as the neighbor set of the target users.
10: From the user-item scoring data and the user scoring reasonable factor δ, select the item set U that the target user needs to predict.
11: predict the target user's score $P'(i, j)$ on the items in the item set according to the scoring formula.
12: Sort the scores $P'(i, j)$ from large to small, and select the top n (Top-n) items as the recommendation set for the target user.

The L-HUMCF algorithm is mainly based on the IHUMCF model. For the problem of the insufficient reason for selecting the neighbor set, that is, calculating the similarity between users, a hotspot impact factor is proposed to obtain more accurate users Neighbor set, so as to achieve a more accurate recommendation effect for users.

3.4   Recommendation Algorithm Based on Heat and Entropy

Compared with the IHUMCF algorithm and the CF algorithm, the L-HUMCF algorithm has significantly improved the recommendation effect when the appropriate neighbor set is used. The impact does not take into account the objectivity of the user. The user's information entropy is objective and a reference for whether the user's scoring of a certain item is reliable. We extend the L-HUMCF algorithm and propose a recommendation algorithm based on attention degree and entropy (EL-HUMCF) using the user's information entropy for prediction and scoring.

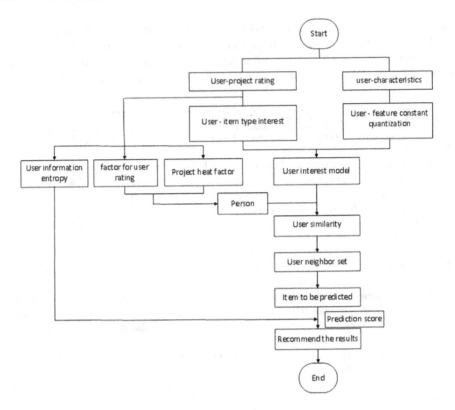

Fig. 1. The flowchart of the EL-HUMCF algorithm.

When predicting the user's scoring of an item, the user's information entropy is introduced to make the predicted score more accurate and the recommendation results better. The recommended working flowchart of the EL-HUMCF algorithm is shown in Fig. 1.

4   Experiments

4.1   Data and Settings

The experiment uses a relatively small 100 K public dataset of MovieLens. This dataset records the relevant information of 943 users, the relevant information of 1682 movies, and the 1, 942 users of these 1, 682 10, 000 pieces of rating information for movies, where the rating value is 1 through 5 with 5 being the most liked. The dataset is divided into two parts, the training set, and the test set, with 80% of the data for training and the remaining 20% for testing. In this article, we use MAE, Precision, Recall, and F1 measure as the evaluation metrics.

4.2   Result Analysis and Discussion

We compared our method with IHUMCF and CF. The results using MAE, Precision, Recall, and F1 are shown in Fig. 2. It can be seen that the MAE value of the L-HUMCF algorithm is smaller than that of IHUMCF and CF after the introduction of hotspot factors. And it is easy to see that the effect is best when the number of neighbor sets is between 20 and 30.

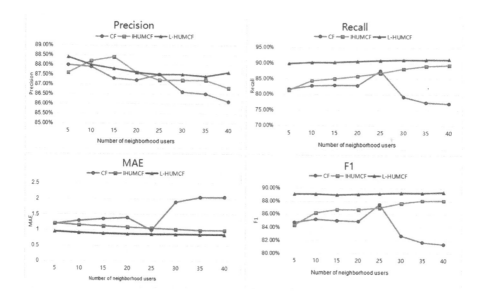

Fig. 2. A comparison with IHUMCF and CF methods.

It can be seen that when the neighbor set is less than 20 and greater than 10, the accuracy of L-HUMCF is not as good as IHUMCF, but when the appropriate neighbor set is selected, the accuracy of L-HUMCF is higher than that of IHUMCF and CF. Better results. It can be seen that the Recall value of the L-HUMCF algorithm is higher than that of IHUMCF and CF, which indicates that the recommendation effect of the L-HUMCF algorithm is better. High and smooth. It can be seen that the F1 value of the L-HUMCF algorithm is higher than that of IHUMCF and CF, which indicates that the L-HUMCF algorithm has a better recommendation effect. It is also easy to see from Fig. 2 that the values of F1 are relatively High and smooth.

We also compared our method with L-HUMCF. The results are illustrated in Fig. 3. The experimental results show that the EL-HUMCF algorithm has a more accurate recommendation effect than the L-HUMCF algorithm. It can be seen that the MA-value of the EL-HUMCF algorithm is smaller than that of the L-HUMCF algorithm, which indicates that the EL-HUMCF algorithm reduces the error between the actual score and the predicted score of the project,

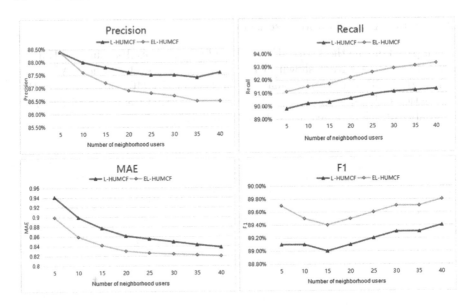

Fig. 3. A comparison between L-HUMCF and EL-HUMCF.

and improves the recommendation result to a certain extent. Although the EL-HUMCF algorithm has a lower Precision value than the L-HUMCF algorithm, both the Recall value and the F1 value are higher, indicating that the recommended effect of the EL-HUMCF algorithm is better than the L-HUMCF algorithm.

5   Conclusion

This article first introduces the advantages of the IHUMCF algorithm compared to the traditional collaborative filtering algorithm and then proposes the remaining shortcomings in the IHUMCF algorithm. In view of the shortcomings of the IHUMCF algorithm in calculating user similarity and predicting user ratings on items, this paper proposes the L-HUMCF algorithm. The innovation of this algorithm is that in the calculation of similarity to select the neighbor set, the selected neighbor set is not sufficient for a certain reason, so this article proposes a hotspot impact factor for this problem; Through experimental verification and comparative analysis of the experimental results from multiple aspects, it is found that the L-HUMCF algorithm has a significant improvement in the recommendation effect compared with other algorithms; then, in this paper, in order to improve the recommendation results, the EL-HUMCF algorithm is proposed. When the user predicts the project score, in order to make the prediction more accurate, the user's information entropy is added; through experimental verification again, the experimental results are compared and analyzed from various aspects, and the EL-HUMCF algorithm is compared with the L-HUMCF algorithm has improved.

Acknowledgements. This work is partially supported by the Natural Science Foundation of China under Grant (31771679, 31671589), the Anhui Foundation for Science and Technology Major Project, China, under Grants 18030901034, 201904e01020006, 201903a06020009, the Key Laboratory of Agricultural Electronic, Commerce, Ministry of Agriculture of China under Grant AEC2018003, AEC2018006, the 2019 Anhui University collaborative innovation project sn: GXXT-2019-013, the Hefei Major Research Project of Key Technology J2018G14.

References

1. Billsus, D., Pazzani, M.J.: User modeling for adaptive news access. User Model. User-Adap. Inter. **10**(2), 147–180 (2000)
2. Burke, R.: Hybrid recommender systems: survey and experiments. User Model. User-Adapt. Interact. **12**(4), 331–370 (2002)
3. Desyaputri, D.M., Erwin, A., Galinium, M., Nugrahadi, D.: News recommendation in Indonesian language based on user click behavior (2013)
4. Gu, L., Han, Y., Wang, C., Chen, W., Jiao, J., Yuan, X.: Module overlapping structure detection in PPI using an improved link similarity-based Markov clustering algorithm. Neural Comput. Appl. **31**(5), 1481–1490 (2018). https://doi.org/10.1007/s00521-018-3508-z
5. Kim, B.M., Qing, L., Park, S., Kim, S., Kim, J.: A new Approach for combining content-based and collaborative filters. J. Intell. Inf. Syst. **27**(1), 79–91 (2006)
6. Li, C., Zhu, Z., Gao, X.: Collaborative filtering recommendation algorithm based on neighbor decision. Comput. Eng. **36**(13), 34–36 (2010)
7. Peng, F., Qian, X.: Personalized news recommendation system based on user attention. Appl. Res. Comput. **29**(03), 1005–1007 (2012)
8. Qiao, D.: Research and implementation of ontology-based News Recommendation Method. Kunming University of Science and Technology (2014)
9. Rao, H., et al.: Feature selection based on artificial bee colony and gradient boosting decision tree. Appl. Soft Comput. J. **74**(1), 634–642 (2019)
10. Xia, Y., Wang, X., Gu, L., Gao, Q., Jiao, J., Wang, C.: A collective entity linking algorithm with parallel computing on large scale knowledge base. Supercomputing **76**, 948–963 (2020)
11. Xiong, L.: Research and design of personalized news recommendation system. Chongqing University of Technology (2017)
12. Xu, Q.: Research and implementation of personalized news recommendation system based on improved collaborative filtering algorithm. Chongqing University (2017)
13. Yang, J., Gao, L.: Dynamic mining algorithm of customer preferences. Inf. Control (01), 125–128 (2007)
14. Yuan, X., Xie, L., Abouelenien, M.: A regularized ensemble framework of deep learning for cancer detection from multiclass, imbalanced training data. Pattern Recognit. **77**, 160–172 (2018)
15. Yuan, X., Buckles, B.P., Yuan, Z., Zhang, J.: Mining negative association rules. In: Proceedings ISCC 2002 Seventh International Symposium on Computers and Communications, pp. 623–628 (2002)

Point Set Registration of Large Deformation Using Auxiliary Landmarks

Amar Maharjan$^{(\boxtimes)}$ and Xiaohui Yuan

University of North Texas, Denton, TX 76207, USA
AmarMaharjan@my.unt.edu, xiaohui.yuan@unt.edu

Abstract. We present a probabilistic non-rigid point set registration method to deal with large and uneven deformations. The registration is treated as a density estimation problem. The main ideas of our method are to add constraints to enforce landmark correspondences and preserving local neighborhood structure. Landmarks represent the salient points in point sets, which can be computed using feature descriptors such as scale-invariant feature transform. By enforcing landmark correspondences, we preserve the overall global shape of the point set with significant deformations. In addition, we incorporate constraints to preserve local neighborhood structure by leveraging Stochastic Neighbor Embedding (SNE), which penalizes incoherent transformation within a neighborhood. We evaluate our method with both 2D and 3D datasets and show that our method outperforms the state-of-the-art methods in a large degree of deformations. In particular, quantitative results show our method is 49% better than the second best result (from the state-of-the-art methods). Finally, we demonstrate the importance of using correct landmark correspondences in registration by showing good registration results in large and uneven deformations point sets.

Keywords: Non-rigid registration · Landmark · Large deformation · Local neighborhood structure

1 Introduction

Point set registration identifies correspondences between two sets of points, from which a transformation function is derived to achieve alignment. It is a fundamental task in many computer vision applications such as range image-based human pose tracking and three-dimensional object reconstruction. In such applications, however, large deformations make point set registration a challenging task [8].

To address non-rigid deformation, Coherent Point Drift (CPD) was proposed to regulate the transformations of the points within a neighborhood [12]. This method assumes that the transformation for points that are in close vicinity is highly similar. Ge et al. [4] extended the CPD method by adding constraints to maintain local neighborhood structure. Ma et al. [11] used shape descriptors

© Springer Nature Singapore Pte Ltd. 2020
X. Yuan et al. (Eds.): ICUIA 2020, CCIS 1319, pp. 86–98, 2020.
https://doi.org/10.1007/978-981-33-4601-7_9

to ensure the local structure of point subsets. Despite the success demonstrated by the aforementioned methods, obtaining accurate correspondences between point sets and maintaining the shape and structure in the case of large and uneven deformation is still an open challenge in non-rigid point set registration. In the applications of tracking humans in actions, for example, deformation from movements of limbs is common. As a consequence, the body shape appears dramatically differently; whereas the local structure of a rigid body part remains unchanged (as shown in Fig. 1(a) and (b)). Such disparity makes the coherency assumption incomplete; registration results of CPD, LSP, and our method are shown in Fig. 1(c), (d), and (e), respectively.

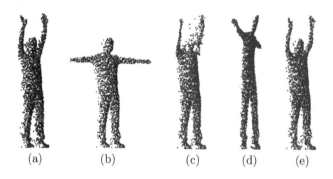

(a)   (b)   (c)   (d)   (e)

Fig. 1. Registration of human body with large and uneven deformation.

In this paper, we present a non-rigid point set registration method by incorporating constraints of corresponding landmarks to register point sets that represent large deformation. Landmarks represent the salient points in point sets, which can be identified using methods such as scale-invariant feature transform [10]. The correspondence between landmarks enables us to regulate the optimization process. In addition, by leveraging Stochastic Neighbor Embedding (SNE) [6], we aim to penalize incoherent transformation within a neighborhood and hence preserve the local structure.

The rest of this paper is organized as follows: Sect. 2 reviews the related methods for non-rigid point set registration. Section 3 presents our proposed method for non-rigid point set registration. Section 4 discusses our experimental results and comparisons with state-of-the-art methods. Section 5 concludes this paper with a summary.

2   Related Work

To register point sets, Chui et al. [3] proposed a general framework based on robust point matching (RPM) [5]. In this framework, the authors used thin-plate spline (TPS) as a non-rigid spatial mapping, which performs a soft assignment, instead of binary assignment, for point correspondence and employs deterministic annealing to favor global rigid transformations at the early stage of the optimization and local, non-rigid transformations in a later stage using thin-plate-splines. Tin et al. [16] proposed Kernel Correlation (KC) by extending the correlation technique to point set registration. This method also used soft correspondence assignment and the correlation of the two kernel density estimates is the main part of the cost function. A similar strategy was used by Jain et al. [7], in which the point sets are modeled as Gaussian mixtures, and the registration problem is formulated as minimizing the L2 distance between the two Gaussian mixtures.

One popular method for non-rigid registration is a probabilistic approach where the registration is mapped into density estimation based on GMM. In this approach, GMM centroids are represented by one point set (template or model) and other point set represents the input data. The template points are transformed with prior constraints so that the point sets are aligned as much as possible by maximum likelihood fashion. Coherent Point Drift (CPD) is a robust probabilistic point set registration method based on GMM and the key idea is moving points coherently to maintain the topological structure of the point set [12]. Extensions to the CPD have been proposed to preserve point set structure and the intrinsic geometry of the data [4,11,13,17]. Panaganti et al. [13] proposed to use proximity weight between the points using shape context [1] to calculate correspondences and graph-Laplacian regularization term to preserve the intrinsic geometry of the point set. Ge et al. [4] extended the CPD method, called Local Structure Preservation (LSP), to handle complex non-rigid and articulated deformations by adding two regularization terms Local Linear Embedding (LLE) [14] and Laplacian coordinate (LC) to maintain the local neighborhood relationship and scale (size) respectively. Instead of using equal membership probabilities to the mixture model such as that in [4,12], recent methods have assigned membership probabilities to the mixture model and show robustness to noises, outliers, occlusions [11,17]. The idea is to match similar local neighborhood structures between point sets with the help of feature descriptors [1,9,15]. However, these methods are vulnerable to a local minimum in case of large and uneven deformations. Also, the assumption of similar local structure in both point sets is problematic as distortions and stretches are always present in real data.

3   Method

Our method takes two sets of points as inputs and corresponding landmarks are used as a strong constraint. The optimization process leverages the Gaussian mixture model that enforces both local coherence using SNE and global constraint through landmarks. Let X and Y denote two sets of points in a D dimensional space. We have $X = \{\mathbf{x}_1, \mathbf{x}_2, \ldots, \mathbf{x}_N\}$ and $Y = \{\mathbf{y}_1, \mathbf{y}_2, \ldots, \mathbf{y}_M\}$, where M and N denote the number of points of the respective set. Assume noise follows the uniform distribution, i.e., $p_n^* = \frac{1}{N}$, we have the probability density function of point $\mathbf{x}_n$ given Y as follows:

$$p(\mathbf{x}_n) = \sum_{m=1}^{M} p(\mathbf{x}_n|\mathbf{y}_m)p(\mathbf{y}_m) + p_n^* \tag{1}$$

where $p(\mathbf{y}_m) = \frac{1}{M}$. Given a set of landmarks $\dot{X} \in X$ and $\dot{Y} \in Y$, we have the correspondence between each pair of points $\dot{x}_j \leftrightarrow \dot{y}_j$, where $\dot{x}_j \in \dot{X}$ and $\dot{y}_j \in \dot{Y}$. Hence, our optimal transformation function must minimize the total distance between all pairs of the corresponding $\dot{x}_j$ and $\dot{y}_j$ as follows:

$$E_G = \sum_j \|\dot{x}_j - \dot{y}_j\|^2. \tag{2}$$

To avoid possible singularity in the matrix inverting operation, we revise Eq. (2) as follows:

$$E_G = \sum_{m,n}^{M,N} \mathbf{A}_{m,n}\|\mathbf{x}_n - \tau(\mathbf{y}_m)\|^2 \tag{3}$$

where $\mathbf{A}_{M \times N}$ is landmark coefficient matrix, $\mathbf{A}_{m,n} = 1$ if $(\mathbf{x}_n, \mathbf{y}_m) \in L$; otherwise 0, and L is a set containing all pairs of landmark correspondences.

To keep points within a neighborhood relatively close after transformation and points far apart remain distant, Stochastic Neighbor Embedding (SNE) [6] is employed. Let r_{ij} be the probability that two points $\mathbf{y}_i$ and $\mathbf{y}_j$ are neighbors before transformation and s_{ij} be the probability that these two points become neighbors after transformation τ. A constraint on local structure is represented as the minimization of cost function which is the sum of Kullback-Leibler (KL) divergences between r_{ij} and s_{ij} distributions over neighbors of each point [6]:

$$E_L = \sum_{ij} r_{ij} \log \frac{r_{ij}}{s_{ij}} = \sum_i KL\left(\mathbf{R}_i \| \mathbf{S}_i\right), \tag{4}$$

where

$$r_{ij} = \frac{\exp(-\beta_2\|\mathbf{y}_i - \mathbf{y}_j\|^2)}{\sum_{k \neq i} \exp(-\beta_2\|\mathbf{y}_i - \mathbf{y}_k\|^2)},$$

and

$$s_{ij} = \frac{\exp(-\|\tau(\mathbf{y}_i) - \tau(\mathbf{y}_j)\|^2)}{\sum_{k \neq i} \exp(-\|\tau(\mathbf{y}_i) - \tau(\mathbf{y}_k)\|^2)}.$$

Following the GMM framework in [12], the objective function of our method integrates local and global constraints as follows:

$$Q(\boldsymbol{\theta}, \sigma^2) = \frac{1}{2\sigma^2} \sum_{n,m=1}^{N,M} p^{i-1}(\mathbf{y}_m|\mathbf{x}_n)\|\mathbf{x}_n - \tau(\mathbf{y}_m)\|^2 + \frac{N_P D}{2} \ln \sigma^2 \tag{5}$$

$$+ \frac{\lambda_1}{2} tr(\mathbf{W}^T \mathbf{G} \mathbf{W}) + \frac{\lambda_2}{2} E_L + \frac{\lambda_3}{2} E_G$$

where

$$p^{(i-1)}(\mathbf{y}_m|\mathbf{x}_n) = \frac{\exp^{(-\frac{1}{2}\|\frac{\mathbf{x}_n - \tau(\mathbf{y}_m)}{\sigma_{(i-1)}}\|^2)}}{\sum_{k=1}^{M}\exp(-\frac{1}{2}\|\frac{\mathbf{x}_n - \tau(\mathbf{y}_k)}{\sigma_{(i-1)}}\|^2) + C}, \tag{6}$$

where $C = \gamma(2\pi\sigma_{(i-1)}^2)^{D/2}M/((1-\gamma)N)$, τ is a transformation function that maps a point $\mathbf{y}_m$ in Y to a new spatial location such that it coincides with a point $\mathbf{x}_n$ in X, i.e., $\mathbf{x}_n = \tau(\mathbf{y}_m)$, $\gamma \in [0,1]$ denotes the rate of noise and outlier in the observed dataset X, $tr(\cdot)$ refers to the trace of a matrix, and $N_P = \sum_{n,m=1}^{N,M} p^{(i-1)}(\mathbf{z}_n = m|\mathbf{x}_n) \leq N$. We use transformation model which moves neighborhood points coherently and helps in maintaining topological structure of the point set [12]. $\mathbf{G}_{M \times M}$ is a kernel matrix with elements $g_{ij} = G(\mathbf{y}_i, \mathbf{y}_j) = \exp(-\frac{1}{2}\|\frac{\mathbf{y}_i - \mathbf{y}_j}{\beta}\|^2)\|$, $\mathbf{W}_{M \times D} = (\mathbf{w}_1, \ldots, \mathbf{w}_M)^T$ is a coefficients matrix, λ_1, λ_2, and λ_3 are regularization weights for motion coherence, local structure, and correspondence constraints, respectively.

We obtain the coefficient matrix $\mathbf{W}$ by taking derivative of Eq. (5) with respect to $\mathbf{W}$ and set it equal to zero

$$(diag(\mathbf{P1})\mathbf{G} + \sigma^2\lambda_1\mathbf{I} + \sigma^2\lambda_2\mathbf{JG} + \sigma^2\lambda_3 diag(\mathbf{A1})\mathbf{G})\mathbf{W} = \tag{7}$$
$$(\mathbf{PX} - diag(\mathbf{P1})\mathbf{Y} - \sigma^2\lambda_2\mathbf{JY} - \sigma^2\lambda_3 diag(\mathbf{A1})\mathbf{Y} + \sigma^2\lambda_3\mathbf{AX})$$

where $\mathbf{J} = (diag(\mathbf{R1}) - 2\mathbf{R} + diag(\mathbf{1}^T\mathbf{R}))$, $\mathbf{1}$ refers to column vector of all ones, $\mathbf{I}$ refers to identity matrix, and $diag(\mathbf{v})$ refers to the diagonal matrix created from the vector $\mathbf{v}$.

We define the transformation function, τ, as the initial position, $\mathbf{y}_m$, plus a displacement function $\mathbf{f}(\mathbf{y}_m)$, $\tau(\mathbf{y}_m) = \mathbf{y}_m + \mathbf{f}(\mathbf{y}_m)$. We adopt the following transformation function [12]:

$$\mathbf{T} = \tau(\mathbf{Y}, \mathbf{W}) = \mathbf{Y} + \mathbf{GW} \tag{8}$$

Similarly, we obtain σ^2 by taking derivative of Eq. (5) with respect to σ^2 and set to zero

$$\sigma^2 = \frac{1}{N_P D}(tr(\mathbf{X}^T diag(\mathbf{P}^T\mathbf{1})) - 2tr(\mathbf{PX}^T\mathbf{T}) + tr(\mathbf{T}^T diag(\mathbf{P1})\mathbf{T})) \tag{9}$$

where $N_P = \mathbf{1}^T\mathbf{P1}$.

4   Results and Discussion

4.1   Experimental Data and Settings

In our experiments, we use publicly available 2D dataset [2] and 3D human pose dataset captured by Microsoft Kinect II [18]. The 2D dataset contains point sets of tools such as scissors, pliers, knives. Each tool has five different shapes. In our 2D tools data experiments, we set the parameters of our method as follows: $\lambda_1 = 8.0$, $\lambda_2 = 1.0$, $\lambda_3 = 120.0$, $\beta_1 = 1.0$, $\beta_2 = 10.0$, and maximum iterations of EM is 50. The 3D human body dataset includes four human subjects with different body shapes and sizes. Each point set consists of more than 12 thousands points. In our experiments on this dataset, the parameters of our proposed method are as follows: $\lambda_1 = 2.0$, $\lambda_2 = 1.0$, $\lambda_3 = 150.0$, $\beta_1 = 1.0$, $\beta_2 = 15.0$, and maximum iterations of EM is 50.

We compute the registration error with a normalized Euclidean distance between points of the input point set and corresponding points of the target point set as follows:

$$\varepsilon = \frac{1}{N} \sum_{i,j} \|\mathbf{x}_i - \mathbf{y}_j\|_2 \tag{10}$$

where $\mathbf{x}_i \in \mathbf{X}$ and $\mathbf{y}_j \in \mathbf{Y}$ is the estimated corresponding point of $\mathbf{x}_i$ after registration, and N is the number of points in point set $\mathbf{X}$. We evaluate our method in the following three aspects: 1) different degrees of deformation, 2) the different number of landmarks, and 3) the impact of incorrect correspondences between landmarks.

4.2   Degree of Deformation

Figure 2 shows a qualitative registration results of both Fig. 2(a) 2D tools and Fig. 2(b) 3D human body datasets of three degrees of deformation (small, medium, and large) in the top, middle, and bottom rows, respectively. In this figure, the first two columns are input and template point sets while the rest of the three columns are the registration results of our method, CPD [12], and LSP [4]. For the 2D tools dataset, both our method and LSP have good registration results than CPD in a small degree of deformation. In the medium degree of deformation, CPD fails to maintain structure in the upper part of the tool. Our method and LSP exhibit better results than CPD in this case but the structure of the tip of the tool (upper part) from our method is better than LSP. Finally, in the large degree of deformation, our method shows good results than the other two methods where both CPD and LSP completely fail to maintain the shape of the tool. For the 3D human body dataset, our method and CPD generate accurate results than LSP in a small degree of deformation. In the medium degree of deformation, CPD fails to maintain the shape of the head and has twisted legs, LSP maintains the local structure but inflexible in this case, and our method generates an accurate result. For a large degree of deformation, both CPD and LSP fail to maintain human body shape but our method shows better results (but has some artifacts in the hand regions). In both datasets, our method shows significantly better results by maintaining both local and global structures especially in a large degree of deformation showing the importance of preserving local neighborhood structure and using landmark correspondences.

Table 1 lists the quantitative registration errors with respect to different degrees of deformation and a comparison with CPD [12] and LSP [4] methods for both 2D tools and 3D human body datasets. We have three degrees of deformation: small, medium, and large (an example of each case is shown in Fig. 2). For each degree of deformation, the best and the second best results are

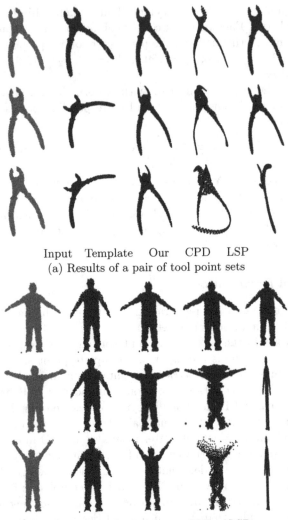

Input   Template   Our   CPD   LSP
(a) Results of a pair of tool point sets

Input   Template   Our   CPD   LSP
(b) Results of a pair of 3D human point sets

Fig. 2. Exemplar registration results with three degrees of deformation. The left two columns of each figure are the inputs and the following three columns are results of our method, CPD, and LSP, respectively.

highlighted in bold and italic fonts, respectively. Each experiment was repeated five times. Our method exhibits the smallest registration error (and stds.) in almost all cases except the case of small deformation in 2D. In this one case, our method's registration error is slightly higher than LSP's registration error by 0.21. The average registration errors, by combining both 2D and 3D deformation results for each method, of our method, CPD, and LSP are 7.64, 15.18, and 83.76, respectively. Our method has the lowest average registration error and is 49% better than the second best result. It is evident that our method has a small registration error (std) than the other methods as the deformation degree increases.

Table 1. Average registration error with respect to three degrees of deformation.

Data	Method	Small	Medium	Large
Tools dataset	Our	*2.54 (0.78)*	**3.11 (1.18)**	**3.49 (1.61)**
	CPD	4.78 (2.65)	6.13 (2.89)	*7.18 (3.10)*
	LSP	**2.33 (0.41)**	*4.71 (3.68)*	12.98 (17.87)
Human body dataset	Our	**11.36 (0.29)**	**12.09 (0.85)**	**13.28 (1.47)**
	CPD	*12.15 (0.66)*	*30.47 (2.44)*	*30.39 (1.97)*
	LSP	70.14 (73.09)	215.92 (22.09)	196.51 (7.90)

4.3   Number of Landmarks

We test our method and compare registration accuracy with other methods to see the effect of the different number of corresponding landmark points in the point sets during registration. In each point set, we marked five landmarks and conducted experiments using $x, x \in \{1, 2, \ldots, 5\}$, number of corresponding pairs of landmarks. In this experiment, we have selected the point sets with large deformations between them (Fig. 3) and the order of corresponding landmark pairs are fixed. For example in human body point sets, we fixed the order of following five pairs of corresponding landmarks between two point sets: heads, right foot, left foot, right hands, and left hands, respectively. For each x, we selected the first x pairs of corresponding landmarks from the fixed order of landmark pairs and repeated the experiment five times. Figure 3 illustrates the registration results using different numbers of landmarks in our method. Figure 3(a) shows the registration results of human body dataset, and Fig. 3(b) shows the registration results of tools dataset. The template and input point sets depict large deformations. Each row depicts a case with the left two columns showing the input and the template point sets. The rest columns in a row show the registration results using an increasing number of landmark pairs from left to right. Figure 3(a) illustrates a challenging case with large and uneven deformations between the input and template point sets. When the number of landmark pairs is less than five, the method resulted in poor registration. In human cases, arms and head were fuzzy or 'vaporized'. As the number of landmark pairs reaches five, the results gained significant improvement due to more precise shape constraints. This trend is also demonstrated in the registration of the Tools case as shown in Fig. 3(b) but shows good registration results even in less than five landmark pairs. In particular, Fig. 3(b) show improved registration results when the number of landmark pairs is four or more. Therefore, it is fair to say the minimum number of landmarks needed depends on the degree of disparity between the point sets.

Table 2 presents the average registration errors and standard deviations of our method using a different number of corresponding landmarks for both 2D tools and 3D human body datasets. As the landmark correspondences increases, the registration accuracy of our method also increases. In particular, registration errors start to decrease sharply after adding four or more landmark correspondences, especially in the case of the 3D human body dataset.

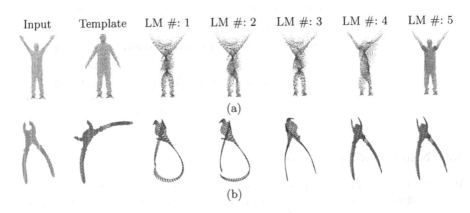

Fig. 3. Registration results of our method using different number of landmarks. The first two left columns show the input and template point sets, respectively. Columns three to seven show the results using different number of landmarks. Row (a) shows the results of human body dataset, and row (b) shows the results of tools dataset.

Table 2. Average registration error of our method with different number of landmarks.

Number of landmarks	Tools dataset	Human body dataset
1	6.06 (2.30)	24.2 (2.05)
2	5.61 (2.81)	24.2 (1.38)
3	5.11 (2.42)	23.48 (0.75)
4	3.85 (1.96)	20.3 (3.14)
5	3.49 (1.61)	13.28 (1.47)

4.4 Incorrect Landmark Correspondence

To evaluate the impact of incorrect landmark correspondence, we create three incorrect correspondence cases for each dataset and repeated each registration five times. Figure 4 shows the results of using incorrect correspondences in our registration method. Figure 4(a) shows registration results of 2D tools point sets and Figure 4(b) shows the registration results of 3D human point sets. The first two columns show the inputs and the corresponding landmarks are shown in the same color. Third and fourth columns are the registration results of using correct and incorrect landmark correspondences respectively.

For the 2D tools dataset, the registration result of the first row shows the thin shape of the tool and is twisted in the middle part of the tool. This is because the left and right landmark correspondences at the top and bottom regions are swapped between input and template point sets. In particular, the left tip landmark (yellow) and right tip landmark (black) of the input point set correspond to the right tip landmark (yellow) and left tip landmark (black) of the template point set. Similar incorrect left and right correspondences between the landmarks at the bottom regions of the tool point set are used. In the second case (middle row), the registration result is similar to the result of the first row, i.e., twisted at the middle part of the tool and thin shape of the tool as a result of incorrect landmark correspondences. In the last case (bottom row), not only left and right landmark correspondences at the top regions but also landmark correspondences at the middle and lower right handle regions between input and template point sets are swapped. In this case, the registration result shows an inaccurate shape of the tool where points from different parts of the tool are mixed together.

Similarly, for the 3D human body dataset, head region points are fused with the right shoulder and the upper body is twisted in the top row. In the middle row, the upper body part is twisted and points from the head are mixed with the left shoulder. The last row is even highly inaccurate with twisted and fusion of the different parts of the body regions.

Table 3 lists the quantitative registration results of using incorrect landmark correspondences in the three different cases. For the 2D tools dataset, all three cases have similar registration errors (and stds.). For the 3D human body dataset, the first two cases have better results than the last case. The average registration errors, when all three cases are combined for each dataset, are 6.78 (2.4) for the 2D tools dataset and 19.74 mm (1.5) for the 3D human body dataset.

Table 3. Registration results (stds.) of our method with different combinations of incorrect landmark correspondences in 2D and 3D datasets.

Incorrect landmark correspondences pair #	Tools dataset	Human body dataset
1	6.47 (3.06)	16.63 (0.85)
2	7.06 (2.07)	18.35 (1.89)
3	6.83 (2.06)	24.24 (1.99)

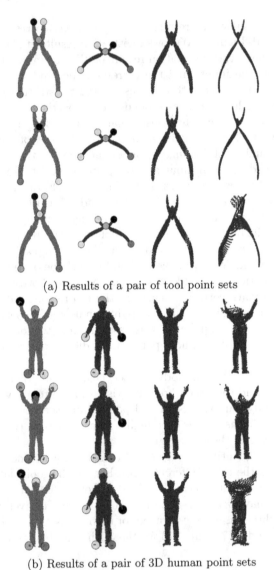

(a) Results of a pair of tool point sets

(b) Results of a pair of 3D human point sets

Fig. 4. Exemplar registration results using incorrect landmark correspondences. The left two columns of each figure are the inputs (and corresponding landmarks have the same color). The third column shows the registration results using correct landmark correspondences and the last column shows the registration results. (Color figure online)

5   Conclusion

In this paper, we present a probabilistic non-rigid point set registration method to register point sets that represent large and uneven deformation. Keys to our method are constraints for enforcing landmark correspondences and preserving local neighborhood structure. Landmarks represent the salient points in point sets, which can be computed using methods such as scale-invariant feature transform. The correspondence between landmarks enables us to regulate the optimization process. In addition, by leveraging Stochastic Neighbor Embedding, we preserve the local structure of the point set by penalizing incoherent transformation within a neighborhood.

We evaluate our method with three different aspects: different degrees of deformation, the number of landmarks in registration, and the impact of incorrect landmark correspondences in registration. Our method shows significantly better results in a large degree of deformation in both 2D and 3D datasets. Quantitative results show our method is 49% better than the second best result in deformation experiments. Our evaluation results show that as the number of landmark correspondences increases, the registration accuracy of our method also increases, highlighting the importance of landmark correspondences in a large degree of deformation. Also, using incorrect landmark correspondences in registration results in a significant degrade in registration accuracy based on our experiments.

References

1. Belongie, S., Malik, J., Puzicha, J.: Shape matching and object recognition using shape contexts. IEEE Trans. Pattern Anal. Mach. Intell. **24**(4), 509–522 (2002)
2. Bronstein, A.M., Bronstein, M.M., Bruckstein, A.M., Kimmel, R.: Analysis of two-dimensional non-rigid shapes. Int. J. Comput. Vision **78**(1), 67–88 (2008)
3. Chui, H., Rangarajan, A.: A new point matching algorithm for non-rigid registration. Comput. Vision Image Understand. **89**(2), 114–141 (2003)
4. Ge, S., Fan, G.: Non-rigid articulated point set registration with local structure preservation. In: IEEE Conference on Computer Vision and Pattern Recognition Workshops, pp. 126–133, June 2015
5. Gold, S., Rangarajan, A., Lu, C., Pappu, S., Mjolsness, E.: New algorithms for 2D and 3D point matching: pose estimation and correspondence. Pattern Recognit. **31**(8), 1019–1031 (1998)
6. Hinton, G.E., Roweis, S.T.: Stochastic neighbor embedding. In: Becker, S., Thrun, S., Obermayer, K. (eds.) Advances in Neural Information Processing Systems, vol. 15, pp. 857–864. MIT Press (2003)
7. Jian, B., Vemuri, B.C.: Robust point set registration using gaussian mixture models. IEEE Trans. Pattern Anal. Mach. Intell. **33**(8), 1633–1645 (2011)
8. Kong, L., Yuan, X., Maharjan, A.M.: A hybrid framework for automatic joint detection of human poses in depth frames. Pattern Recognit. **77**(C), 216–225 (2018)
9. Ling, H., Jacobs, D.W.: Shape classification using the inner-distance. IEEE Trans. Pattern Anal. Mach. Intell. **29**(2), 286–299 (2007)
10. Lowe, D.G.: Object recognition from local scale-invariant features. In: Proceedings of the Seventh IEEE International Conference on Computer Vision, vol. 2, pp. 1150–1157 (1999)
11. Ma, J., Zhao, J., Yuille, A.L.: Non-rigid point set registration by preserving global and local structures. IEEE Trans. Image Process. **25**(1), 53–64 (2016)

12. Myronenko, A., Song, X.: Point set registration: coherent point drift. IEEE Trans. Pattern Anal. Mach. Intell. **32**(12), 2262–2275 (2010)
13. Panaganti, V., Aravind, R.: Robust nonrigid point set registration using graph-Laplacian regularization. In: IEEE Winter Conference on Applications of Computer Vision, pp. 1137–1144, January 2015
14. Roweis, S.T., Saul, L.K.: Nonlinear dimensionality reduction by locally linear embedding. Science **290**(5500), 2323–2326 (2000)
15. Rusu, R.B., Blodow, N., Beetz, M.: Fast point feature histograms (FPFH) for 3D registration. In: 2009 IEEE International Conference on Robotics and Automation, pp. 3212–3217, May 2009
16. Tsin, Y., Kanade, T.: A correlation-based approach to robust point set registration. In: Pajdla, T., Matas, J. (eds.) ECCV 2004. LNCS, vol. 3023, pp. 558–569. Springer, Heidelberg (2004). https://doi.org/10.1007/978-3-540-24672-5_44
17. Wang, G., Chen, Y.: Fuzzy correspondences guided gaussian mixture model for point set registration. Knowl.-Based Syst. **136**, 200–209 (2017)
18. Yuan, X., Kong, L., Feng, D., Wei, Z.: Automatic feature point detection and tracking of human actions in time-of-flight videos. IEEE/CAA J. Automatica Sinica **4**(4), 677–685 (2017)

Model-Based Intelligent Non-linear Signal Recognition for Gearbox Condition Monitoring

Hanxin Chen[1,2(✉)], Lang Huang[1,2], Yuzhuo Miao[1,2], Qi Wang[1,2], Liu Yang[1,2], and Yao Ke[1,2]

[1] School of Mechanical and Electrical Engineering,
Wuhan Institute of Technology, Wuhan 430073, China
pg01074075@163.com
[2] Hubei Provincial Key Laboratory of Chemical Equipment,
Intensification and Intrinsic Safety, Wuhan, China

Abstract. In this paper, a method for equipment fault diagnosis of gearbox using principal component analysis (PCA) and sequential probability ratio test (SPRT) is proposed. The method is to study and monitor the working state of the gearbox by studying the original vibration signal of the gearbox, and establish a corresponding experimental model by using the normal gear and the fault gear, respectively. Firstly, the vibration signal of the gearbox is preprocessed by wavelet packet transform (WPT). Then the time domain signal analysis method is used to extract the characteristic parameters of the vibration signal and the data is reduced by PCA. After the data are reduced in dimension, the principal element with the highest contribution rate are selected as the input parameter of SPRT. Test parameters to verify the proposed SPRT algorithm and Root Mean Square Error (RMSE). The results show that the proposed method is effective and practical.

Keywords: PCA · SPRT · RMSE · Condition monitoring

1 Introduction

Gearbox is commonly used in industrial production [1]. Gearbox is an important part of the power transmission of many mechanical devices. It is used to change the transmission ratio, direction of change, and power transmission. In the actual production life, the operating state of the gearbox is closely related to the operating state of the equipment, while the gears, shafts and other components in the gearbox work under high load for a long time, and the probability of mechanical failure is higher [2–4]. According to relevant statistics, the gear failure is about 60% of the failure of the gearbox components. Therefore, research on gear fault diagnosis in gearboxes has become very valuable and necessary [5, 6].

As early as 1901, PCA was first proposed by Pearson. The basic idea of the method is to compress multiple linear correlation variables into a multivariate statistical method of a few unrelated variables [7, 8]. Ding et al. reduced the amount of data dimension

© Springer Nature Singapore Pte Ltd. 2020
X. Yuan et al. (Eds.): ICUIA 2020, CCIS 1319, pp. 99–106, 2020.
https://doi.org/10.1007/978-981-33-4601-7_10

by PCA [9]. PCA reduced the multidimensional correlated variable to be low dimensional independent eigenvector. PCA has advantages in the simple concept, convenient calculation. It has been widely used in numerous areas such as data compression, feature extraction, image processing, signal analysis etc. al [10].

In 1947, Wald introduced SPRT in his book. Because of its simplicity and high efficiency, this method has been widely used in the field of fault diagnosis in recent years. Ray et al. applied SPRT to fault detection and identification in nuclear power plants and aircraft [11]. Chen et al. used SPRT for gearbox fault diagnosis [12, 13]. Compared with the traditional method, Compared with the traditional method, sequential probability ratio test differs from the fixed sample test in that this algorithm requires a smaller average sample size, but it has a higher test efficiency [14].

This paper proposes a new gear multi-fault monitoring method based on PCA and SPRT. The gear vibration signal is denoised by wavelet packet transform, and then PCA is taken to remove the characteristic data of the signal and select the appropriate principal element as the substitute data of SPRT. Finally, SPRT algorithm is used to identify the fault state of the gearbox. With the aim for corroborating the potency of SPRT algorithm for fault diagnosis of the gearbox, the equipment fault diagnosis of the gearbox is diagnosed by jointing the root mean square error (RMSE) and the binary SPRT. The final consequences show that the strategy is effective and dependable.

2 SPRT Algorithm of Gearbox

In the likelihood ratio test, the change in mean and standard deviation has a greater impact on the results. The test sequence selected after pre-processing and PCA basically conforms to the Gaussian distribution, and the mean value is $c\mu$, and the standard deviation is σ. Suppose that the probability distribution of one of the groups to be tested satisfies the initial hypothesis: $H_j : \mu = \mu_j$; the probability distribution of another group of sequences to be tested satisfies the alternative hypothesis: $H_j : \mu = \mu_j$. The standard deviation σ does not change. When the both hypotheses are reality, the joint probability density function (PDF) of the two sets of sequences is as follows:

$$P_{ik}(y_k) = \frac{1}{\sigma\sqrt{2\pi}} \exp\left(-\frac{1}{2\sigma^2}(y_k - \mu_i)^2\right) \qquad (1)$$

$$P_{jk}(y_k) = \frac{1}{\sigma\sqrt{2\pi}} \exp\left(-\frac{1}{2\sigma^2}(y_k - \mu_j)^2\right) \qquad (2)$$

Where $P_{jk}(y_k)$ represents PDF under selective hypothesis; $P_{ik}(y_k)$ represents PDF under null hypothesis.

We could calculated the likelihood ratio of SPRT as follows:

$$\lambda_{i,j}(Y_{Sm}) = \frac{\prod\limits_{k=1}^{n} P_{jk}}{\prod\limits_{k=1}^{n} P_{ik}} = \frac{p_{j1}(y_1)p_{j2}(y_2)\cdots p_{jk}(y_k)}{p_{i1}(y_1)p_{i2}(y_2)\cdots p_{ik}(y_k)} \times \frac{p_{j0}}{p_{i0}} \qquad (3)$$

Where $S_m = \{S_1, S_2, S_3, S_4\}$, P_{j0} and P_{i0} are prior probability functions under selective and null hypothesis. SPRT probability ratio $\lambda_{i,j}(Y_{Si})$ and $\lambda_{i,j}(Y_{Sj})$ are computed by inputting the testing data (Y_{Si}, Y_{Sj}) of the signal waveform for gearbox Si and Sj conditions to Eq. (3). SPRT probability ratios $\lambda_{i,j}(Y_{Si})$ and $\lambda_{i,j}(Y_{Sj})$ are expressed in the following section. The Eq. (3) can be simplified:

$$\Delta_{i,j}(Y_{Sm}) = \ln \lambda_{i,j}(Y_{Sm}) = \ln \frac{\prod\limits_{k=1}^{n} p_{jk}}{\prod\limits_{k=1}^{n} p_{ik}} = \sum_{k=1}^{n} \ln \frac{p_{jk}}{p_{ik}} \tag{4}$$

$$E_{i,j}(Y_{Sm}) = \left(\frac{1}{k} \sum_{t=1}^{k} \left(\lambda_{i,j}(Y_{Sm}) - \lambda_{i,j}(Y_S) \right)^2 \right)^{\frac{1}{2}} \quad m = i, j \tag{5}$$

3 Experiment System

The normal gear F1 and the cracked fault gears F2, F3, and F4 were selected for the experiment. The full depth of the gear crack is $a = 2.4$ mm, the full width of the crack is $b = 25$ mm, the thickness of the gear crack is 0.4 mm, and the angle of the gear crack is 45°. In the experiment, the gearbox was in no-load state and the speed was 800 r/min. The parameters of the three sets of gears are shown in Table 1.

Table 1. Four gear failure modes

Gear	Crack parameter			
	Depth/mm	Width/mm	Thickness/mm	Crack angle/°
F1	0	0	0	45°
F2	(1/4)a	(1/4)b	0.4	45°
F3	(1/2)a	(1/2)b	0.4	45°
F4	(3/4)a	(3/4)b	0.4	45°

Figure 1 is a structural diagram of a gearbox. Vibration is generated between the running gears 3 and 4, so one of them is selected to simulate the fault. In this experiment, the gear 3 was selected for the simulation experiment.

The experimental signal acquisition is obtained from the gearbox SpectraQuest dynamic simulator. A PCB352C67 accelerator is fixed in the vertical and horizontal directions of the gearbox. The collected initial vibration signals are input into the PC and stored by the DSP20-42 signal analyzer. This paper only studies the analysis of signals in the horizontal direction. S1, S2, S3, and S4 are used to represent the signals under normal conditions and three fault conditions.

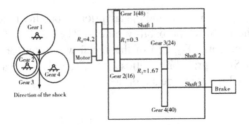

Fig. 1. Gearox structure

4 Multi-fault State Recognition of Gearbox Based on Three-Layer SPRT

4.1 Diagnosis of Gearbox in Fault State F1

The Eqs. (1–3) are used to calculate the variable $\lambda_{1,2}(Y_{S1})$. The parameters μ_0 and μ_1 are the means of the waveform under $(F1, F2)$ condition. The variables $\lambda_{1,2}(Y_{S1}(N))$, $\lambda_{1,2}(Y_{S2}(N))$, $\lambda_{1,2}(Y_{S3}(N))$, $\lambda_{1,2}(Y_{S4}(N))$ are calculated by Eqs. (4–5) by using ten waveforms (Y_{S1}) under $F1$ and one testing waveform of the $F2, F3, F4$.

Figure 2(a) shows the establishment of the unequal relationship $\lambda_{1,2}(Y_{S1}(N)) < b$. Figure 2(b) shows the variables $\left(E_{1,2}(Y_{S1})\right)$ for $\lambda_{1,2}(Y_{S1}(N))$, $N = 1, \cdots, 10$ are compared with $\left(E_{1,2}\left(Y_{Sj}\right)\right), j = 2, 3, 4$ for $\lambda_{1,2}(Y_{S1}(N))$ with $\lambda_{1,2}\left(Y_{Sj}\right), j = 2, 3, 4$. The parameters $\left(E_{1,2}\left(Y_{Sj}\right)\right), j = 2, 3, 4$ are bigger than $\left(E_{1,2}(Y_{S1})\right)$.

Figure 3(a) shows the establishment of the unequal relationship $\lambda_{1,2}(Y_{S1}(N)) < b$. Figure 3(b) shows the unequal relationship are established, which is $E_{1,3}(Y_{S1}(N)) < E_{1,3}\left(Y_{Sj}\right), j = 2, 3, 4$.

Figure 4(a), the unequal relationship $\lambda_{1,4}(Y_{S1}(N)) < b$ is established. In Fig. 4(b), the parameters $E_{1,4}(Y_{S1})$, $E_{1,4}(Y_{S3})$ and $E_{1,4}(Y_{S4})$ are less than the threshold E_{C1} and RMSEs $E_{1,4}(Y_{S2})$ are more than E_C.

As shown in Figs. (2, 3 and 4), if $E_{1,2}(Y_{S1}) < E_C$ and $\lambda_{1,2}(Y_{S1}) < b$ or $E_{1,3}(Y_{S1}) < E_C$ and $\lambda_{1,3}(Y_{S1}) < b$ are satisfied, then $F1$ could be diagnosed.

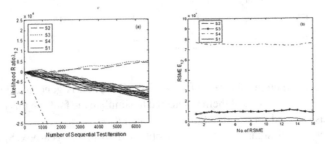

Fig. 2. Three-layer SPRT results: (a) likelihood ratio $\lambda_{1,2}(Y_{S1}(N))$, $\lambda_{1,2}(Y_{S2})$, $\lambda_{1,2}(Y_{S3})$, $\lambda_{1,2}(Y_{S4})$ versus sequential test iteration number. (b) RMSEs $E_{1,2}(Y_{S1}(N))$, $E_{1,2}(Y_{S2})$, $E_{1,2}(Y_{S3})$, $E_{1,2}(Y_{S4})$.

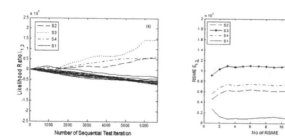

Fig. 3. Three-layer SPRT results: (a) likelihood ratio $\lambda_{1,3}(Y_{S1}(N))$, $\lambda_{1,3}(Y_{S2})$, $\lambda_{1,3}(Y_{S3})$, $\lambda_{1,3}(Y_{S4})$ versus sequential test iteration number. (b) RMSEs $E_{1,3}(Y_{S1}(N))$, $E_{1,3}(Y_{S2})$, $E_{1,3}(Y_{S3})$, $E_{1,3}(Y_{S4})$.

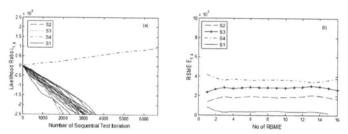

Fig. 4. Three-layer SPRT results: (a) likelihood ratio $\lambda_{1,4}(Y_{S1}(N))$, $\lambda_{1,3}(Y_{S2})$, $\lambda_{1,3}(Y_{S3})$, $\lambda_{1,3}(Y_{S4})$ versus sequential test iteration number. (b) RMSEs $E_{1,3}(Y_{S1}(N))$, $E_{1,3}(Y_{S2})$, $E_{1,3}(Y_{S3})$, $E_{1,3}(Y_{S4})$.

4.2 Diagnosis of Gearbox in Fault State F2

If the waveform is not $S1$ and falls into one of the other three waveforms that is $(S2, S3, S4)$, the variables $\lambda_{2,3}$ and $\lambda_{2,4}$ are used to identify $F2$ by classifying $(S2, S3, S4)$.

As is shown in Fig. 5(a), the inequality that $\lambda_{2,3}(Y_{S2}) < b$ is satisfied. Figure 5(b) shows that $E_{2,3}(Y_{S2}(M)) < E_C$ and $E_{2,3}(Y_{S4}(M)) > E_C$. The inequality $E_{2,3}(Y_S) < E_C$ is satisfied means the condition is $F2$ or $F3$. The variable $\lambda_{2,4}$ is used to classify the waveform $S2$ and $S4$. Figure 6(a) shows $\lambda_{2,4}(Y_{S2}(M)) < b$ is satisfied. Figure 6(b) shows RMSEs $E_{2,4}(Y_{S2}(M)) < E_C$. The condition $F2$ is classified among the three conditions by the variable $\lambda_{2,4}$. The inequalities $E_{2,4}(Y_{S2}) < E_C$ and $\lambda_{2,4}(Y_{S2}) < b$ are the index to diagnose $S2$ from $(S2, S3, S4)$, which is effective to classify $F2$ among $(F2, F3, F4)$.

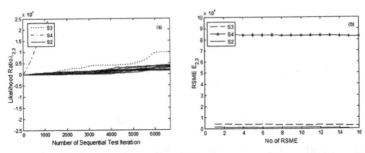

Fig. 5. Three-layer SPRT results: (a) likelihood ratio $\lambda_{2,3}(Y_{S2}(N))$, $\lambda_{2,3}(Y_{S3})$, $\lambda_{2,3}(Y_{S4})$ versus sequential test iteration number. (b) RMSEs $E_{2,3}(Y_{S2}(N))$, $E_{2,3}(Y_{S3})$ and $E_{2,3}(Y_{S4})$.

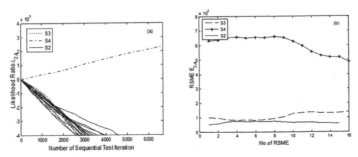

Fig. 6. Three-layer SPRT results: (a) likelihood ratio $\lambda_{2,4}(Y_{S2}(N))$, $\lambda_{2,4}(Y_{S3})$, $\lambda_{2,4}(Y_{S4})$ versus sequential test iteration number. (b) RMSEs $E_{2,4}(Y_{S2}(N))$, $E_{2,4}(Y_{S3})$ and $E_{2,4}(Y_{S4})$.

4.3 Diagnosis of Gearbox in Fault State F3

Calculate the likelihood ratios of the sequences to be tested according to the formulas (1) to (5), labeled $\lambda_{3,4}(Y_{S1}(1))\cdots\lambda_{3,4}(Y_{S3}(10))$ and $\lambda_{3,4}(Y_{S4})$, and the test results are shown in Fig. 7(a). It can be seen from the figure that the likelihood ratio $\lambda_{3,4}(Y_{S3}(M)) < b$ of the vibration signal $S3$ in the fault state $F3$ and the likelihood ratio $\lambda_{3,4}(Y_{S4}) < b$ of the vibration signal $S4$. Figure 7(b) shows that if $E_{3,4}(Y_{S3}) < E_{3,4}(Y_{S4})$ and $E_{3,4}(Y_{S3}) < E_C$ are satisfied, the inequalities $\lambda_{3,4}(Y_{S3}(M)) < b$ and $E_{3,4}(Y_{S3}) < E_C$ are used

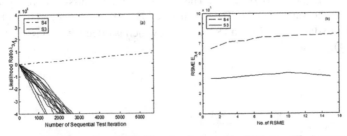

Fig. 7. Three-layer SPRT results: (a) likelihood ratio $\lambda_{3,4}(Y_{S3}(N))$, $\lambda_{3,4}(Y_{S4})$ versus sequential test iteration number; (b) RMSEs $E_{3,4}(Y_{S3}(N))$ and $E_{3,4}(Y_{S4})$.

to categorize the waveform $S3$ from the waveform $S4$. The gearbox condition $F3$ is diagnosed from the gearbox condition $F4$.

5   Conclusions

In this paper, a gearbox fault diagnosis method based on PCA and SPRT is proposed. Firstly, WPT is used to denoise the initial vibration signal, and the time domain analysis method is utilized to extract the characteristic parameters of the signal. Then PCA is used to reduce the extracted feature parameters. The principal component with the biggest contribution rate is chosen as the monitoring sequence. Finally, SPRT algorithm is used to analyze the running state of the gearbox and combine the root mean square algorithm to classify the fault. Subsequently, detailed fault diagnosis experiments and analysis were carried out on the gearbox. SPRT was used to identify different faults and combined with the root mean square error to further give the identification criteria. The experimental results show that the fault diagnosis of the gearbox is accurate and effective.

Acknowledgement. The experimental data is provided by the Reliability Research Lab in the Department of Mechanical Engineering at the University of Alberta in Canada. This work was supported by the National Natural Science Foundation of China (Grant 51775390).

References

1. Zeng, L., Chen, G., Chen, H.: Comparative study on flow-accelerated corrosion and erosion-corrosion at a 900 carbon steel bend. Materials **12**, 1780 (2020). https://doi.org/10.3390/ma1 3071780
2. Yang, L., Chen, H.: Fault diagnosis of gearbox based on RBF-PF and particle swarm optimization wavelet neural network. Neural Comput. Appl. **31**(9), 4463–4478 (2018). https://doi.org/10.1007/s00521-018-3525-y
3. Chen, H.: Model-based method with nonlinear ultrasonic system identification for mechanical structural health assessment. Trans. Emerg. Telecommun. Technol. e3955 (2020). http://doi.org/10.1002/ett.3955
4. Chen, H.: Nonlinear Lamb wave analysis for microdefect identification in mechanical structural health assessment. Measurement **164**, 108026 (2020). https://doi.org/10.1016/j.measurement.2020.108026
5. Zeng, L., Guo, X.P., Zhang, G.A., Chen, H.X.: Semiconductivities of passive films formed on stainless steel bend under erosion-corrosion conditions. Corros. Sci. **144**, 258–265 (2018)
6. Zeng, L., Shi, J., Luo, J., Chen, H.: Silver sulfide anchored on reduced graphene oxide as a high -performance catalyst for CO2 electroreduction. J. Power Sources **398**, 83–90 (2018)
7. Chen, H., Chen, Y., Yang, L.: Intelligent early structural health prognosis with nonlinear system identification for RFID signal analysis. Comput. Commun. **157**, 150–161 (2020). https://doi.org/10.1016/j.comcom.2020.04.026
8. Yang, L., Hanxin, C.: A novel time-frequency-space method with parallel factor theory for big data analysis in condition monitoring of complex system. Int. J. Adv. Robot. Syst. **17**(2) (2020). https://doi.org/10.1177/1729881420916948
9. Ding, J., Zhao, L., Huang, D.R.: Incipient fault feature extraction method of gearbox based on wavelet package and PCA. In: IEEE International Conference on Data Driven Control and Learning Systems, pp. 656–660 (2017)

10. Chen, H., Fan, D., Huang, J., Huang, W.: Finite element analysis model on ultrasonic phased array technique for material defect time of flight diffraction detection. Sci. Adv. Mater. **12**(5), 665–675 (2020)
11. Ray, A.: Sequential testing for fault detection in multiply-redundant systems. J. Dyn. Syst. Meas. Control Trans. ASME **111**(2), 329–332 (1989)
12. Hanxin, C., Dong, L.F., Lu, F.: Particle swarm optimization algorithm with mutation operator for particle filter noise reduction in mechanical fault diagnosis. Int. J. Pattern Recognit. Artif. Intell. https://doi.org/10.1142/S0218001420580124
13. Hanxin, C., Wenjian, H., Jinmin, H.: Multi-fault condition monitoring of slurry pump with principle component analysis and sequential hypothesis test. Int. J. Pattern Recognit. Artif. Intell. https://doi.org/10.1142/S0218001420590193
14. He, Y., Xiong, W., Chen, H.: Image quality enhanced recognition of laser cavity based on improved random hough transform. J. Vis. Commun. Image Representation (2020). https://doi.org/10.1016/j.jvcir.2019.102679

Brain Tumor Segmentation Algorithm Based on Attention Mechanism and Hybrid Cascaded Network

Yitong Li[✉]

School of Information and Electronics, Beijing Institute of Technology, Beijing 100081, China
Yinxing_tx2@163.com

Abstract. Brain tumors have different sizes and can be found anywhere of the brain; the edges of tumors are unclear and incoherent. Therefore, the segmentation of the tumor sub-region is always difficult to achieve accurate results. Under that background, a brain tumor and sub-region segmentation method based on the hybrid cascaded network and the attention mechanism is proposed. According to the idea of location and segmentation, the framework of the hybrid cascaded model was constructed. Through the first stage segmentation, the foreground range was narrowed. Through the classification of parallel network structure, the task of second stage segmentation was simplified to avoid the inter-class competition. A three-dimensional U-Net with the attention module was used as the basic network of segmentation; multi-modal semantic information was extracted to obtain the terminal to terminal tumor image segmentation results. Brain MRI images of 285 patients which were provided by the BraTS2017 Competition were used to segment brain tumors as well as their sub-regions. The accuracy of segmenting the whole tumor region, the tumor core region, and the enhancing tumor region were 0.907, 0.836, and 0.741. Compared with the existing counter neural network segmentation method, the cascaded V-Net segmentation method made improvements. By combining the convolution neural network and the attention mechanism, the approach proposed can extract multi-modal characteristics of MRI features with targets, and make the brain tumor and sub-region segmentation more accurate.

Keywords: Brain tumor segmentation · MRI image processing · 3D convolution neural network · Attention mechanism

1 Introduction

Brain tumors, which originate from the undisciplined growth and reproduction of abnormal cells, have developed into one of the common causes that increased the mortality of children and adults. The quantitative evaluation of brain tumor parameters, such as the volume of sub-regions, is closely related to the follow-up treatment and the determination of operation plans. Segmenting tumors as well as sub-regions precisely is the premise of quantitative evaluation. Therefore, it is of great significance to realize segmentation through the magnetic resonance imaging (MRI) technique. The automatic segmentation

© Springer Nature Singapore Pte Ltd. 2020
X. Yuan et al. (Eds.): ICUIA 2020, CCIS 1319, pp. 107–114, 2020.
https://doi.org/10.1007/978-981-33-4601-7_11

of multi-modal brain MRI features is also a challenge in the field of medical image processing.

Wang [1] and others fused multiple reference maps and obtained the results of segmenting brain anatomical regions by clustering and weighted majority voting. Pereira [2] proposed a brain segmentation algorithm based on the conditional random field. Using the random forest coding likelihood function, this algorithm gets competitive segmentation results in normal and sick brains. The above methods improve the accuracy of brain image segmentation in different degrees, but due to the lack of resolution in manual design features, registration errors produce great impacts on segmentation results. It is difficult to further improve the indicators.

The deep learning model directly learns the hierarchical structure of task-specific features from the data, in which the convolutional neural network improves the computational efficiency through the operation of the local connection [3]. At that time, Kayalibay and others [4] used the improved U-Net [5] network to make the tumor segmentation more accurate. In recent years, the Attention Mechanism is applied in image vision. Combining the attention module with the existing neural network becomes a popular research direction. Kaiming [6] and others confirmed the effectiveness of the non-local operation in the space-time dimension. The non-local operation is a kind of attention mechanism.

To improve the segment accuracy, a hybrid cascaded network on the basis of the attention mechanism is put forward. In this method, the three-dimensional U-Net with the attention module is used as the basic segmentation network, and a hybrid cascaded structure is constructed. The target area is located by the preliminary segmentation, and then the tumor is segmented according to the target area classification. Information provided by the BraTS2017 Competition was used as the training and test data to guarantee the effectiveness of the algorithm. According to the results, this method can achieve accurate brain tumor and sub-region segmentation.

After the introduction, the first part of this paper introduces the hybrid cascaded segmentation model on the basis of the attention mechanism; the second section is the experiment of brain tumor segmentation through MRI images and result analysis; the third section explains the conclusion.

2   Hybrid Cascaded Model Based on the Attention Mechanism

2.1   Attention Mechanism

The attention mechanism uses the mask to selectively focus on information related to the target task in input data. The core purpose of the attention mechanism is to invest more computing resources in the focus of global input through filtering. It also simplifies the task by suppressing the background information and improves the computing efficiency. When the attention mechanism is combined with the convolutional neural network, the main function is to learn a new layer of weight distribution and apply the learned weight distribution to the input data or the existing feature map. To obtain the model of available gradient descent, the neural network usually combines with the soft attention mechanism to retain all components for weighting and achieve the trainability of parameters.

In the soft attention mechanism, the output value is calculated as follows. A query vector related to the target task is given (Query); the address or the value of the query key is recorded as Key; the attention distribution of Query and Key is calculated as the weight and then attached to the Value to be processed. Then the value after the attention process is output, the Key and Value correspond to each other. Using $X = [x_1,..., x_N]$ to represent N input information and given $Key = Value = X$, the attention distribution can be expressed as follows.

$$\alpha_i = soft \max(s(X_i, query)) \, (i \in [1. \, N]) \tag{1}$$

α_i is the attention weight of the ith information learned; $s(X_i, query)$ is a kind of attention scoring mechanism, which is used to judge the relevance. After selecting and encoding the input information with the weight, we can get the final output.

$$Attention(query, X) = \sum_{i=1}^{N} \alpha_i X_i \tag{2}$$

In addition, there is another attention mechanism in computer vision called the task focus. The initial task is divided into several sub-tasks; different sub-tasks correspond to different algorithm branches. The single branch focuses on processing decomposed sub-tasks, which reduces the difficulty of task processing while supervising the allocation of computing resources.

The algorithm uses two kinds of attention mechanisms at the same time and adds the attention module in the 3D U-Net to filter local semantic information in the shallow feature map. At the same time, in the second phase of the cascade, the multi-level segmentation network is transformed into multiple single class segmentation networks, which can reduce the competition among classes in segmentation training.

2.2 Three-Dimensional U-Net Combined with the Attention Module

Brain MRI images have three dimensions of numerical information. The single-mode MRI data cannot provide complete information on brain tumor segmentation. In order to fuse sufficient multi-modal context information, the basic network of the algorithm is a three-dimensional convolution network based on U-Net [7], which treats multi-modal information as different channels of the input network.

The network structure is shown in the picture. The coding path is composed of convolution blocks and down-sampling modules. Each convolution block contains a convolution filter of 3*3*3 and an Instance Normalization. The neural activation unit adopts the Parametric Rectified Linear Unit (PReLU). Each layer contains two consecutive convolution blocks. Sufficient receptive fields are ensured by the concatenation of convolutional blocks to obtain more context information. A dropout layer is put between two convolution blocks to deal with overfitting. The decoding path of the network is composed of convolutional filtering and upsampling modules with a size of 3*3*3 (Fig. 1).

The Attention module in the network is added between the encoding path and the decoding path and in front of the long hop layer connection of the network. Setting l as the current layer of the neural network. The input information X of the attention module

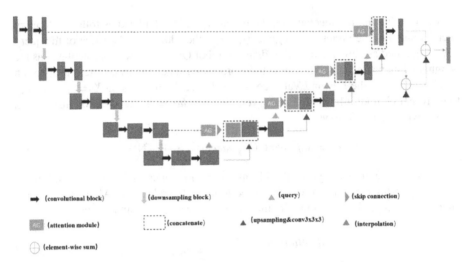

Fig. 1. Structure of the 3D attention U-Net mode

is the feature map of the l layer encoding path; the query vector Query is the feature map of the $l+1$ layer decoding path. Using addition as the scoring mechanism, the correlation between the two feature maps is calculated to get the weight, which is superimposed on the shallow coded feature map after inputting information and outputting attention. The structure can be seen in reference [8].

To improve output accuracy, a deep supervision system is introduced into the decoding path [9]. The resolution of the output characteristic map of the last layer of the decoding path is recorded as $S*S*S$, and the resolution of one dimension of the l layer characteristic map is $S/2^{(l-1)}$. The final output feature map of the last layer is obtained by adding three adjusted feature maps pixel by pixel. The sigmoid function is used to activate the feature map to get the segmentation result of a single network.

2.3 Hybrid Cascaded Model

Figure 2 shows the overall structure of the hybrid cascaded mode. It is composed of two parts of sub-networks. In the first part, the sub-network is a single Attention U-Net. The Area of interest (ROI) is extracted by preliminary segmentation; target classification boxes of different categories are output. The second part of the molecular network is multiple Attention U-Nets in parallel. The number of parallels depends on the number of target classification boxes.

Firstly, the NMR image after processing is input into the first sub-network as training data, and the preliminary multi-class segmentation results are output. If the number of regions to be segmented is recorded as CN, the number of target classification boxes to be generated will also be CN. According to different volumes of target regions, CN target classification boxes of different sizes are generated, and then the original training figure is cropped to generate the input of the next stage sub-network. In parallel network training, each network only carries out single class segmentation training, and the input is the cut image corresponding to the network target class. The network does not affect each other;

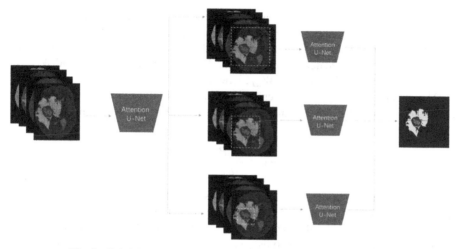

Fig. 2. Hybrid cascaded structure based on the attention mechanism.

it outputs the segmentation image of each class. The output result of the hybrid cascaded model is obtained by superposition of multiple single class segmentation results.

3   Experimental Results and Analysis

To verify the proposed algorithm, public brain tumor segmentation data of the BraST2017 competition is used. The information includes MRI images of 285 patients with glioma. The original segmentation data of each patient are composed of MRI images obtained through four different imaging methods, including T1, T1Gd, T2, and FLAIR images, with the modal image size of 240*240*150. The target segmentation area is divided into three parts, the whole tumor (WT), and the tumor core (TC), and the enhancing tumor (ET) [10, 11].

First, the initial data is registered with ANTs, the advanced normalization toolkit. Then the difference in brightness of the MRI image is corrected by the bias field. The data were divided as a training set and test set, in which 228 patients' data is used in training and cross-validation, and 57 patients' data are used for testing. In view of a large number of parameters of the three-dimensional network model and the small amount of data, there will be overfitting phenomenon. After preprocessing, the training set image is expanded through elastic deformation, random rotation, and Gaussian noise adding. The algorithm is based on the implementation of the Keras library with Tensorflow in the back-end and is trained on the 64 bit Linux operating system.

The Adaptive Motion Estimation (Adam) updates the parameters of the optimized network. Researchers set the initial learning rate as $5*10^{-4}$; the weight attenuation is 10^{-7}. One batch has 1 sample; the Tversky [12] loss function is used. The specific training time is divided into two phases. To begin with, the Attention U-Net is trained separately and iterated 20000 times to generate a pre segmentation positioning network with fixed parameters of W_0. Afterward, the training is divided into three times; one target segmentation area is processed each time. The network parameters are recorded as W_{WT},

W_{TC} and W_{ET} respectively. The sizes of target classification frames of different areas are 128*128*128, 96*96*96, and 64*64*64. For the Attention U-Net of the training cascade, the first network parameter of the cascade is fixed to W_0, and only the second network parameter is updated according to the loss. When training W_{WT} and W_{TC}, it iterates 40000 times; when training W_{ET}, it iterates 30000 times.

The experiment uses a 5 fold cross-validation (5-fold) method in training. The evaluation index is the Dice similarity coefficient (DSC). Its specific meaning is as follows.

$$Dice = \frac{2|P \cap G|}{|P| + |G|} \tag{3}$$

In the formula, P represents the predicted result of the algorithm; G represents the standard segmentation result; $|\cdot|$ is the total voxel of the target region.

Figure 3 shows the algorithm segmentation results, the standard segmentation results, and the visual images of the superposition of the two. The first row is the horizontal section of case Brats17_TCIA_151_1; the second row is the sagittal section; the third row is the coronal section. Table 1 compares the average segmentation accuracy of the algorithm proposed in this paper with typical algorithms, including the cascaded V-Net algorithm, [13] the adaptive feature semantic segmentation algorithm, [14] the multi-task generation counter network algorithm [15], and the improved residual U-Net segmentation algorithm [16]. From Fig. 3 and Table 1, the proposed algorithm realizes the segmentation accuracy of 91% in the whole tumor area; its performance in the tumor core area is also better, with the improvement of 4% to 16%. The reasons are as follows. First, references [14] and [15] use a two-dimensional network; they input three-dimensional MRI images into the network one by one. Only pixels in the slice can be convoluted; the receptive field in one direction is missing. The three-dimensional network can aggregate axial context information from three dimensions, and extract more distinguishing features. Under the same conditions of using the Sigmoid layer as the classifier, the accuracy of pixel classification can be improved. Second, when using the three-dimensional network, the U-Net and its variants can be trained directly for semantic segmentation [17]. To maintain the overall accuracy of classification, the network tends to ignore small probability labels. The algorithm in this paper uses the

Table 1. Quantitative evaluation of different models (algorithms).

Model (Algorithm)	Dice indicator		
	Whole tumor	Tumor core	Enhancing tumor
Cascaded V-Ne algorithm t [13]	0.869	0.685	0.671
Adaptive feature semantic algorithm [14]	0.866	0.766	0.698
Multi-task generation counter - network algorithm [15]	0.88	0.77	0.76
Improved residual U-Net algorithm [16]	0.896	0.797	0.732
Algorithm in this paper	0.907	0.836	0.741

target area frame to narrow the foreground range, reduces the category imbalance of data, and reduces missing reports. Third, the algorithm classifies the task according to the label category. Therefore, it simplifies the task, reduces the competition among parameters, and improves the segmentation accuracy.

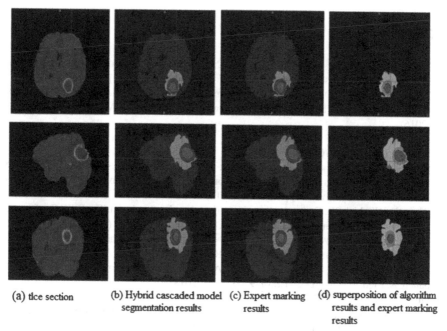

(a) tlce section   (b) Hybrid cascaded model   (c) Expert marking   (d) superposition of algorithm
                        segmentation results   results   results and expert marking
                                                                          results

Fig. 3. Comparing the segmentation results of the proposed model and the manual method.

In the above picture, the first row represents axial segmentation results; the second row shows the sagittal view segmentation results; the third row shows the coronal segmentation results.

4 Conclusion

The algorithm put forward in this paper combines the attention mechanism and the convolution neural network and improves the accuracy of segmenting brain tumors and sub-regions through the hybrid cascaded segmentation model. Compared with mainstream tumor segmentation methods, the advantages are as follows. Firstly, it aims at the category imbalance of brain tumor images; the attention module and the cascaded structure can highlight the foreground and weaken the background, and reduce the false positive (FP) in pixel classification. Secondly, multi-class tasks are coupled. Each label class corresponds to a separate segmentation network, which processes the binary tasks. The segmentation task is simplified, which is conducive to training and convergence. Thirdly, the segmentation sub-network adopts a parallel structure; the single class output results do not act on each other, which reduces the inter-class competition and cumulative error of training. The following researches can introduce this proposed model into the segmentation of pathological and physiological structures such as the stroke and renal cortex. At the same time, the weak supervision method can also be introduced to solve the problems of the high cost of medical image labeling and insufficient samples and improve the segmentation accuracy of the enhancing tumor region.

References

1. Wang, J.H., Clement, V., Ashley, R., et al.: Multi-atlas segmentation of subcortical brain structures via the autoseg software pipeline. Front. Neuroinform. **8**(7), 432–440 (2014)
2. Sérgio, P., Pinto, A., Oliveira, J., et al.: Automatic brain tissue segmentation in MR images using random forests and conditional random fields. J. Neurosci. Methods **270**, 111–123 (2016)
3. https://arxiv.org/abs/1811.02629
4. https://arxiv.org/abs/1701.03056
5. Ronneberger, O., Fischer, P., Brox, T.: U-Net: convolutional networks for biomedical image segmentation. In: International Conference on Medical Image Computing and Computer-Assisted Intervention, vol. 3, pp. 234–241(2015)
6. Wang, X., Girshick, R., Gupta, A., et al.: Non-local neural networks. In: The IEEE Conference on Computer Vision and Pattern Recognition, vol. 1, pp. 7794–7803 (2017)
7. He, J.J., et al.: Adaptive pyramid context network for semantic segmentation. In: The IEEE Conference on Computer Vision and Pattern Recognition, vol. 1, pp. 7519–7528 (2019)
8. Oktay, O., Schlemper, J., Folgoc, L.L., et al.: Attention U-Net: learning where to look for the pancreas. Med. Imaging Deep Learn. **9**, 605–615 (2018)
9. https://arxiv.org/abs/1701.03056v2
10. Menze, B.H., Jakab, A., Bauer, S., et al.: The multimodal brain tumor image segmentation benchmark (BRATS). IEEE Trans. Med. Imaging **34**(10), 1993–2024 (2015)
11. https://doi.org/10.1038/sdata.2017.117
12. Abraham, N., Mefraz, N.K.: A novel focal tversky loss function with improved attention U-Net for lesion segmentation. In: 2019 IEEE 16th International Symposium on Biomedical Imaging, vol. 1, pp. 683–687 (2019)
13. Casamitjana, A., Cata, M., Sanchez, I., et al.: Cascaded V-Net using ROI masks for brain tumor segmentation. In: International MICCAI Brainlesion Workshop, vol. 4, pp. 381–391 (2018)
14. Pereira, S., Alves, C.V., Silva, A.: Adaptive feature recombination and recalibration for semantic segmentation: application to brain tumor segmentation in MRI. In: International Conference on Medical Image Computing and Computer-Assisted Intervention, vol. 2, pp. 706–714 (2018)
15. https://arxiv.org/abs/1811.10419v1
16. Isensee, F., Kickingereder, P., Wick, W., et al.: Brain tumor segmentation and radiomics survival prediction: contribution to the BRATS 2017 challenge. In: International Conference on Medical Image Computing and Computer-Assisted Intervention, vol. 1, pp. 287–297 (2018)
17. Fu, J., Liu, J., Tian, H., et al.: Dual attention network for scene segmentation. In: The IEEE Conference on Computer Vision and Pattern Recognition, vol. 1, pp. 3146–3154 (2019)

Planning and Design of Distributed Power Grid Based on Weed Algorithm

Jieyun Zheng[1]([⊠]), Chao Xun[2], Xiangjing Qiu[2], Shicheng Huang[2], and Chao Huang[3]

[1] State Grid Fujian Provincial Electric Power Co., Ltd., Institute of Economics and Technology, Fuzhou 350012, Fujian, China
whjunfei@163.com
[2] State Grid Fujian Electric Power Co., Ltd., Fuzhou 350003, Fujian, China
[3] State Grid Fujian Nanjing County Power Supply Company, Nanjing 363600, Fujian, China

Abstract. In recent years, the penetration rate of distributed power sources such as photovoltaics, wind turbines, and micro gas turbines in the distribution network has been increasing. Distributed generation has the advantages of low carbon environmental protection, renewable and flexible control. Meanwhile, affected by wind speed and light intensity, wind turbines, and photovoltaic output have random volatility, which makes the operation of active distribution networks more complex. Network reconfiguration can determine the on and off state of the power grid, to improve the reliability and economy of power supply. Based on the above point of view, it is very important to reduce the power loss and distribution effectively. Taking weeds as an example, this paper analyzes the mathematical model of distribution network transformation. The algorithm theory is analyzed with IEEE33 single feeder node system was proposed, and the effectiveness and practicability of the algorithm in the re-planning of the distribution network with distributed power supply are discussed.

Keywords: Distribution network planning · Weed algorithm · Distributed power supply

1 Introduction

In recent years, the increasingly severe energy crisis and increasingly serious environmental pollution have triggered a new energy revolution worldwide. Distributed power generation has low carbon environmental protection, flexible control, local consumption, and can reduce the economy caused by long-distance transmission. Loss of many other benefits [1]. As an important supplement to the traditional power supply, distributed power sources have made significant contributions to improving energy structure and mitigating environmental pressure, and have a certain effect on the distribution network. With the development of power systems, distributed power access to the distribution network has evolved from a single target with only minimal network loss to a multi-objective optimization problem that considers the voltage distribution index, short-circuit level, and power shortage. The operation of a traditional distribution network is simpler than

© Springer Nature Singapore Pte Ltd. 2020
X. Yuan et al. (Eds.): ICUIA 2020, CCIS 1319, pp. 115–122, 2020.
https://doi.org/10.1007/978-981-33-4601-7_12

that of an active distribution network, and the reconstruction can be used as both a planning tool and a real-time control tool to optimize the safety and economy of the grid operation. In this context, it is very important to study the active reconfiguration of the distribution network.

In this article, the mathematical model of distribution network reconstruction is discussed from the aspects of the objective function, constraint condition, and multi-objective processing method. Then we introduce the weed algorithm concept and process and finally introduce the IEEE 33 single feeder node system as a case. Calculation and verification were performed.

2 Distribution Network Reconstruction Mathematical Model

2.1 Objective Functions and Constraints

From the two perspectives of distribution system operation efficiency and environmental benefit, this paper considers the reconstruction of new energy after accessing the distribution network [2]. To this end, the system's active power loss, node voltage deviation, and indicators are selected as optimization targets. First, the minimum Ploss of the active power loss of the system is as shown in Eq. (1):

$$f_1 = \min p_{loss} = \min \sum_{s=1}^{N_x} p_s \sum_{l=1}^{N_b} \alpha_k R_k |I_k|^2 \tag{1}$$

In the formula, N and p respectively represent the total number of scenes, and the scene probability of the scene s divided according to the scene analysis method. Nb represents the total number of branches of the system [3]. Ak denotes the state of the branch switch, and 0 and 1 respectively correspond to the opening and closing of the switch. Rk and Ik represent the magnitudes of the branch resistance and the branch current, respectively.

We minimize the node voltage deviation ΔU as follows:

$$f_2 = \min \Delta U = \min \sum_{s=1}^{N_x} p_s \max\{U_{ref} - U_j\} \tag{2}$$

The reference voltage and the actual voltage of the node are expressed by Uref and UJ respectively. Constraints for distribution network reconfiguration include power flow constraints, node voltage constraints, branch power constraints, DG output constraints, and network topology constraints.

The trend constraint is:

$$\begin{cases} P_{i_n} = U_{i_n} \sum_{j_n \in G(i_n)} U_{j_n} \left(G_{i_n j_n} \cos \theta_{i_n j_n} + B_{i_n j_n} \sin \theta_{i_n j_n} \right) \\ Q_{i_n} = U_{i_n} \sum_{j_n \in c(i_n)} U_{j_n} \left(G_{i_n j_n} \sin \theta_{i_n j_n} - B_{i_n j_n} \cos \theta_{i_n j_n} \right) \\ \qquad\qquad i_n = 1, 2, 3 \dots, i, N \end{cases} \tag{3}$$

In Eq. (3), Pin is the active and reactive power of node in, respectively. Uin and Ujn are the node voltages of nodes in and jn, respectively, and G(in) is the node directly connected to node i. Ginjn and Binjn are the branch conductance and susceptance of the node machines in and jn respectively; The phase angle difference between the middle node and the jn node is θ in jn, where the total number of system nodes is N.

The node voltage constraint is as follows:

$$U_{i_n \min} \leq U_{i_n} \leq U_{i_n \max} \tag{4}$$

In Eq. (4), Uin min and Uin max are the upper and lower limits of the node in voltage.

2.2 Multi-target Processing Method

In the actual optimization problem, most of the optimization goals are often more than one, but multi-objective optimization problems. Compared with single-objective optimization, the advantage of multi-objective optimization is that it can simultaneously optimize the optimization of multiple indicators. Distribution network reconfiguration is a multi-objective optimization problem [4, 5]. At the same time, four indicators are selected as the objective function of optimization. For this reason, the maximum and minimum methods based on fuzzy membership functions are used to deal with multi-objective optimization problems. This method not only solves the problem of dimension and magnitude difference of each objective function value but also avoids the artificial selection of the weight coefficient. First, convert each objective function value into a membership function value. The conversion formula is as follows:

$$MF_j(x) = \begin{cases} 1 & f_j(x) \leq f_j^{\min}(x) \\ \frac{f_j^{\max}(x) - f(x)_j}{f_j^{\max}(x) - f_j^{\min}(x)} & f_j^{\min}(x) < f_i(x) \\ 0 & f_i(x) \geq f_j^{\max}(x) \\ j = 1, 2, 3, 4 \end{cases} \tag{5}$$

In Eq. (5), f(x) represents the function value of the jth objective function, MF(x) corresponds to the membership function value, fjmin(x), fjmax(x) represents the minimum and maximum values under the single objective function respectively. Because the four objective functions selected in this paper are all to find the minimum. Therefore, the larger the MF (x) value is, the closer the objective function value is to the optimal solution under single-objective optimization, and the better the decision-making effect. Due to the possible contradictions and constraints between the various objective functions, the overall satisfaction f of each set of solutions takes the minimum of all membership functions, namely:

$$f = \min\{MF_j(x)\} \tag{6}$$

3   Weed Algorithm

In recent years, more and more scholars have proposed a series of intelligent algorithms inspired by the natural environment to solve the problem of multi-objective optimization.

The algorithm of weed invasion optimization proposed by foreign scholars for the first time is a numerical random search algorithm which simulates the natural growth behavior of weeds in the optimized living space. The IW0 algorithm in this paper simulates the robustness, adaptability, and randomness of weeds in the breeding process in a simple way. The natural evolution of plants mainly has two main choices: r selection and human selection. r selection and k selection correspond to the global exploration mode and the local search mode of the IW0 algorithm, respectively. This allows the particles to have a higher convergence rate and is less prone to a local optimum. Figure 1 shows the steps of the weed algorithm.

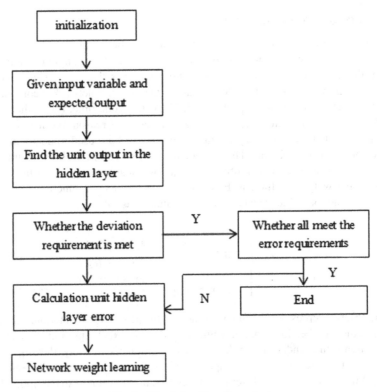

Fig. 1. Weed algorithm flow chart

In the last step of the competitive survival rule process, after a certain number of iterations, the weed population will reach the maximum number of ethnic groups allowed for rapid reproduction. However, we hope that the more adaptable plants are better. The competitive survival rule is: when the number of weeds in the population reaches the maximum, each weed is propagated and spatially distributed in the above manner. Sort the resulting offspring and initial plants according to the fitness value, select the Qsize individuals with the highest fitness value, and clear the other individuals with small adaptation values. This way, individuals with low initial fitness value have the opportunity to reproduce. If their offspring adapt to better values, this offspring can survive. This way of letting plants grow faster and then retain more competitive individuals in a relatively stable environment corresponds to the biological r choice and k. options. It not only ensures the diversity of the population but also makes the optimal value of the algorithm reasonable.

4   Results and Case Analysis

This paper uses the IEEE33 single feeder node system for simulation. The rated voltage of the system is 12.66 kV, including 37 branches and 5 tie switches S33-S37. The total system load is 3715 kW + j2300 kvar. The system has a reference capacity of 10MVA, a rated voltage of 12.66 kV, a total active load of 3 715 kW, a total reactive load of 2300 kvar, and an initial network loss of 0.203 MW. The load nodes 2-33 in the network can run a distributed power supply, and only one DG can be installed in each node [6–8]. DGS is treated as PQ node, and each node is allowed to install DG, at this time, the power factor λ is 0.9. The capacity is 50 kVA, the maximum capacity is 200 kVA, and the investment cost per unit of DG unit is Cxc = 1 200 yuan/kW. The maintenance cost per unit of DG unit is Cw = 50 yuan/kW, and the unit price is C, = 0.5 yuan/kWh. The annual maximum load loss hour Tmax = 3000 h, the total DC access capacity is limited to 10% of the total capacity of the distribution network system, and the voltage deviation is specified at ±7%.

The specific parameters of the algorithm are shown in Table 1.

Table 1. Weed IWO algorithm parameter settings

P_{size}/One	Initial population	20
Iter $_{max}$/time	The maximum number of iterations	200
Q_{size}/One	Maximum allowable number of ethnic groups	30
S_{max}/One	Maximum number of seeds per weed	5
S_{min}/One	Minimum number of seeds per weed	1
λ	Nonlinear modulation index	3
δstart	Initial interval step	3
δstop	Final interval step	0.5

The simulation results for different scenarios are shown in Table 2. The results show that the power loss of the power grid can be effectively reduced by the improved algorithm and the access of distributed generation.

Reconstruction of the distribution network by the weed algorithm in Case2 reduced the network loss of the distribution network from 202.67 kW before reconstruction to 139.53 kW. In Case3, the weed algorithm with existing research was used to reconstruct the distribution network containing DG, reducing the network loss to 62.08 kW. In Case4, the weed algorithm modified by this paper is used to reconstruct the distribution network

Table 2. IEEE33 node simulation reconstruction results

Contrast indicator	Case1	Case2	Case3	Case4
Network loss	202.67	139.53	62.08	53.28
Reduction ratio	–	31.15%	69.37%	73.71%
Contact switch	33, 34, 35, 36, 37	7, 9, 14, 32, 37	11, 14, 32, 33, 37	7, 9, 1114, 24, 33
DG position	–	–	6	6
DG capacity	–	–	2468.5	2468.5

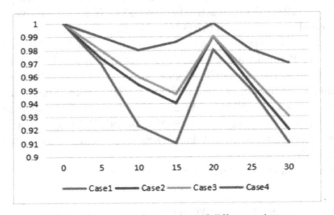

Fig. 2. voltage distribution curve of different schemes

with DG to reduce the network loss step to 53.28 kw. The voltage distribution index of different schemes is shown in Fig. 2.

As shown in Fig. 3, due to the introduction and improvement of distributed power supply in the curve, the voltage distribution of each node is greatly improved, so as to make the system run more stable, thus ensuring the reliability and balance of power supply. At the same time, Fig. 3 shows that the weed algorithm can reduce the network loss more effectively after introducing the multi-objective solution method. Meanwhile, the iteration number of the algorithm in this paper is significantly reduced, which verifies that the algorithm in this paper has higher search efficiency and can quickly converge to obtain the global optimal solution [9–11].

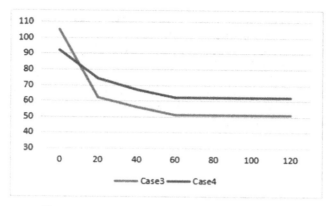

Fig. 3. Comparison of Case3 and Case4 network loss

5 Conclusions

According to the planning simulation of distributed power supply in IEEE33 node distribution network system, the weed IWO algorithm proposed in this paper uses the theory of optimal solution to establish a set of non-dominant optimal solutions, and then uses fuzzy decision to select the optimal solution according to different target weight factors. By introducing the multi-agent system into the traditional algorithm, the convergence speed and accuracy of the algorithm are effectively improved. It is feasible and effective to apply IWO algorithm to the distribution network planning and optimization with distributed power supply while improving the node voltage of the distribution network.

References

1. Liang, T., Xie, Q., Liu, C., et al.: Comprehensive benefit evaluation of distribution network planning based on the life cycle cost theory and the cloud matter element theory. **45**(19), 12–17 (2017)
2. Liu, W., Zhou, Z., Liu, H.: Research on auto disturbance rejection of PMLSM based on chaos algorithm and invasive weed optimization algorithm. J. Jilin Univ. **35**(5), 102–103 (2017)
3. Huang, X., Ye, C., Cao, L.: Chaos invasive weed optimization algorithm for multi-objective permutation flow shop scheduling problem. Xitong Gongcheng Lilun yu Shijian/Syst. Eng. Theory Pract. **37**(1), 253–262 (2017)
4. Ghadiri, A., Haghifam, M.R., Larimi, S.M.M.: A novel approach for hybrid AC/DC distribution network planning using genetic algorithm. IET Gener. Transm. Distrib. **11**(16), 32–35 (2017)
5. Xia, C., Zhang, Y., Chen, I.-M.: Learning sampling distribution for motion planning with local reconstruction-based self-organizing incremental neural network. Neural Comput. Appl. **31**(12), 9185–9205 (2019). https://doi.org/10.1007/s00521-019-04370-y
6. Pan, Z., Liu, J., Shi, M., et al.: Static voltage stability and weak bus analysis of islanded microgrids considering static voltage/frequency characteristics. **4**(35), 1012–1014 (2017)
7. vom Brocke, J., Maedche, A.: The DSR grid: six core dimensions for effectively planning and communicating design science research projects. Electron. Mark. **29**(3), 379–385 (2019). https://doi.org/10.1007/s12525-019-00358-7

8. Feng, L., Feng, Q.I., Lu-Jie, Q.I., et al.: Design of business collaboration oriented power grid planning and intelligent decision platform. **8**(13), 58–59 (2018)
9. Lai, Q., Wu, Z., Cui, K., et al.: Key technology analysis and prospect of microgrid planning and design. Electr. Power Constr. **51**(1), 51–52 (2018)
10. Birchfield, A.B., Xu, T., Overbye, T.J.: Power flow convergence and reactive power planning in the creation of large synthetic grids. IEEE Trans. Power Syst. **21**(99), 1 (2018)
11. Arfeen, Z.A., Khairuddin, A.B., Larik, R.M., Saeed, M.S., et al.: Control of distributed generation systems for microgrid applications: a technological review. Int. Trans. Electr. Energy Syst. (2) (2019)

Classroom Engagement Evaluation Using Multi-sensor Fusion with a 180° Camera View

Ramya Sri Gadaley[1(✉)], Prakash Duraisamy[1], James Van Haneghan[1], and Steve Jackson[2]

[1] University of South Alabama, Mobile, AL 36688, USA
rg1921@jagmail.southalabama.edu
[2] University of North Texas, Denton, TX 76203, USA

Abstract. Classroom engagement is a challenging task in modern days due to a lot of digital distractions, but keeping students engaged is one important factor that determines whether students learn from lectures. Globally, many schools and colleges force students not to bring any digital devices to the class. Even though they force them to listen but professors could not get the insights of the student's engagement due to daydreaming and they cannot monitor the students if the classroom size is larger. In this paper, we focus on classroom engagement with all digital devices and observe their level of attention in the class. We recorded the facial gestures of the students during the lecture from the front end (180° view of the camera). Most of the traditional classroom assessment tools are based on summary judgments of students in the form of student surveys filled out in class or online once a semester. Such ratings are often biased and do not capture the real-time teaching of professors. In addition, they fail for the most part to capture the locus of teaching and learning difficulties. They cannot differentiate whether the ongoing poor performance of students is a function of the instructor's lack of teaching skill or the student's lack of engagement in the class. So, in order to streamline and improve the evaluation of classroom engagement, we introduce human gestures as an additional tool to improve teaching evaluation along with other techniques. In this paper, we report the results of using a novel technique that uses a semi-automatic computer vision-based approach to obtain an accurate prediction of classroom engagement in classes where students can have digital devices like laptops and, cellphones during lectures. We conducted our experiment in various classroom sizes at different times of the day.

Keywords: Classroom · Engagement · Camera · Computer vision

1 Introduction

Maintaining classroom engagement is a challenging task in modern days due to an abundance of digital distractions, but keeping students engaged is one impor-

Supported by University of South Alabama.

X. Yuan et al. (Eds.): ICUIA 2020, CCIS 1319, pp. 123–131, 2020.
https://doi.org/10.1007/978-981-33-4601-7_13

tant factor that determines whether students learn from lectures [4]. Globally, many schools and colleges require students not to bring any digital devices to the class. Even though they force the students to listen, the professors cannot accurately determine the degree of student engagement due to factors such as daydreaming and they cannot monitor the students closely if the classroom size is larger.

In this paper, we focus on assessing classroom engagement in environments with permitted digital devices and observe the student level of attention in the class. We recorded the facial gestures of the students during the lecture from the front end (180° camera view) in addition to recording the audio interaction. We note that most of the traditional classroom assessment tools are based on summary judgments of students in the form of student surveys filled out in class or online once a semester. Such ratings are often biased and do not capture the real-time teaching of professors. In addition, they fail for the most part to capture the locus of teaching and learning difficulties. They cannot differentiate, for example, whether ongoing poor performance of students is a function of the instructor's lack of teaching skills or the student's lack of engagement in the class. So, in order to streamline and improve the evaluation of classroom engagement, we introduce the use of human gestures as additional tools to improve teaching evaluation along with other techniques. In this paper, we report the results of using a novel technique that uses a semi-automatic computer vision-based approach to obtain an accurate prediction of classroom engagement in classes where students can have digital devices such as laptops and cellphones during lectures. We conducted our experiment in various classroom sizes at different times of the day.

Classroom Engagement deals with the degree of attention, enthusiasm, activeness, passion to learn by the students from the professor. It varies with the classroom environment, courses, time duration, professor, or timings of the lecture. For example, a student who was not engaged in the early morning class might be engaged in the afternoon class because of the class timings. Similarly, a student who was engaged in the class for the first 30 min might be distracted later due to the long duration of the class. Therefore, classroom engagement depends upon various attributes.

Classroom Engagement Evaluation is assessing how well the students are engaged when a professor is delivering a lecture in a classroom environment. Maintaining classroom engagement is important to solving many of the difficulties of students such as low grades, boredom, high dropout rates, and so on. Students who are more engaged in the class seem to achieve better grades in the course than those who are not. Effective Classroom engagement paves the way to develop two-way communication between the professor and the students. This learning process of the students in the classroom increases their curiosity and focuses them on the subject, motivates them to practice great brainstorming problems, and promotes them to achieve their learning goals which in turn makes them successful. Student engagement also plays a critical role in the success of the university and future enrollment.

A traditional method for evaluating classroom engagement is through the use of student evaluations. Student evaluations typically are computed only once at the end of the semester. This evaluation will explore the insight of the students and the evaluation results give the professor's lagging areas. It may be a good tool for novice professors and it can also aid experienced professors to validate new courses or to find the response rate of complex portions of the courses. However, the evaluation is not sampled much, so the professor cannot find their mistakes in the early or middle part of the semester which may result in both the students and professors not being on the same page.

Other traditional methods used to assess classroom engagement are through assignments, exams, or other performance assessments. The students who achieved the best grades were considered to be more engaged and students who achieved the low grades were considered as less engaged. Later, student engagement was evaluated through the use of a questionnaire given to the students. The questionnaire includes questions about the student's interest in the topic, their participation in the class, the professor's teaching style, and various other entities. But the answers provided by the students can be biased or depend upon several external factors. So, that is not the optimal solution to evaluate classroom engagement (Fig. 1).

(a) Texting   (b) Cellphone

(c) Sleeping   (d) Facebook

Fig. 1. Different distractions in classroom environment

In modern days, students are allowed to bring their digital devices such as mobile phones and laptops into the classroom. These devices act as distractors during the lectures. This might result in lower grades. So, professors need to notice this and certain measures need to be taken to rectify it. Here we are introducing a new method where student engagement is calculated by facial emotions. The facial emotions and gestures are scored by a semi-automated procedure [3]. This will produce a continuous-time calculation of an engagement index, useful even for larger classes. This helps professors to observe the activity of each student after completion of the class. By the result of the evaluation, professors will be able to identify less engaged students and make them engaged in the upcoming classes by slightly modifying the teaching style or eliminating the root cause for their distractions.

2   Related Work

Student Engagement is often calculated by recognizing emotions. Emotion Recognition is the process of identifying human emotions. Human emotions are mainly classified into six. They are anger, disgust, fear, happiness, sadness, and surprise. Emotions are the primary aspect in determining student engagement in the class.

In earlier days, most of the researchers have used global super-segmental or prosodic features as their acoustic cues for emotion recognition. They implemented three different classifiers for emotion classification. The classifiers are the Maximum Likelihood Bayes classifier (MLB), Kernel Regression (KR), K-nearest neighbors (KNN) [1]. Then, researchers used three different systems based on audio, video, and bimodal information to calculate human emotions. The most widely used speech cues for audio emotion recognition are global-level prosodic features such as the statistics of the pitch and the intensity. In a video-based system, the captured video is divided into frames and the extracted information from every frame is fed into the PCA algorithm. In the bimodal system, both acoustic cues and facial expressions are used to calculate human emotion. Two approaches named feature level fusion and decision level fusion are used in which the acoustic cues and facial data are fed into the single classifier and two separate classifiers respectively.

This was overcome by adding K-Nearest Neighbor (KNN) to the PCA algorithm [5]. PCA algorithm was used for feature extraction and the KNN algorithm was used for classifying facial emotions. The main drawback of this method is accuracy when the population becomes large [8].

To improve accuracy, a new method is introduced which is a combination of the PCA reconstruction algorithm and Snapsort algorithm on the eigenfaces [2]. This combination of algorithms achieved greater accuracy than the previous algorithms. The disadvantage of this method is it works only on still images and dimensionality needs to be reduced. Later, a neural Adaboost based facial expression recognition system was introduced [6]. In this recognition system, Viola and Jones algorithm for face detection, Gabor feature extraction, Adaboost feature reduction algorithms were used. This system reduced the image dimensions and preserved the perceptual quality of the original image. The limitation of this method is that it faces the difficulty of recognizing mild expressions.

By considering all the limitations and drawbacks of previous methods, the Haar Cascades method Sobel edge detection method is introduced in [7]. In this system, higher efficiency and accuracy are achieved. But the problem is it does not involve illumination. Recently, wearable devices are introduced to analyze students' attention and evaluate classroom engagement. For this, a Rule-based approach and a Data-driven approach are used. It cannot be used for larger class evaluation as it is difficult to provide a wearable device to each student [9]. Later, Image processing came into the picture. To overcome all the drawbacks and limitations of previous methods, we are introducing a novel method for the evaluation of classroom engagement.

The novelty of our proposed method includes the following aspects:

- As the system develops, it can be used as an additional evaluation tool for classroom evaluation on a daily basis.
- The success and failure of a course outcome can be known with much deeper analysis.
- Students who are exceptionally out of sync with the lecture can be identified from this algorithm.
- The system can be used to identify when students are lack of engagement in lecture is a source of learning problems.

3 Proposal Method

The data set for this is derived from observations of the students. Students are placed in different classroom environments such as different levels of students (undergraduate and graduate) and different timings. We record the students' emotions during a lecture in a modern classroom environment using a conventional digital camera. The attributes which are supplied as the inputs to our approach are (a) Audio (b) Facial Expressions (c) Eyeball movements (d) Body gestures (e) Neighborhood Influence.

The entities such as classroom environment, specific course, time duration, professor, or timings of the lecture on which the student engagement depends are also observed along with the student's movements.

3.1 Observation of Student Attention

Once the video is recorded, we extract from the sensor audio data (1D data) and video frame data (2D data) specific attribute values corresponding to human face gestures related to signs of distraction such as body position, eye moments (all attributes mentioned in Tables 1 and 2).

We try to classify all the gestures for the available student data in the video. We give scores to every attributes from sensors based on the distraction level. Every student is evaluated based on attributes mentioned in Table 1 and Table 2 (undergraduate and graduate students). We sampled video clips for every 30 sec for a total duration of 45 min. On each sample, starting and ending times

(a) Data set 1

(b) Dataset 2

Fig. 2. Student attention in the classroom

were labeled, and actions related to engagement (attributes) were calculated. For each of the attributes in Tables 1 and 2, and, for each of these video samples, a binary assessment score was given: 0 for not engaged and 1 for engaging. These scores were summed over the course of the video to obtain an engagement score for that particular attribute. We calculated the mean values of every attribute behavior from the video samples (Fig. 2).

In addition to this attribute data which was extracted manually from the video frames, automated feature extraction was performed using Microsoft Azure. The selected video frames were passed to Azure which performed facial recognition on the images and assigned attribute valued for the categories "anger", "contempt", "disgust", "fear", "happiness", "neutral", "sadness", and "surprise." We currently used the "happiness' and "neutral" attributes as indicators of positive engagement, with the others signs of negative engagement. We added these positive engagement attributes and subtracted the negative attribute values to arrive at an engagement index. In this way, we computed for all students an attention/engagement level and related the students' observable behavior to an attention level.

4   Experiments

From Tables 1, 2, and 3, we correlate the relations between student's attention level and professor's lecturer style. This study helps to find the root cause for student's distraction. For each of the student attributes which are being measured through the various sensor modalities, an aggregate time-dependent function $f_i(t)$ (where $i = 1, \ldots, n$ ranges over the possible attributes) is computed which measures the amount to which this attribute at time t is a factor in student distraction. For some of the attributes (such as body position), $f_i(t)$ will be computed by measuring a corresponding value $f_i^j(t)$ for each individual student (indexed by j), and then averaging over the student population $f_i(i) = \frac{1}{N} \sum_j f_i^j(t)$. For other attributes (such as background noise) the aggregate value $f_i(t)$ will be measured directly. For example, $f_i^j(t)$ might represent the angular deviation from vertical of the head position of student j at time t. A mathematical modeling function $g(x_1, \ldots, x_n)$ will be developed which accesses the degree of student distraction from the values of $x_i = f_i(t)$. Thus we will have the function $u(t) = g(f_1(t), \ldots, f_n(t))$ which is the time-dependent measurement of student distraction.

Table 1. Student's observation from undergraduate students 11.00 A.M.

Attention Level of Students (Dataset - 1)
Time Duration: 45 min, Number of participants - 8

Behavior	Poor	Average	Test results
Positive facial gestures	–	87.5%	12.5%
Eye position		20%	80%
Active devices	25%	–	75%
Body positions	–	12.5%	87.5% (gaze)
Audio interaction	87.5% (no response)	12.5% (low interaction)	–
Neighborhood influence	–	–	100%

In a similar manner, we will, by sensor measurements, have determined functions $h_k(t)$ for each of the attributes (indexed by k) being assessed for the lecturer (see Table 2). The next step is to correlate the function $u(t)$ with the functions $h_k(t)$. This will be done through both a regression/correlation and a clustering

Table 2. Student's observation from graduate students (3.30 P.M.)

Attention Level of Students (Dataset - 2)
Time Duration: 45 min, Number of participants - 5

Behavior	Poor	Average	Test results
Positive facial gestures	–	100%	–
Eye position	10%		90%
Active devices	10%		90%
Body positions	–	–	100% (gaze)
Audio interaction	–	–	–
Neighborhood influence	–	–	100%

Table 3. Professor's teaching style attributes

Classroom Lecturer (45 min)

Teaching attributes	Time
Using classroom boards	9 min (20%)
Slides	36 min (80%)
Video	0 min
Tone of lecturer	50% variation in modulation

analysis. The regression analysis will seek to determine the coefficients $a_1, \ldots, a_n$ so that

$$\int \left(u(t) - \sum (a_i h_i(t)) \right)^2 dt$$

is minimized. This will then determine how student distraction is affected by the various performance attributes of the instruction. The cluster analysis will cluster the time-series data into clusters determined by ranges of values for the faculty attributes. For example, one clustering could be determined by whether the faculty member is speaking, writing on the board, or showing a presentation to the class. An overall assessment of student distraction for the class will be computed as $\int |u(t)| \, dt$.

5   Conclusion

From our experiment, we conclude that our experiment has both positive outcomes and negative outcomes. We conducted the above experiments in different classrooms at different timings. Overall, the students seemed to be engaged in the lecture. We did notice a few distractions in both classrooms. The experiment which we have conducted only covers a 180-degree view of the classroom. So, there is some degree of ambiguity in determining the students' engagement in the classroom by considering only facial expressions and body gestures attributes from this view. For example, students can have positive facial expressions and body gestures when they are using a mobile phone or when they are playing games on the laptop. Students can also be daydreaming while having positive facial expressions and body gestures. The other attributes such as eyeball movement and head movement seem to be more realistic when calculating student engagement.

5.1 Limitation

- Most of the students show their facial gestures are neutral (not happy nor sad) and most of their eye moments are all focused on the laptop. Since our camera covers only 180-degree, we have no exact knowledge if students follow the powerpoints along with the professor or distracted by other social media from the internet.
- The interaction level being too low also indicates the student may get distracted by the internet.

5.2 Future Work

We plan to place another camera on the backside of the students which can cover the uncovered scenes from the first camera (180° view) which can give a better visualization about class climate.

References

1. Busso, C., et al.: Analysis of emotion recognition using facial expressions speech and multimodal information. In: Proceedings of the 6th International Conference on Multimodal Interfaces, vol. 123, pp. 205–211(2004)
2. Chakrabarti, D.D.: Facial expression recognition using eigenspaces. Proc. Technol. **10**, 755–761 (2013)
3. Chen, T., et al.: Emotion recognition using empirical mode decomposition and approximation entropy. Comput. Electr. Eng. **72**, 383–392 (2018)
4. Liu, Y., Xie, Z., Yuan, X., Chen, J., Song, W.: Multi-level structured hybrid forest for joint head detection and pose estimation. Neurocomputing **266**, 206–215 (2017)
5. Ou, J.: Classification algorithms research on facial expression recognition. Proc. Technol. **25**, 1241–1244 (2012)
6. Owusu, E., Zhan, Y., Mao, Q.R.: A neural-adaboost based facial expression recognition system. Exp. Syst. Appl. **41**, 3383–3890 (2014)
7. Yang, D., Alsadoon, A.: An emotion recognition model based on facial recognition in virtual learning environment. Proc. Comput. Sci. **125**, 2–10 (2018)
8. Yuan, X., Abouelenien, M., Elhoseny, M.: A boosting-based decision fusion method for learning from large, imbalanced face data set. In: Hassanien, A.E., Elhoseny, M., Kacprzyk, J. (eds.) Quantum Computing: An Environment for Intelligent Large Scale Real Application. SBD, vol. 33, pp. 433–448. Springer, Cham (2018). https://doi.org/10.1007/978-3-319-63639-9_18
9. Zhang, X., Wu, C.: Analyzing students' attention in class using wearable devices. In: IEEE Conference, vol. 13, pp. 123–125 (2017)

Mobility and Transportation

Urban Scene Recognition via Deep Network Integration

Zhinan Qiao[1(✉)], Xiaohui Yuan[1], and Mohamed Elhoseny[2]

[1] University of North Texas, Denton, TX 76207, USA
ZhinanQiao@my.unt.edu, xiaohui.yuan@unt.edu
[2] Mansoura University, Mansoura 35516, Egypt
mohamed_elhoseny@mans.edu.eg

Abstract. Scene understanding remains a challenging task due to the complex and ambiguous nature of scene images in defiance of several networks pre-trained on large-scale benchmark datasets are available. In this paper, we proposed a multi-scale, discriminative integrating method to aggregate both context and multi-scale object information of urban scene images. Our model is formulated as the integration of both patches and networks. Our scene-centric network is built upon the network fine-tuned on scenery dataset; our object-centric is an aggregation of multi-scale networks pre-trained on object-centric networks. We show that the integration of networks leads to an improvement in performance and achieved a 6.63% boost on overall accuracy comparing with the best-performed base model.

Keywords: Classification · Multi-scale · Decision fusion

1 Introduction

Scene recognition remains a challenging problem mostly due to the complexity and variety of the enclosed objects and background [3,15]. A typical scenery image contains multiple objects of different scales. Hence, getting an accurate classification of a scenery image relies on both an understanding of the objects and the knowledge of the background. This predicament is more conspicuous for urban scenery understanding, which is often cluttered and complex in nature, and calls for improved methods to learn both the dominant objects and the surrounding context in images.

Deep convolutional neural networks (CNNs) such as AlexNet [7] and ResNet [4] demonstrated a superior performance for generic classification tasks. However, understanding a scenery is beyond recognizing a single object or a collection of objects; an image is not simply an assembly of objects (i.e., object-level information). The spatial arrangement of objects, their scales, and frequencies (number of occurrences), and the interactions between objects and background (i.e., scene-level information) are factors for deciding what an image presents.

© Springer Nature Singapore Pte Ltd. 2020
X. Yuan et al. (Eds.): ICUIA 2020, CCIS 1319, pp. 135–149, 2020.
https://doi.org/10.1007/978-981-33-4601-7_14

It was demonstrated that CNNs trained with ImageNet dataset [2] (i.e., object-centric CNN) performs well for generic object recognition and CNNs trained with Places dataset [16] (i.e., scene-centric CNN) exhibits improved performance for scene recognition [15].

The success of inferring scene categorizing by integrating multiple CNNs for object and scene recognition demonstrated that aggregating knowledge derived from separate CNNs helps to gain a comprehensive understanding of an image and encourages the development of a coherent object- and scene-centric model for improved accuracy [1,17]. Inspired by these studies, we developed a discriminative CNN integration method to aggregate image features learned by various networks. Our method leverages the scene-centric CNNs to learn scene features and adopts multi-scale object-centric CNNs to learn object features at different scales and integrates these features via a discriminative fusion strategy.

In our paper, we extend the multi-branch network [5] and propose a method to integrate object-level features with scenery features extracted with object-centric and scene-centric networks, respectively. Scene-centric networks are fine-tuned on the Place365 dataset [15]. The Fully Connected (FC) layers of the CNNs are re-trained using urban street view images. Object-centric networks are developed on the networks trained with ImageNet [2], which consist of networks for multi-scale inputs. The final scene recognition result is obtained by aggregating the object- and scene-centric models via discriminative integration.

The rest of this paper is organized as follows. Section 2 reviews the related works. Section 3 describes the proposed method and network architecture. Section 4 discusses the experimental results. Section 5 concludes the paper with a summary.

2   Related Work

To accommodate objects in various scales and the disparity among models trained with datasets emphasizing different aspects, Herranz et al. [5] presented a method to integrate object and scene information for scene recognition. The semantic features of a scenery image were extracted by CNNs, which were concatenated to train a Support Vector Machine (SVM) classifier. Wang et al. [12] extended this idea by training two PatchNet models for recognizing objects and the entire scene using the cropped patches from images of the ImageNet [2] and the Places dataset [14]. The two models extract activation maps and probability distributions, which are used to form image descriptors for training an SVM. These methods use all the cropped patches for training the network and the sub-networks are treated equally, i.e., having the same weights at the integration.

Using all the cropped patches to train an object-centric network faces indispensable 'noise' because the informative part may only exist in a small region of an image. To filter out the futile parts of the training images, methods have been proposed to identify the most informative local features to guide patch cropping from the dataset of the target applications. Cheng et al. [1] presented a method that identifies the most discriminative object-level patches. An object distribution is computed and patches that contain objects frequently appeared in various images are discarded. Xia et al. [13] used the Grad-CAM [9] method to capture class-specific regions in an image and applied object- and scene-centric models to the identified regions for extracting multi-scale features, which are concatenated for classification. Despite the improvements, these methods require a separate step to identify the informative patches and remove the rest parts, which is time-consuming and could result in information drop.

Besides concatenation, trainable integration methods have been devised. Seong et al. [10] proposed an Object-to-Scene Class Conversion module (CCM) that unifies the class probability vectors (i.e., the output of the Softmax layer of CNNs) of an object-centric network and a scene-centric network. The unified probability vectors are integrated via summation for the final decision. A later work of the authors extended CCM by adding a correlative context gating (CCG) model to object-centric branch [11]. The output of the CCG model was fused with the output of the scene-branch by element-wise multiplication. Inspired by the recent development, we hypothesize that learning and fusing multi-scale features using networks fine-tuned with datasets of local and global emphasis improves scene recognition. In addition, automatic discriminative integration helps to learn complex scenery images without an expensive training process.

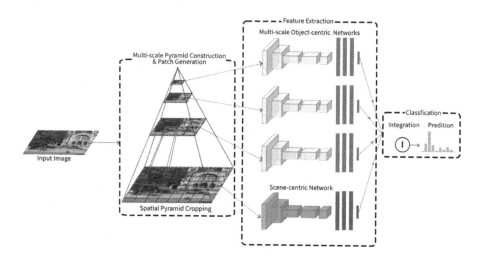

Fig. 1. The flowchart of our proposed method.

3   Method

Figure 1 illustrates the flowchart of our proposed method. Without loss of generality, this flowchart depicts the convolutional network architecture of AlexNet [7].

The input image is used to train the scene-centric network, which is also resized to different scales following the Gaussian pyramid decomposition. These re-scaled versions are used to train object-centric networks, which consists of three networks trained with patches at different scales. The outputs of these three networks are integrated with the output of the scene-centric network via discriminative integration to make the final prediction.

3.1 Multi-scale Feature Extraction

Our method generates multi-scale patches using a spatial pyramid patch generation approach. The input image is re-scaled to various sizes and we use a fixed-size window to slide over the input image. The regions enclosed within the window are cropped as the multi-scale patches. In our implementation, we resize the input image and get the patches using a fixed-sized window to simplify the patch sampling process.

We use the AlexNet [7], ResNet18 and ResNet50 [4] trained with ImageNet [2] and Places [16] datasets as our backbone models. To maintain the generic feature extraction capability of the pre-trained models, we keep the convolution groups and re-train the FC layers of our models using an eight-class urban scene dataset. In the training phase of the scene-centric network, un-cropped training images are used to capture the overall features. The patches of different scales are fed into CNNs to learn the patch-level descriptors at each scale. The datasets provide no annotation of the objects within the scenery images. Labeling the objects using bounding boxes is time-consuming and difficult because a patch may contain multiple objects or parts of an object. Our method retrains the FC layers of base models and the Softmax score vector extracted by both scene- and object-centric networks are $1 \times N$ vector, where N denotes the class number of the training dataset.

3.2 Discriminative Integration and Scene Recognition

Our proposed discriminative integration method is inspired by the traits of generalized average function and the inherent noisy and information sparsity of patches. Figure 2 use $x^i + y^i$ as an example of the generalized average formula. When i increases, the equation trends to encourage the relatively large values of x and y and penalize the small values. As scenery images are always complex and noisy, the number of cropped patches that contain useful information is limited. To effectively making use of more informative patches and reduce the influences of the noisy patches, we adopted a variant of generalized average formula to perform discriminative integration of Softmax predictions of patches for the patch-based networks.

Similarly, as the training procedure, we adopt the cropped group of patches for every testing image and integrate the Softmax outputs of all the patches and compute the overall score, S_n, as follows:

$$S_n = \frac{1}{N} \sum_{i=1}^{N} y\left(C_n | P_i\right)^k, \tag{1}$$

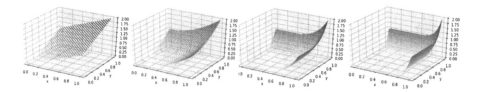

Fig. 2. Landscape of the exponent factor of 1, 2, 5, and 10 (from left to right).

where $y\left(C_n|P_i\right)$ is the Softmax prediction of patch P_i for class C_n, N is the number of patches generated by the input image, and k is a parameter that controls the aggregating preference. This discriminative integration method is designed to emphasize the patches, which contain informative objects at multiple scales and eliminate the patches that make a limited contribution to scene understanding. A higher value of k will emphasize the most discriminative patches, which have more distinct prediction scores and ignored the patches with evenly distributed scores.

The multi-scale patch-based networks are integrated as follows:

$$O_n = \frac{1}{N}\sum_{i=1}^{N} S\left(C_n|N_i\right)^j, \tag{2}$$

where O_n is the resulting score of multi-scale, object-centric network integration, N is number of networks, $S\left(C_n|N_i\right)$ is the Softmax prediction of network N_i for class C_n. After integrating multi-scale object-centric networks, the result of the multi-scale integration is aggregated with the Softmax prediction of the scene-centric network via averaging to make the final prediction.

4   Experimental Results

4.1   Dataset and Settings

In our experiments, we use the building instance classification dataset (BIC GSV) [6], which contains 17,600 training images and 2,058 testing images collected from Google Street View. The dataset consists of eight classes including apartment, church, garage, house, industrial, office building, retail, and roof. Figure 3 illustrates exemplar images of the dataset. Most of the images contain multiply objects at various scales. We used 75% of the examples of each class for training and the rest for validation. We trained the networks with SGD optimizer (momentum is 0.9) using Pytorch [8] on four Nvidia Tesla K80 GPUs with a batch size of eight for 100 epochs (for patch-based networks batch size is 256). The learning rate was initialized to 0.001 and reduced to 1/10 every seven epochs.

(a) apartment   (b) church   (c) garage   (d) house

(e) industrial   (f) office bldg   (g) retail   (h) roof

Fig. 3. Examples of images in the BIC GSV dataset.

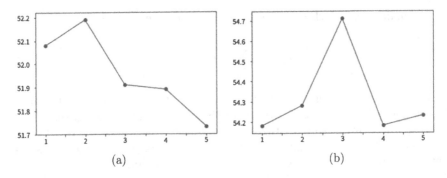

(a)   (b)

Fig. 4. Accuracy (y-axis) w.r.t. different exponent factors (x-axis). (a) Accuracy using Eq. (1). (b) Accuracy using Eq. (2).

4.2 Performance of Patch Integration

In this section, we evaluate the discriminative patch integration. We use AlexNet in our experiments for analysis. We crop each training image to the size of s × s, where s ∈ {100, 150, 200}, and each patch is re-scale to the size of 224 × 224 to ensure a consistent input size to the deep networks. We train a network for each scale of patches. We also train a hybrid AlexNet, which uses all the cropped images as the input (Hybrid in Table 1). The testing images are cropped in the same manner as that of the training images, e.g., for the AlexNet trained using patches of size 100 × 100, we use the patches of size 100 × 100 for testing and aggregate the Softmax prediction of sampled patches using discriminative integration.

Figure 4(a) shows the accuracy of the patch integration using different exponent factor k in Eq. (1). This plot shows the results of an AlexNet trained with patches of size 200 × 200. It is clear that as the exponent factor increases, the accuracy decreases slightly. The trend of reduction is probably due to the over-emphasis of the large values of the Softmax sores. We obtain the highest overall accuracy when k equals 2, which is used in the following experiments. Table 1 presents the overall accuracy (for all classes) of our proposed method with and without the discriminative integration. The hybrid network is trained using all the patches in three scales. With discriminative integration, the patch-based net-works demonstrated improved accuracy. The best accuracy (52.6%) was achieved by the hybrid AlexNet, which exhibits a 5.2% improvement. AlexNet trained using patches of size 100 × 100 obtained the largest improvement of 28.8%. Without using discriminative integration (i.e., using the uncropped images), the performance is trampled down. This is because the training data are inconsistent with the testing data and the best accuracy (50.0%) was achieved by the hybrid AlexNet. The AlexNet trained using a patch size of 100 × 100 yielded low accu-racy. This is because when the patches are small, the number of non-informative patches increased.

Table 1. Accuracy (%) of our proposed method with and without the discriminative integration (DI).

Network	Patch size	Without DI	With DI	Imp. (%)
Hybrid AlexNet	–	50.0	52.6	5.2
AlexNet	100	36.4	46.9	28.8
AlexNet	150	44.3	52.1	17.6
AlexNet	200	48.5	52.2	7.6

4.3   Performance of Network Integration

Figure 4(b) shows the integration accuracy using Eq. (2) with different exponent factors. As the exponent factor increases, the accuracy increases and then drops. The best performance was achieved when j was 3. For Eq. (1) and Eq. (2), the accuracy will decrease when the exponent factors are greater than 5, thus we plot the result when k and j are ranged from 1 to 5 and report the best parameter by observation. Hence, we use 3 for the exponent factor of the network integration function in the rest of our experiments.

Table 2 lists the overall accuracy of the object-centric network, multi-scale object-centric networks, scene-centric network, and our proposed method. Three different base deep networks were used in these variations. The object-centric network used only a single scale patch in the training process; whereas multi-scale object-centric used three scales. Our proposed method essentially integrates multi-scale object-centric networks and scene-centric network. By examining the results of the object-centric and multi-scale object-centric networks, it is clear that the multi-scale object-centric network consistently achieved better accuracy. On average, the overall accuracy achieved 50.4%, which is about 1% improvement. Hence, the multi-scale strategy helps the recognition of scenes.

Our proposed method uses network integration that fuses the outputs of a multi-scale object-centric network with that of the scene-centric network. The overall accuracy of our method is greater than that of all the other variants based on different base networks. The average accuracy of our method achieved 51.8%, which is about 2.8% of improvement. It is evident that the discriminative network integration improves the overall accuracy.

Table 2. Accuracy (%) of proposed single/integrated networks.

Base network	Object-centric	Multi-scale obj.-centric	scene-centric	Proposed method
AlexNet	50.2	54.4	51.3	54.7
ResNet18	43.2	45.7	47.7	49.3
ResNet50	44.3	51.1	47.6	51.3
Average	45.9	50.4	48.9	51.8

4.4   Comparison with the State-of-the-art Methods

We compare our method with the most recent methods by Seong et al. [10,11]. For the CCM model, a network pre-trained on ImageNet [15] was used as the base model for an object-centric network, and, similarly to our method, the network retrained using Places dataset [15] was used as the underlying network for a scene-centric branch. The FC layers of the scene-centric model are retrained using the BIC GSV dataset to fine-tune to the scene recognition. In the CCM-CCG model, the CCM model is applied to the scene-centric model. Thus to calibrate the dimension of the object- and scene-centric models, we used the network pre-trained with Places [15] as the backbone model, and use our retrained ImageNet model as the object-centric model. Softmax score fusion was used in all the aforementioned models.

Table 3 presents the overall accuracy of the compared methods using three different deep networks: AlexNet, ResNet18, and ResNet50. Among all cases, our method achieved the best performance using AlexNet and the overall accuracy is 54.7%. Compared to the second best accuracy by CCM-CCG using ResNet50, the improvement is about 4%. This table also reports the average accuracy of using the three base networks. The average accuracy is 51.6% for our method, which is about 1% improvement to the second best model (CCM-CCG).

To understand class-wise performance, Figs. 5, 6, 7 show the confusion matrix of the compared methods using the three base networks. Each row of the subfigures shows the confusing matrix of one method using AlexNet, ResNet18, and ResNet30 from left to right. In each confusion matrix, a row represents the true class and a column represents the predicted class. Among all classes,

Table 3. Overall accuracy of our proposed method and the state-of-the-art methods (CCM [10] and CCM-CCG [11].).

Base Network	Proposed	CCM	CCM-CCG
AlexNet	54.7	46.1	49.0
ResNet18	49.3	49.7	51.7
ResNet50	51.3	49.0	52.6
Average	51.6	48.3	51.1

Church, Garage, Roof, and Retail are the classes that have the highest accuracy. However, it is clear that the accuracy for each class varies when a different deep network was used. This is consistent with our observation that the hybrid network exhibits better performance.

By computing the average error rate of three deep networks for each method, we identified four pairs of most confused classes. The major miss-classifications are between houses and garages. This is because a garage is often part of a house and the urban scenery image of garages also captures a part of or even an entire house, and vice versa (see Fig. 8 (a) and (b) for examples). The second dominating miss-classification case occurs when the models try to distinguish industrial and office buildings from retail stores. The differences are mainly decided by whether there is a signboard in the scene (see Fig. 8 (c) and (d) for examples).

Table 4 shows the error rate of the four most confusing classes. The table reports the average error rate of each method using the three deep networks (AlexNet, ResNet18, and ResNet50). In this table, each column stands for a pair of miss-classed cases, e.g. "garage-house" stands for the error rate that an image of a garage is miss-classified as a house. Our model achieved a lower error rate for differentiating industrial-retail and office building-retail, and a similar error rate when classifying garage-house pair (with an 0.2% difference on error rate). When comparing to the CCM-CCG model, our model has a reduction in error rate on the confusing classes. Our methods achieved an error rate reduction of 16.2% and 39.7% comparing with CCM and CCM-CCG methods. This demonstrates that multi-scale features help capture class-specific local features, and further assists the classification of ambiguous images.

Table 4. Error rate of our model, CCM [10], and CCM-CCG [11] of the four most confusing class pairs.

Model	Garage-house	House-garage	Industrial-retail	Office bldg-retail
Proposed	24.2	26.5	27.9	20.4
CCM	24.0	24.7	31.2	23.7
CCM-CCG	22.9	30.7	34.0	28.5

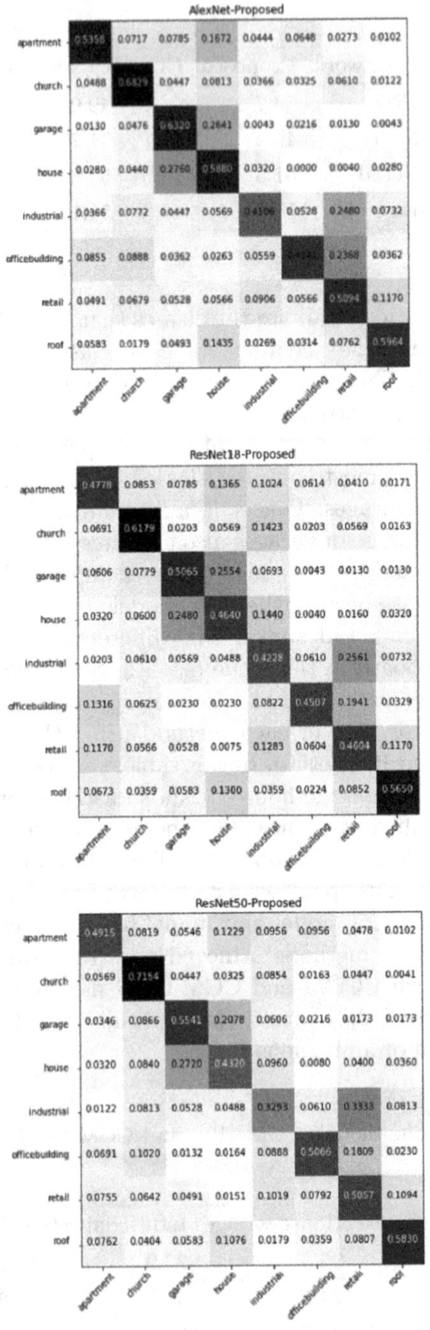

Fig. 5. Confusion matrix of the proposed method using different deep networks.

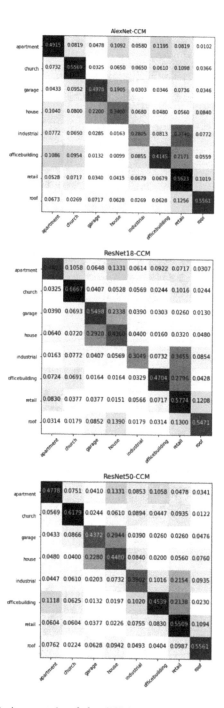

Fig. 6. Confusion matrix of the CCM using different deep networks.

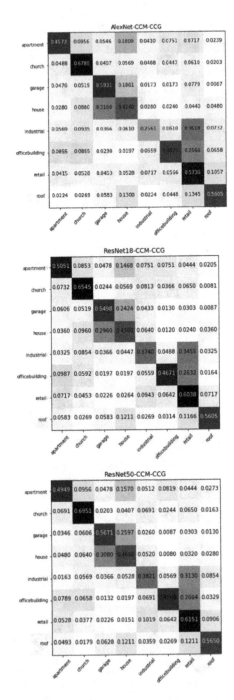

Fig. 7. Confusion matrix of the CCM-CCG using different deep networks.

(a) garage

(b) house

(c) industrial and office building

(d) retail

Fig. 8. Examples of the most confused categories.

5 Conclusion

In this paper, we present a multi-scale, deep network integration framework to tackle the challenging problem of recognizing complex urban scenery imagery. Our model uses both scenery contextual information and multi-scale object information. The scenery information is learned by training a deep network using the Places dataset; whereas the object information is learned using networks trained with the ImageNet dataset. The scene- and object-centric networks are integrated to achieve the final recognition.

The experimental results demonstrated our multi-scale, discriminative integration method enhanced the scenery image recognition in both patch integration and network integration procedures in all cases across various backbone CNN models. Specifically, using patches integration on testing images obtained an accuracy improvement of 18.0% on our example model; integration of multi-scale networks achieved a performance boost of 9.8%; the integration of object- and scene-centric models obtained an accuracy improvement of 5.9% comparing with single scene-centric models. In the comparison with state-of-the-art models, our multi-scale AlexNet model achieved the best performance (54.7% on overall accuracy) and demonstrated the ability to capture class-specific local features and further assist scene recognition by differentiating the most ambiguous classes.

In the future, we plan to develop trainable models to extract and integrate multi-scale features in a learnable manner. We will continue investigating more effective and efficient methods to jointly make use of multi-scale, multi-stream convolutional features in CNN-based models for urban scene understanding and other challenging computer vision problems.

References

1. Cheng, X., Lu, J., Feng, J., Yuan, B., Zhou, J.: Scene recognition with objectness. Pattern Recogn. **74**, 474–487 (2018)
2. Deng, J., Dong, W., Socher, R., Li, L.J., Li, K., Fei-Fei, L.: ImageNet: A large-scale hierarchical image database. In: IEEE Conference on Computer Vision and Pattern Recognition, pp. 248–255 (2009)
3. Fang, F., Yuan, X., Wang, L., Liu, Y., Luo, Z.: Urban land-use classification from photographs. IEEE Geosci. Remote Sens. Lett. **15**(12), 1927–1931 (2018)
4. He, K., Zhang, X., Ren, S., Sun, J.: Deep residual learning for image recognition. In: Proceedings of the IEEE Conference on Computer Vision and Pattern Recognition, pp. 770–778 (2016)
5. Herranz, L., Jiang, S., Li, X.: Scene recognition with cnns: objects, scales and dataset bias. In: Proceedings of the IEEE Conference on Computer Vision and Pattern Recognition, pp. 571–579 (2016)
6. Kang, J., Körner, M., Wang, Y., Taubenböck, H., Zhu, X.X.: Building instance classification using street view images. ISPRS J. Photogram. Remote Sens. **145**, 44–59 (2018)
7. Krizhevsky, A., Sutskever, I., Hinton, G.E.: ImageNet classification with deep convolutional neural networks. In: Advances in Neural Information Processing Systems, pp. 1097–1105 (2012)
8. Paszke, A., et al.: Pytorch: an imperative style, high-performance deep learning library. In: Advances in Neural Information Processing Systems, pp. 8024–8035 (2019)
9. Selvaraju, R.R., Cogswell, M., Das, A., Vedantam, R., Parikh, D., Batra, D.: Grad-CAM: visual explanations from deep networks via gradient-based localization. In: Proceedings of the IEEE International Conference on Computer Vision, pp. 618–626 (2017)
10. Seong, H., Hyun, J., Chang, H., Lee, S., Woo, S., Kim, E.: Scene recognition via object-to-scene class conversion: end-to-end training. In: International Joint Conference on Neural Networks, pp. 1–6 (2019)
11. Seong, H., Hyun, J., Kim, E.: FOSNET: an end-to-end trainable deep neural network for scene recognition. arXiv preprint arXiv:1907.07570 (2019)

12. Wang, Z., Wang, L., Wang, Y., Zhang, B., Qiao, Y.: Weakly supervised patchNets: describing and aggregating local patches for scene recognition. IEEE Trans. Image Process. **26**(4), 2028–2041 (2017)
13. Xia, S., Zeng, J., Leng, L., Fu, X.: WS-AM: weakly supervised attention map for scene recognition. Electronics **8**(10), 1072 (2019)
14. Zhou, B., Khosla, A., Lapedriza, A., Torralba, A., Oliva, A.: Places: An image database for deep scene understanding. arXiv preprint arXiv:1610.02055 (2016)
15. Zhou, B., Lapedriza, A., Khosla, A., Oliva, A., Torralba, A.: Places: a 10 million image database for scene recognition. IEEE Trans. Pattern Anal. Mach. Intell. **40**(6), 1452–1464 (2017)
16. Zhou, B., Lapedriza, A., Xiao, J., Torralba, A., Oliva, A.: Learning deep features for scene recognition using places database. In: Advances in Neural Information Processing Systems, pp. 487–495 (2014)
17. Zhu, Y., Deng, X., Newsam, S.: Fine-grained land use classification at the city scale using ground-level images. IEEE Trans. Multimedia **21**(7), 1825–1838 (2019)

Simulation of Ship Path Prediction and Remote Control Based on UE4 Next Generation Rendering

Mingsheng Huang[1(✉)] and Huawen Zhang[2]

[1] Graduate School of Information, Production and System, Waseda University,
Kitakyushu, Japan
huangmingsheng@fuji.waseda.jp
[2] Department of Mechanical Engineering, Tsinghua University, Peking, China

Abstract. This paper analyzes the hardware requirements and communication requirements of the immersive unmanned boat remote control system and makes a preliminary design. Subsequently, one of the key technologies of remote control system for immersive unmanned boat, motion prediction, was researched. In this regard, the Abkowitz model was used to perform the unmanned boat motion prediction, and the two-dimensional motion prediction was implemented in MATLAB software. The simulation of the ship motion prediction was performed through the joystick and keyboard input response, and the two-dimensional motion prediction was performed using the GUIDE module Interface implementation. Finally, a three-dimensional interface design and implementation of the UE4 game engine for two-dimensional motion prediction simulation is implemented, and the integrated display of motion prediction trajectory and multi-source heterogeneous data under keyboard input response and joystick input response is realized.

Keywords: Immersive · Unmanned boat · Remote control system · Virtual reality · Motion prediction

1 Introduction

1.1 3D Visual Simulation Technology Based on UE4

UE4 game engine [1–3] is an open source game engine for commercial development developed by Epic Game. Its functional modules are very powerful and complete, and the graphical user interface design is friendly, and the 3D rendering effect is very powerful. The research on the remote control of unmanned boats using UE4 is limited and has not been applied. Developers use the terrain tool that comes with the UE4 engine to create terrain and other landscape models [4]. On this basis, the UE4 game engine has real-time lighting dynamic rendering function, which is implemented by real-time GI, which can realistically simulate the real environment, weather, light and shadow effects. For the marine environment, it is possible to realistically simulate sea surface fluctuations, color changes under light, shadows, and changes in sea hydrological conditions under weather effects and special effects weather. And can simulate the real ocean waves through dynamic methods, inversion, geometric modeling and other methods.

© Springer Nature Singapore Pte Ltd. 2020
X. Yuan et al. (Eds.): ICUIA 2020, CCIS 1319, pp. 150–158, 2020.
https://doi.org/10.1007/978-981-33-4601-7_15

1.2 Theoretical Basis of Unmanned Boat Motion Prediction

There are four basic assumptions for ships [5]: 1. The sea surface is infinitely extended. 2. The value of gravity acceleration and the density of seawater remain unchanged. 3. The hull is a rigid body with uniform and constant mass. 4. The ship is symmetrical about its longitudinal section. The nonlinear model established by Abkowitz in 1964 applies the following four assumptions [6]: 1. The control of most ships can be described by third-order Taylor expansion, where the initial steady-state condition is u = u0. 2. Consider only the acceleration component of the first order. 3. Except for the effects of constant torque and constant force from a single propeller, the standard simplification of the standard port and starboard sides of the hull is simplified. 4. The coupling between acceleration and velocity terms can be ignored.

1.3 Three Degree of Freedom System Matrix

$$x = (u, v, r, x, y, psi, \delta) \tag{1}$$

$$x = \left(\dot{u}, \dot{v}, \dot{r}, u, v, r, \dot{\delta}\right) \tag{2}$$

Among them, u is the deviation between the current longitudinal speed and normal speed, v is the lateral speed, and r is the heading angular speed. The last three terms are the derivatives of the first three terms, and the last term is the true rudder deflection angle. In our calculations, instead of the three-term derivative, the position in the x direction, the position in the y direction, and the yaw angle are used to replace the three derivatives to form the state vector of formula (1). Its derivatives are as (2) Shown.

The initial state vector is

$$x_0 = (U, 0, 0, 0, 0, 0, 0) \tag{3}$$

According to the state variables and forces, we can get the equations needed for our motion prediction. Since it is blueprint programming in UE4, the equations are the same as MATLAB, for convenience we show the writing of MATLAB code. In the above modeling, we mainly used the seven-dimensional vector X of the state variable, which is the amount representing the current position, speed, and attitude of the ship. The remaining factors affecting it are the current target rudder angle and speed. We temporarily set it as Ui and U0. To control the hull, we are observing the change of state quantity while constantly changing the speed and rudder angle. Therefore, in this code, we mainly output the change rate of the state variable, that is, the derivative of the state variable, and the current ship speed value.

The current ship speed is shown in formula (4), and the derivative of the current state variable is shown in formula (5). Repeated derivation and integration in this way can continuously update the current ship speed and state variables.

$$U = \sqrt{(U_0 + u)^2 + v^2} \tag{4}$$

$$\dot{x} = \begin{pmatrix} \frac{X \cdot U^2}{L(m-X_{\dot{u}})} \\ \frac{U^2[Y(I_z-N_{\dot{r}})-N(mx_g-Y_{\dot{r}})]}{L[(m-Y_{\dot{v}})(I_z-N_{\dot{r}})-(mx_g-Y_{\dot{r}})(mx_g-N_{\dot{v}})]} \\ \frac{U^2[N(m-Y_{\dot{v}})-Y(mx_g-N_{\dot{v}})]}{L[(m-Y_{\dot{v}})(I_z-N_{\dot{r}})-(mx_g-Y_{\dot{r}})(mx_g-N_{\dot{v}})]} \\ U \cdot [\cos(psi) \cdot (\frac{U_0}{U}+u) - \sin(psi) \cdot v] \\ U \cdot [\sin(psi) \cdot (\frac{U_0}{U}+u) + \cos(psi) \cdot v] \\ \frac{rU}{L} \\ \dot{\delta} \end{pmatrix} \tag{5}$$

2 Method

2.1 Overview of the Architecture Design of Unmanned Remote Control System

Unmanned boat remote control system is mainly divided into shore-based control system and ship-based control system [7]. Figure 1 shows the structure of the relationship between the two systems and the transfer between them. Among them, 4G is used as the transmission method [8].

The ship-based control system mainly receives the instructions sent by the shore-based control system to control the unmanned boat, and collects the current data of the unmanned boat to feed back to the shore-based control system [9]. The shore-based control system mainly visualizes the data sent by the ship-based control system and provides operation guidance to remote operators. In the remote control system of immersive unmanned boats, the design of shore-based control systems is particularly important, and the main design of immersion is also reflected in this aspect [10].

As mentioned earlier, the visualization of the immersive unmanned boat remote control system is mainly helmet-type and large-screen multi-person mode [11, 12], which mainly presents the information transmitted by the ship-based control system to controller of the shore-based console visually in a system. The display system here is not only three-dimensionally processing the ship-based control system with the image information collected by the on-board camera to the interface of the immersive unmanned remote control system, but also includes radar map, temperature, humidity, wind speed and wind direction and other information. The system integrates this information with a visual presentation [13] of the control guidance of the shore-based console controller. The controller of the shore-based control system sends instructions to the ship-based control system by manipulating the joystick, keyboard, mouse, and the like. Because the wireless ad hoc network expands quickly and can temporarily form a network that is highly resistant to interference and damage, we use wireless ad hoc network equipment to complete the data transmission between the two systems.

shore-based
remote control system

Vessel-based
remote control system

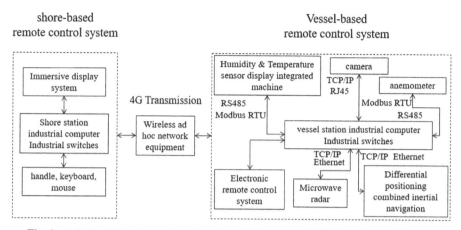

Fig. 1. Relationship between shore-based control system and ship-based control system

2.2   Overview of Unmanned Remote Control Module Design

For the entire remote control system, we can divide it into five parts [14]: sensing module, control module, communication module, power module, and navigation module. The sensing module is responsible for collecting information about the drone itself and its environment. The control module is responsible for sending control instructions to achieve remote control of the unmanned boat. The communication module is responsible for transferring a lot of information between the shore-based control system and the ship-based control system. The power module provides energy for unmanned boat movement and control. The navigation module is responsible for navigation of the hull.

3   Implementation

3.1   Motion Prediction and Simulation of Unmanned Boat on MATLAB

Figure 2 shows the interface of motion prediction simulation. The main callback function is set under the "Start" button. The main callback function uses a large loop for real-time function implementation of drawing. There are six in the large loop. The small loops are all performed by a mariner. m script function loop on different state variables, speeds, rudder angles, etc., which are the original trajectory of the ship, the motion prediction within 30 s in the original motion state, and a left hit of 5° in the original motion state. Rudder angle, 10° rudder angle left, 5° rudder angle right, 10° rudder angle right prediction. The right side shows the current speed and rudder angle, and the following instructions are used to implement keyboard input to change the rudder angle and speed. We re-read the current rudder angle and speed value in each input, that is, we can update the current state in real time to make a new prediction. As shown in Fig. 2, the GUI interface is finally connected to the joystick and can be operated with the keyboard.

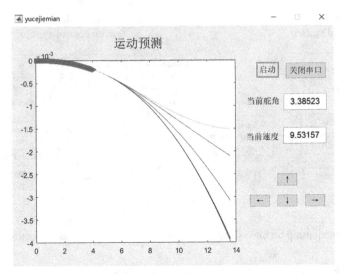

Fig. 2. GUI interface motion simulation

3.2 Development of Immersive Control Interface of 3D Unmanned Boat on UE4

UE4 Engine (Unreal Engine 4) is a powerful game engine with excellent effects in models and special effects. It has very powerful functions in 3D game development. The blueprint language is a visual language by which functions can be easily written using various elements and nodes. The C++ programming language is the underlying language of UE4, and some functions of UE4 can be implemented through C++ programming [15].

We imported a boat model and performed motion simulation in a state without wind and waves. Figure 3 shows the interface of the immersed unmanned remote control system after the establishment.

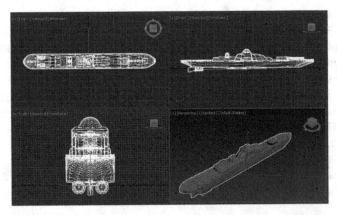

Fig. 3. Trimaran model for 3D unmanned boat remote control system based on UE4

The position information, wind direction, wind speed, temperature, humidity, speed, radar, etc. all show the sensor data in the immersive unmanned boat remote control system, which makes people have a more intuitive experience to control. Figure 3 shows the interface of the 3D immersive unmanned remote control system.

First, we used the mariner. m function of the hull itself and wrote it into the code of UE4, where U is the real speed of the current ship and Ψ is the current yaw angle (yaw angle of the heading in the initial state is 0). The movement of the ship is thus achieved, so that the movement of the ship can be achieved independently. At the same time, the predicted points are drawn using the coordinates (x, y) in the seven-dimensional matrix. And if further realized, the position of the ship should be constantly corrected by radar and combined inertial navigation positioning. The upper left corner shows a global map, which shows the ship's scheduled and predicted routes and the global position of the ship from a global perspective. The ship itself can use directional control and speed control through WASD. The C key can switch between free view and hull view. The hull cockpit view is the basic view of immersive remote control. Press V can switch the first perspective and the third perspective, suitable for observation in different situations.

Fig. 4. Immersive unmanned boat remote control system interface implemented by UE4 game engine

After the ship model is hidden, it is shown in Fig. 5. In this figure, we can observe five lines well, so the function of several lines is explained according to this figure. The longest one on the far right is the scheduled route, that is, the route that the ship is supposed to travel, which is a semi-circular line in the global map. A short line at the bottom left is the track that the ship has currently traveled, and it will also be displayed in the global map. From the left to the right, the three lines starting from the bow are the predicted trajectory lines with a rudder angle of 10° to the left, sailing in the original movement state, and 10° to the right.

Fig. 5. Interface of immersive unmanned boat remote control system from free perspective

Figure 5 and Fig. 6 are the immersive unmanned boat remote control system interface in the free perspective and the first perspective, respectively, and Fig. 4 is the observation chart in the third perspective.

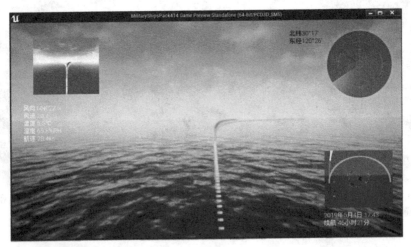

Fig. 6. Interface of Immersive unmanned remote control system from the first perspective

The movement of the ship itself is determined in accordance with the heading and speed of the ship as described above. A method of determining is to continuously update the coordinates of the position where the ship appears at each moment, that is, to process the hull as a blinking discrete point. In this case, even if the number of frames is high, there will be a noticeable lag, so only the realization The continuous movement of the ship itself can be realized. In the trajectory prediction and tracking program, we set a refresh frequency of 10 ms, that is, the current position information of the ship is updated every 10 ms. Then the simulation of the course and speed of the ship actually applies the refresh value of each short time, in another words, the continuous movement of the unmanned boat is divided into many tiny micro-elements for processing, which is not completely continuous, so it will also generates a small cumulative error, which can be corrected by radar and inertial navigation positioning. Figure 7 the blueprint codes of course and speed respectively.

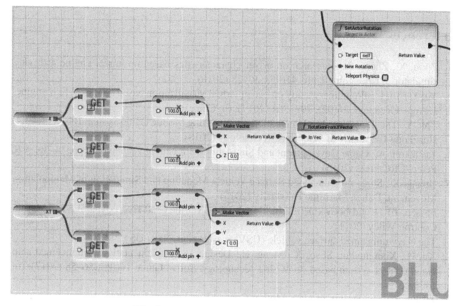

Fig. 7. Blueprint code to control heading

4 Conclusion

The paper mainly completed the modeling and code writing of the unmanned boat, the design of the unmanned boat hardware, the data format arrangement, and the design of the communication protocol, and the keyboard input response and the joystick input response were used to perform the motion prediction simulation. −2D motion prediction simulation and UE4 based 3D model motion prediction simulation.

In the two-dimensional motion prediction simulation, the movement and prediction of the ship are controlled by establishing a dynamic model, and the interface is compiled and the motion prediction simulation is performed through the GUIDE module. First, the keyboard is used to input the response, and then the serial data is used to read the control. So the real-time control and motion prediction of the ship under the above two input responses can be realized.

The development of 3D unmanned immersion control system based on the above content is the core of the paper. Innovatively the current powerful 3D rendering engine UE4 is used to develop the immersive unmanned boat remote control system. Finally, a three-dimensional unmanned immersion control system capable of real-time maneuvering and motion prediction was established.

At present, there is still a lot of room for growth of unmanned boats, and the remote control system for immersive unmanned boats is rarely studied. The thesis creatively designed and simulated the 3D immersive unmanned boat remote control system with the current powerful UE4 game engine, which provided some ideas for the subsequent development of unmanned boat remote control system.

References

1. Zhou, X., Zheng, L.: Research on driver characteristics based on unreal engine 4 driving simulator. J. Chongqing Univ. **41**(09), 30–38 (2018)
2. Yu, X., Yu, L.: Preliminary study on ocean virtual visualization based on unreal four engine. J. Appl. Oceanogr. **36**(02), 295–301 (2017). (in Chinese)
3. Zhu, Y.: The design and Implementation of a Shooting Mobile Game System Based on UE4. Huazhong University of Science & Technology (2018)
4. Tavakkoli, A.: Game Development and Simulation with Unreal Technology, pp. 34–36. A K Peters/CRC Press (2015)
5. Huang, X.: Study on Unmanned Surface Vehicle Modeling and Simulation of Manipulation Movement. Dalian Maritime University (2015)
6. Fossen, T.I.: Rigid-body kinetics. In: Handbook of Marine Craft Hydrodynamics and Motion Control. Wiley (2011)
7. The Navy unmanned surface vehicle (USV) master plan. Navy US (2007)
8. Xu, H., Xianghuihui, Shao, X., Meng, H.: Design and implementation of unmanned ship cloud control system based on 4G IoT technology. Softw. Guide **16**(06), 56–58 (2017). (in Chinese)
9. Zhang, X.: The Design of USV Motion Control System Based on ROS. Jiangsu University of Science and Technology (2015)
10. Zhao, M.: Large Screen, Multi-user and Immersive Stereo Display System. Dalian Maritime University (2010)
11. Wang, S.: The Research on Somatosensory Visual Tele-presence and Tele-operation Technology of USV. Harbin Engineering University (2014)
12. Zhen, L.: Modeling and Motion Control System Design of Unmanned Surface Vehicle. South China University of Technology (2016)
13. Fossen, S.: Visualization of Ships in a Mixed-Reality Environment and Automated Situational Awareness using Live AIS Data (2018)
14. Zhu, W., Zhang, L.: Development of unmanned surface vehicle. Marine Technol. (02), 1–6 (2017)
15. Sherif, W.: Learning C++ by creating Games with UE4. Packt Publishing, pp. 52–53 (2015)

Highway Network Traffic Survey Point Layout Planning Method Based on Machine Learning-Optimization Hybrid Algorithm

Liting Shi[✉]

CCCC First Highway Consultants Co., Ltd., Xi'an 710075, Shaanxi, China
305078654@qq.com

Abstract. Due to the backward observation and treatment methods of existing expressway traffic survey points, the observation and treatment system simply cannot match with the expressway network survey points and play its own due traffic observation function. The main purpose of this paper is to solve a problem with the overall layout planning of expressway network planning traffic survey observation points on the network. This paper mainly studies and designs a hybrid analysis method, which is a convex nonlinear programming traffic distribution problem and is solved by a frank-wolfe hybrid algorithm. Secondly, in order to fully verify the effectiveness of the design of a supervised machine learning-network optimization hybrid algorithm, a real machine learning large-scale data set is used for testing. The results of mixed data analysis show that ml-op's mixed analysis algorithm still has a good performance in terms of computational capability and reliability when it is used to deal with large scale bi-level convex nonlinear programming traffic distribution problem.

Keywords: Discrete traffic network design · Bi-level programming model · Traffic distribution · Machine learning · Hybrid algorithm

1 Introduction

In recent years, highway traffic construction of modernization and development to promote our country highway construction, especially highway construction project economic survival and progress in the development of surrounding areas played a very important role, the highway has become project surrounding area and the survival and development of local economy and economic lifeline in the main. However, the operation status of the expressway traffic statistics survey and management work is seriously too lagging behind, which has become the bottleneck and obstacle of the expressway network construction and development strategic planning, maintenance and management, safety monitoring, information construction, and local economic development. Traffic volume statistics is one of the foundation and important work for highway construction and modern management. Since 2002, the highway traffic operation status survey has been included in the national statistical management system. The layout of the highway

© Springer Nature Singapore Pte Ltd. 2020
X. Yuan et al. (Eds.): ICUIA 2020, CCIS 1319, pp. 159–165, 2020.
https://doi.org/10.1007/978-981-33-4601-7_16

traffic statistics investigation point is to conduct statistics and data analysis on the investigation of highway traffic operation condition, it provides the direction and source of data, and the accuracy and quality of the data directly affect the final result of traffic statistics and data analysis. Obviously, traffic statistics site layout and use are reasonable will directly affect involving a survey of highway traffic operation condition, which directly affect the highway around the local economy and construction of project planning and management decisions in the survival and development of correctness and reliability of data, the effect involved in highway construction can effectively satisfy the safety of the highway traffic modernization construction and management and so on various aspects of the target and requirements.

Artificial intelligence algorithms have been applied to the prediction, classification, or optimization of building energy consumption. However, there is a significant gap in the literature on energy optimization problems for hybrid objective function development, including qualitative and quantitative data sets. To solve this problem, Saeed Banihashemi proposed a machine learning algorithm with a mixed objective function, which optimizes residential energy consumption by considering both continuous and discrete energy consumption parameters. To do this, a set of comprehensive data, including the important parameters of palisade structure, established the architectural design of the layout and hvac, artificial neural network as prediction and decision tree classification algorithm through cross-training the whole create mix function and equation model is validated by weighted average error separation performance [1]. Automated sentiment analysis and opinion mining is a complex process that involves extracting useful subjective information from text. The explosion of user-generated content on the web, especially the millions of users who, every day, express their opinions about products and services on blogs, wikis, social networks, message boards, and so on, presents the key to reliable, automatic export of emotions and opinions from unstructured text to some business applications. Stalidis, Panagiotis proposed a new method of vectorization of text resources, which combines the weighted variant of popular Word2Vec notation with lexical notation and lexical emotion-based vectors. By applying several machine learning classification algorithms on a data set widely used for emotion detection, the text representation method is evaluated [2]. The choice between using a second-generation or third-generation sequencing platform can be a trade-off between accuracy and reading length, and several studies require long and accurate readings. In such cases, researchers often combine the two techniques and use short reads to correct long reads. The current approach relies on various graph-based or aligned techniques and does not take into account the error profile of the underlying technology. Efficient machine learning algorithms that address these shortcomings have the potential to achieve a more precise integration of the two technologies. Firtina Can proposed the first long read error correction algorithm Hercules based on machine learning. Every once in a while this model is interpreted as a hidden Markov model with an error profile of the underlying platform. The algorithm learns the posterior transition/emission probability distribution of each long read to correct errors in these reads [3].

The two-layer programming problem of discrete traffic network is np-hard because of its high computational difficulty. The research USES unconventional methods to mix the concepts and techniques of machine learning with classical optimization methods. The core of this idea is to learn from successive iterations to target functions with variables and constraints. In other words, the approach in this article is to separate the original problem from some variables and constraints and make it a much easier problem to solve. Then, the supervised training technique is used to learn from the previous iteration to establish a new objective function to replace the original objective function. The emergence of machine learning and deep learning provides a large number of tools and technologies, which provide a very effective technical approach for dealing with complex optimization problems in the field of operations research.

2 Proposed Method

2.1 Optimization Using Hybrid Algorithm

SLA is a training method widely used by machines in supervised learning. The function of an estimated target variable is approximately analyzed based on some decision variable functions, which effectively limits the constraints and makes the problem analysis easier to deal with. A simple SLA function can be directly assumed as a nonlinear function of a decision variable. In order to better form a decision variable function with good problem analysis performance, we call a simple nonlinear function SLA (multivariate nonlinear function regression) [4].

One of the main ideas and purposes of researching and designing hybrid solutions is to make full use of the advantages of the mathematical characteristics of the two hybrid solutions to tailor a feasible hybrid solution for this integer programming problem, which can also be regarded as a decomposition method. In addition, this method does not require the bi-level-programming problem itself to have a high content of mathematical information attributes (such as integer gradient), nor does it require any specific mathematical characteristics of the functions of the original bi-level-programming problem and the mathematical attribute types of the upper decision variables [5]. As a result, the mixed method has no complex requirements for the mathematical properties of functions and variables, so it can be widely studied and applied to large-scale practical problems. Based on the mixed integer factorization method of design thinking, the hybrid method proposed method the bi-level programming problem of mixed-integer nonlinear programming problem can be decomposed into two sub-problems, a difficult problem (integer programming problem, contains all the integer continuous variables), a simple integer programming problem (nonlinear integer programming problem, NLP contains all the integer continuous variables). On the basis of this method, all continuous variables (including the following reactions) can be directly calculated [6].

2.2 Highway Network Traffic Survey Points Layout Planning

As the next step of expressway information network construction scale and the improvement of the infrastructure construction to further expand and function, through the highway informationization construction and management to improve the level of management of the highway, to enhance the capacity of road network traffic infrastructure, and improve the efficiency of road network traffic, and in the future of the constant change

and growth development of highway traffic demand is the next step of highway informationization management in one of the important basic content [7, 8]. Survey of highway
dynamic traffic management work of highway system infrastructure dynamic traffic data
collection, analysis, and information collection, and processing, to the timely monitoring
operation condition of the highway system, the effective measures for highway traffic
control and induced traffic infrastructure work to provide the support of information
technology, the next step is the important technical basis of highway traffic information
construction. Further investigation and management of the dynamic traffic volume of
expressways are of great guiding significance for improving the construction and management level of expressways in the next step and adapting to the development of the
constantly changing and growing expressway traffic demand in the future [9, 10].

3 Experiments

3.1 Experimental Scenario

China's highway traffic survey work began in the 1970s, after more than 20 years of
development, the preliminary establishment of the intermittent survey, intermittent survey, and continuous survey, covering the national, provincial, county, township highway
survey system. According to statistics, by the end of 2016, there were 930 observation stations on expressways, among which 115 were continuous observation stations,
accounting for 5.1% of the total number of observation stations on the national road
network. Even in a station of the highway, because involves many aspects, such as
maintenance of equipment, electric power, and other reasons, usually will be the station layout in urban highway entrances, large hub type, the exchange between the large
and medium-sized cities, such as traffic flow is easy to change the position, lead to the
observation site distribution uniformity is poor, the survey data can't reflect the actual
running condition of the road network.

3.2 Experimental Design

In this paper, a real data set is used to test the road network. This data set mainly
includes the data of a major directional trunk road in a certain region. It consists of 861
data containing CSV files, each of which may exceed 1 million pieces of data. China's
road Internet is composed of 74 alternative node regions, 74 alternative hub nodes and
258 nodes mainly connected to the trunk roads. The travel data demand of the main
trunk roads per hour is 65,576, the travel speed is 50 km/h, and the capacity density is
1700 vph (vehicles per hour). The road network has 22 main nodes connected to hubs.
This includes eight projects with major options for connecting nodes to hubs. Table 1
below lists the actual construction costs of each of these alternative node projects, as well
as the respective times and volumes of traffic for all projects under construction (without
considering any budget). The total budget cost of the optimal hub construction is 22 (unit
cost), and the projects to be invested in the optimal hub construction are selected under
different budget cost levels of 20%, 40%, 60%, 80%, and 100% respectively. In order to
better obtain an accurate numerical calculation result of convergence rate, when solving
the function tap, it is assumed that the relative gap of convergence rate is about 0.001
(boyce, ralevic-dekic and) (bar-gera, 2004), which takes at least 3 s.

Table 1. The construction cost of alternative projects

Hub project	The connection	Traffic	Construction costs
1	0, 1, 2, 3	754, 65, 924, 32, 774, 524	1.9
2	0, 1, 4, 5, 6, 7	754, 65, 924, 32, 683, 71, 998, 34, 833, 787	2.5
3	2, 3, 4, 5, 8, 9, 10, 19	774, 524, 545, 78, 683, 71, 998, 34, 1761, 04, 1600, 24, 386	2.9
4	6, 7, 12, 13, 16, 17	833, 558, 787, 744, 1555, 34, 1598, 9, 483, 186, 389, 567	2.0
5	8, 9, 12, 13, 14, 15, 18, 19	1600, 24, 1761, 04, 1555, 34, 1598, 9, 562, 273, 424, 579, 1793, 058, 1115, 84	3.2

4 Discussion

4.1 Analysis of Traffic Survey Point Layout

As shown in Fig. 1, the numerical results demonstrate that the heuristic method, which combines machine learning techniques with traditional optimization methods, can directly perform more efficient analysis and calculation for large-scale problems. It enriches the basic theory that the traditional machine learning theory and technique are widely used in optimizing the bi-level programming problem. Ml-op basically adopts a traditional heuristic programming method, whose main purpose is to find a good (not always the best) solution to a problem in a time when a large-scale problem is computable. When we started to study how to effectively deal with large-scale problems,

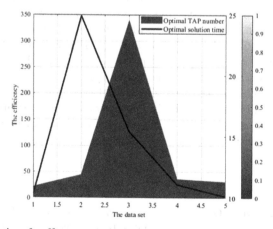

Fig. 1. Statistics of traffic survey point layout under machine optimization algorithm

ml-op has sought an effective solution to solve the problem of practical bilevel programming. Ml-op does not necessarily have to enforce any specific bilevel programming requirements, unlike most heuristic bilevel programming methods that require as much rigor as the accuracy of the problem. In fact, ml-op considers a bilayer programming problem as a black box (that is, a variable in the decision process) and inputs it into a box, which makes ml-op widely applicable to real-world problems.

4.2 Suggestions on the Layout of Traffic Survey Points

Through scientific and rational layout category, the category of basic traffic data stations, building a universal coverage network, have the ability of dynamic traffic data collection, conform to the highway traffic volume survey could satisfy the requirement of survey statistics function orientation, basic traffic dynamic data acquisition system, to reflect the characteristics of freeway traffic flow and operation characteristics, monitoring the running state of the road, promote the construction of highway intelligent transportation, building highway public travel information service platform provides dynamic traffic data. On the basis of fully considering the layout principle, the layout idea of the observation station is to make use of the idea of a total volume control method to layout a class of observation station which mainly meets the macroscopic needs of users. Then, according to the traffic flow theory, the second class observation station which mainly meets the real-time discrimination requirements of road operation status is arranged, and the first-class observation station is compatible with the second class observation station, and the two coordinate with each other to form the traffic quantity observation station of the whole network.

5 Conclusions

In this paper, a nonlinear user equilibrium mixed-integer system BPP is established. By referring to the design idea of the decomposition method, the upper problem is how to minimize the cost of a nonlinear user equilibrium system with mixed-integer variables (such as decision integer variables), while the lower problem is how to program the mixed-integer NLPP for the user equilibrium nonlinear system at a higher level. The lower levels will make it easier to solve the problem. As mentioned above, the decomposition algorithm in this study avoids some tedious system design procedures, including narrowing the gap between the upper and lower layers, which is almost impossible for large np-hard problems. On this basis, this paper provides an optimized calculation model for solving the problem of the distribution of traffic survey points and provides more reasonable Suggestions for the distribution of survey points.

References

1. Banihashemi, S., Ding, G., Wang, J.: Developing a hybrid model of prediction and classification algorithms for building energy consumption. Energy Procedia **21**(1), 110 (2017)
2. Stalidis, P., Giatsoglou, M., Diamantaras, K.: Machine learning sentiment prediction based on hybrid document representation. Comput. Sci. **26**(2), 251 (2015)

3. Can, F., Ziv, B.-J., Can, A.: Hercules: a profile HMM-based hybrid error correction algorithm for long reads. Nucleic Acids Res. **12**(21), 21 (2018)
4. Dipnall, J.F., Pasco, J.A., Berk, M.: Fusing data mining, machine learning and traditional statistics to detect biomarkers associated with depression. PLoS ONE **11**(2), e0148195 (2016)
5. Rudolph, G., Martinez, T.: Finding the real differences between learning algorithms. Int. J. Artif. Intell. Tools **24**(3), 1550001 (2015)
6. Natarajan, R., Subramanian, J., Papageorgiou, E.I.: Hybrid learning of fuzzy cognitive maps for sugarcane yield classification. Comput. Electron. Agric. **127**(1), 147–157 (2016)
7. Malhotra, A.: A hybrid econometric-machine learning approach for relative importance analysis: food inflation. Papers **6**(3), 45–48 (2018)
8. Houborg, R., McCabe, M.F.: A hybrid training approach for leaf area index estimation via Cubist and random forests machine-learning. Isprs J. Photogramm. Remote Sens. **135**(1), 173–188 (2018)
9. Apolloni, J., Leguizamón, G., Alba, E.: Two hybrid wrapper-filter feature selection algorithms applied to high-dimensional microarray experiments. Appl. Soft Comput. **15**(3), 38 (2015)
10. Li, L., Ren, H., Li, X.: Machine learning-based spectrum efficiency hybrid precoding with lens array and low-resolution ADCs. IEEE Access **PP**(99), 1 (2019)

Measurement and Empirical Analysis of Hangzhou Smart City Development Index

Lingchen Liu[✉]

North China Electric Power University, Baoding 071000, Hebei, China
llc9917@163.com

Abstract. Through quantitative analysis of the development level of smart cities, we can accurately determine the development status of smart cities, and provide quantitative support for the government to formulate future development strategies and related policies. This paper refers to the research at home and abroad on the evaluation index of the development level of smart cities, reconstructs a comprehensive evaluation system for smart cities, and uses a comprehensive index evaluation method to measure the level of smart development in Hangzhou. The results show that the level of Hangzhou's smart development is in the acceleration stage from 2013 to 2017 but the growth rate slowed down in 2018. In these past years, smart applications, development effects, and environmental support have made rapid progress, and infrastructure increased a little small with a good foundation.

Keywords: Hangzhou · Smart city · Development index

1 Introduction

IBM proposed a smart city in 2010. IBM believes that smart cities are made up of six core systems: organization (people), government affairs, transportation, communications, water, and energy. These systems are not decentralized but interconnected collaboratively. The construction of smart cities requires the application of next-generation information technologies, such as the Internet of Things and cloud computing represented by mobile technologies, to make operation more smooth, urban management more efficient, city life more convenient [1].

Currently, two methods for the evaluation of smart cities are adopted: one is to divide the smart city system into sections according to different modules, and then evaluate them separately, such as the evaluation methods of IBM and EU Vienna University of Technology [2, 3]; the another is to consider the city as a complete system for an overall evaluation. The specific method borrows models from other disciplines and introduces it into the assessment system of smart cities, such as the Beijing Smart City Evaluation System [4]. A common concern of the study on the evaluation index framework of smart cities in various countries is the development level and innovative power of the information industry, e-commerce. However, the existing indicator system often ignores the characteristics of cities and the huge differences between cities.

© Springer Nature Singapore Pte Ltd. 2020
X. Yuan et al. (Eds.): ICUIA 2020, CCIS 1319, pp. 166–171, 2020.
https://doi.org/10.1007/978-981-33-4601-7_17

In 2012, Hangzhou was included in the first batch of pilot cities for smart cities, and the construction of smart Hangzhou began. Hangzhou has a good foundation in the digital economy and industrial development. Against this background, the Hangzhou Municipal Government has formulated a series of smart city development plans, guided by sound city management and providing convenient services to the public. This paper draws on the research results of China's Information Development Index and Beijing Smart City Development Index (SCDI) and rebuilds the evaluation system with the characteristics of Hangzhou to access the level of Hangzhou's smart development.

2 Method

2.1 Principles of Smart City Development Index

This study selects the comprehensive evaluation index method to calculate the development level of a smart city. The linear weighted model can be used to calculate the samples with relatively balanced importance of each evaluation index, little difference in index value, and a weak correlation of each index [4]:

This study selects the comprehensive evaluation index method to calculate the development level of a smart city. The comprehensive index method can be divided into a linear weighted model, multiplicative evaluation model, and multiplicative mixed evaluation model. The linear weighted model can be used to calculate the samples with relatively balanced importance of each evaluation index, little difference in index value, and a weak correlation of each index.

$$SDI = \sum_{i=1}^{n} W_i \left(\sum_{j}^{m} W_{ij} P_{ij} \right) \tag{1}$$

where SDI is the value of smart city development level index, n is the number of classifications for SDI, m is the number of indicators for the category i index of SDI, W_i is the weight of the category i index in the overall index while $\sum_{i=1}^{n} W_i = 1$, P_{ij} is the dimensionless value of the j-th index of the i-th index, and W_{ij} is the weight of index j in index i while $\sum_{j=1}^{m} W_{ij} = 1$.

2.2 Dimensionless Data Processing

The preprocessing of the indicator system data is dimensionless. To make the indicators comparable, a threshold method was used to pre-process the original indicator data. After the threshold method is used for transformation, the data will all fall within the range of 0–1, and the data comparison is relatively obvious. Threshold calculation is divided into two cases:

If the value distribution of the indicator sample is relatively uniform, and the data is not significantly different, the general formula is used for calculation:

$$Z_i = \frac{X_i - X_{min}}{X_{max} - X_{min}}$$

where Z_i is the dimensionless pre-processed value, X_{min} is the minimum threshold, X_{max} is the maximum threshold, and X_i is the raw data of each indicator of the assessment index system.

If the value of each indicator sample in the indicator system is significantly different, it can be calculated using a logarithmic method to eliminate the effect of the large data difference on the final value. The calculation formula is as follows:

$$Z_i = \frac{lgX_i - lgX_{min}}{lgX_{max} - lgX_{min}}$$

3 Evaluation of Smart Hangzhou Development Index

3.1 Construction of the Smart City Assessment Index System

Since the smart city assessment index system has not been formally formed, and considering the availability of data, this paper reconstructed the Smart Development Index (SDI) based on the Beijing smart city development index (SCDI) [4] and European smart city indicator system [2, 3, 5–7] to measure the smart city development level of Hangzhou. The SDI index constructed in this paper also uses the IDI index as the basic basis and adds some indexes in combination with the latest smart city construction and it considers four aspects: environmental support, infrastructure, intelligent application, and development effect. The specific indicators are as follows (Table 1):

3.2 Determination of the Threshold

For continuous annual evaluation, the evaluation model and method required to be established must meet the requirements of sustainability and comparability of the evaluation results. In the mid-to-long-term continuous evaluation of the smart city development level, this article determines the minimum and maximum thresholds for each evaluation index with reference to national mid- and long-term development planning target values and international advanced levels.

There are two types of thresholds: for relative indicators, the minimum threshold is determined to be zero, and the maximum threshold is determined with reference to international advanced levels. For absolute indicators, the minimum threshold can be determined with reference to the minimum value of the base period, and the maximum threshold is referenced to the target value of the indicator.

3.3 Calculation of Indicator Data Weights

Based on the research on the significance of the four secondary indicators to the overall index, the relatively important intelligent application index and development effect index are given an average weight of 30%, and the environmental support index and the infrastructure index are given 20% respectively. For the four-level specific indicators under the two-level indicator, the internationally-used average weight method is adopted [4].

Table 1. Smart city development level indicator system

First-level indicator	Secondary indicators	Tertiary indicators	Fourth level indicators
Smart city development index	Environmental support index	Technology investment	The proportion of scientific research funds to regional GDP
		Regional economic development level	Per capita output value
		Smart innovation ability	Education index
			Invention patent applications per million people
			The proportion of employees in the tertiary industry
	Infrastructure index	Broadband network construction level	Number of internet broadband access users
		Smart terminal popularity index	Internet-connected phone ownership rate
			Computer ownership rate
			TV ownership rate
	Intelligent application index	Smart government services	Comprehensive application level of government websites
		Digital residential life	Residents' online shopping consumption
		Networked enterprise operations	Online retail sales as a percentage of total merchandise sales
	Development effect index	Living standard	Economic income per capita
		Information level	Proportion of information industry output value to regional GDP

3.4 Calculation of Smart Hangzhou Development Index

Based on the Hangzhou smart city development level evaluation system, this study selects the relevant index data of Hangzhou city from 2012 to 2018 (data sources are Hangzhou Statistical Yearbook and Zhejiang Internet Development Report) to calculate and evaluate the development level of smart Hangzhou (Table 2).

Table 2. Calculation results of Hangzhou SCDI index and sub-index

	2018	2017	2016	2015	2014	2013
SCDI index	0.876	0.814	0.707	0.599	0.529	0.457
Environmental support index	0.829	0.714	0.678	0.601	0.508	0.475
Infrastructure index	0.886	0.891	0.812	0.667	0.641	0.643
Intelligent application index	0.929	0.868	0.705	0.604	0.553	0.436
Development effect index	0.847	0.776	0.660	0.546	0.443	0.344

3.5 Analysis of Evaluation Results

As a leading city in China's informatization and digitalization, Hangzhou, China, has been using digitalization and intelligence to drive technology, management, service, and industrial innovation over the years. The development of smart Hangzhou has the following characteristics:

1) Hangzhou's smart cities are generally in the stage of accelerated improvement. Among them, the fastest development occurred between 2015 and 2017, increasing by 11 points each year. After that, the growth rate slowed down slightly. Calculated at the slowest growth rate, the total SCDI index of Hangzhou will also reach 1.0 (the target value of 1.0) by 2020, indicating that the construction goals of Hangzhou's smart cities can be fully achieved through hard work.
2) Smart applications, development effects, and environmental support have made rapid progress, and infrastructure has progressed steadily.

   - The construction of smart city infrastructure refers to network construction, and it is the key foundation and guarantee for smart cities to play a role. The level of infrastructure in Smart Hangzhou is not low in 2013. From 2013 to 2018, the infrastructure classification index of Hangzhou has improved, especially from 2015 to 2017 increased by 11.3 points.
   - The environmental support classification index is a comprehensive index reflecting the level of scientific and technological investment, regional economic development, and relevant talents in smart cities. In the past 6 years, the index of environmental support in Smart Hangzhou has improved significantly with 35 points increase.
   - The smart application classification index reflects the degree to which mobile technology is applied by various departments in the smart city, and is the core part of the smart city evaluation index system. From 2013 to 2018, the acceleration rate and change trend of this index ranked second among the four categories, which reflected that the smart application growth in Hangzhou is relatively ideal.
   - The development effect classification index reflects the final objectives of smart development, that is, to achieve sustainable urban development through intelligent management and operation. Such indicators mainly reflect the promotion of smart cities to the economic structure and the improvement of residents' quality

of life. Surprisingly, the development effect index of smart Hangzhou has been improved the most with 50 points increase in 6 years.

3) In recent years, Hangzhou has increased its investment in science and technology and focused on supporting the development of the information economy industry, including e-commerce, mobile Internet, digital content, software and information services and so on. Not only have they become the main engine of economic development, but they have also tremendously promoted the efficiency and convenience of the government and the people, and realized service upgrading and consumption upgrading.

4 Conclusion

This paper used the development index method to measure the overall construction level and development trend of Smart Hangzhou. The evaluation results are basically consistent with the current status of Hangzhou, indicating that this method can effectively measure the development level of smart Hangzhou. The construction of smart Hangzhou is highly concerned by the government and the information industry, and the infrastructure construction is further improved. Smart cities should form a sustainable development model. In the future, the construction of Smart Hangzhou should concentrate on people's livelihood, comprehensively improve the application level and construction effectiveness of smart Hangzhou, accelerate the formation of industrial clusters, and strengthen Hangzhou's comprehensive competitiveness. At the same time, the smart construction of small and medium-sized cities around Hangzhou should be promoted to accelerate the process of intelligentization in the Yangtze River Delta.

References

1. Song, G., Wu, L.: Innovation in the smart city vision 2.0. Urban Dev. **19**(09), 53–60 (2012). (in Chinese)
2. Paroutis, S., Bennett, M., Heracleous, L.: A strategic view on smart city technology: the case of IBM smarter cities during a recession. Technol. Forecast. Soc. Change **89**(11), 262–272 (2014)
3. Dall'O, G., Bruni, E., Panza, A., Sarto, L., Khayatian, F., et al.: Evaluation of cities' smartness by means of indicators for small and medium cities and communities: a methodology for Northern Italy. Sustain. Cities Soc. (10), 193–202 (2017)
4. Yang, J., Chen, Y., Hou, X., Ni, D.: Research on evaluation index system of smart city in Dongcheng District, Beijing. Research on Smart City Development Index - Measurement and Empirical Analysis of Beijing Smart City Development Index .Research World (11), 8–14 (2013). (in Chinese)
5. García-Fuentes, M.Á., Quijano, A., et al.: European cities characterization as basis towards the replication of a smart and sustainable urban regeneration model. Energy Procedia (3), 836–845 (2017)
6. Dameri, R.: Smart City Implementation: Creating Economic and Public Value in Innovative Urban Systems, vol. 2, pp. 7–8. Springer, Gewerbestrasse (2017). https://doi.org/10.1007/978-3-319-45766-6
7. Caird, S.: City approaches to smart city evaluation and reporting: case studies in the United Kingdom. Urban Res. Pract. (2), 159–179 (2018)

Boundary Enhanced Network
for Improved Semantic Segmentation

Chengyuan Zhuang[1(✉)], Xiaohui Yuan[1], and Wencheng Wang[2]

[1] University of North Texas, Denton, TX 76203, USA
{cz0056,xiaohui.yuan}@unt.edu
[2] Weifang University, Weifang 261061, China
wwcwfu@126.com

Abstract. Deep convolutional neural networks (DCNNs) have become the state-of-art methods for semantic segmentation of very high-resolution remote sensing imagery nowadays. However, the downsampling and upsampling stage in encoder and decoder components have caused inaccurate localization of objects, especially at boundaries. To mitigate this spatial inaccuracy, we propose boundary enhanced network for improved semantic segmentation based on the state-of-art DeepLabV3+ network to reinforce the object class boundary information by jointly learning semantic segmentation and edge detection. Preliminary results demonstrate that our method improves the state-of-the-art network of DeepLabV3+ in overall accuracy, mean F1 score, and IoU score at a high level on the two famous ISPRS 2D Semantic Labeling datasets, indicating it is an effective method for semantic segmentation of very high-resolution remote sensing imagery.

Keywords: Boundary enhancement · Semantic segmentation · Multi-task learning · Deep convolutional neural networks

1 Introduction

Semantic segmentation is the task of assigning a class label to each pixel of an input image, which has been applied to remote sensing imagery of the urban area. In recent years, deep convolutional neural networks (DCNNs) such as FCN [13], SegNet [2], U-Net [16] and DeepLab [5] demonstrated much improved performance for semantic segmentation. Built upon pooling and downsampling operations, DCNNs often face inaccurate segmentation of objects, especially at the boundaries [3,14]. To mitigate this issue, a number of techniques that extend DCNNs have been developed, e.g., skip connections [13], max-pooling indices reusing [2], and atrous convolution [4]. However, boundary location is more critical in remote sensing image analysis and needs to be retained in the segmentation results [14,20].

To address this problem, Marmanis et al. [14] used object class boundaries to train an edge detection network Holistically-Nested Edge Detection (HED) [18]

© Springer Nature Singapore Pte Ltd. 2020
X. Yuan et al. (Eds.): ICUIA 2020, CCIS 1319, pp. 172–184, 2020.
https://doi.org/10.1007/978-981-33-4601-7_18

and the predicted boundaries were then used as a supplementary input for the ensemble semantic segmentation network of FCN and SegNet. Liu et al. [11] trained a multi-task network based on HSNet (hourglass-shaped network [12]) for both semantic segmentation and edge detection. Class boundaries were used as extra supervision to guide the boundary prediction from the encoder component and decoder component of the semantic network separately. Cheng et al. [7] adopted a similar strategy based on SegNet, but combined the boundary prediction from both components as a whole. The semantic prediction result was further refined with edge regularization. All these methods rely on early semantic segmentation networks and some model is complex [11]. Alternatively, Xu et al. [19] used an image filter to enhance edges for the input image before feeding into ResUnet [21] and then applied a guided filter [9] to fine-tune the network output for building extraction. This method does not reinforce edge learning inside the network, which limits its performance. Despite the improvement, the predicted boundaries are still blurry with edge enhancement according to the authors. The guided filter further to sharpen the result could not handle complex scenes such as tree occlusion, blurry, irregular boundaries, and more accurate methods are needed [19].

In this paper, we present improved semantic segmentation with boundary enhancement based on an advanced network. We use object class boundaries as extra supervision, and adapt the state-of-the-art semantic segmentation network of DeepLab V3+ [6] with boundary enhancement structures upon both encoder and decoder components to simultaneously learn semantic segmentation and edge detection. Preliminary results demonstrate that we have improved the overall accuracy and mean IoU (Intersection over Union) of the state-of-art DeepLabV3+ from 90.41% to 90.60% and 74.60% to 75.76% respectively on Vaihingen Dataset, as well as 90.98% to 91.19% and 78.07% to 79.12% on Potsdam Dataset. It also outperforms another state-of-the-art network of PSPNet [22] on these two famous ISPRS 2D Semantic Labeling datasets.

We organize the rest of this paper as follows: Sect. 2 introduces related work, Sect. 3 describes the proposed method in detail, Sect. 4 presents the results and the comparison with other methods, Sect. 5 provides the conclusion and future work.

2   Related Work

Semantic segmentation networks usually extend image classification models by incorporating a decoder process to restore the original image resolution for pixelwise classification. While pooling and downsampling are useful for image classification, these operations are unsuitable for segmentation where spatial accuracy is expected [4,5]. To address this issue, Long et al. [13] proposed Fully Convolutional Network (FCN) to introduce middle-level features from the encoder component using skip connections. The class scores derived from these features were then integrated with simple summation in the upsampling process. Badrinarayanan et al. [2] proposed SegNet to store max-pooling indices at the encoder stage, which were reused at the decoder stage to upsample corresponding features at those indices more accurately. Ronneberger et al. [16] proposed U-Net to introduce low-level features to corresponding decoder component levels using skip connections. The fine-grained features were concatenated with high semantic features at the same level for upsampling. Chen et al. [4,5] proposed series DeepLab especially the advanced DeepLabV3+ [6] to apply atrous convolution at the last few layers of the encoder component to replace downsampling for better localization, while the expensive memory cost preventing the usage on more layers.

To improve the semantic segmentation of remote sensing images, Marmanis et al. [14] supplemented the input of the semantic segmentation networks with class boundary prediction. An edge detection network HED (Holistically-Nested Edge Detection [18]) was trained with class boundaries (boundaries between different class regions) using satellite image and DSM image (with height information) together to predict pixel-wise class boundary likelihoods. The boundary prediction was then used as an additional input to make class boundaries explicit for the ensembled semantic segmentation network of SegNet [2] and FCNs [13]. Liu et al. [11] introduced a multi-task semantic network to learn both semantic segmentation and edge detection by sharing features using HSNet (hourglass-shaped network [12]). The edge loss reinforced structures predicted class boundaries from two levels of the encoder component and decoder component separately by convolution after upsampling the features, then the edge loss from each component was added to the semantic loss as the total loss to optimize the entire network. Cheng et al. [7] used a similar strategy by applying a parallel edge detection network for jointly learning semantic segmentation and edge detection for sea-land-ship segmentation. They proposed FusionNet (based on SegNet [2]) to perform dimensionality reduction first then upsample features from two levels of the encoder component and three levels of the decoder component together to predict the class boundaries. The boundary prediction was further used to refine the final result with edge regularization. These methods are built upon early semantic segmentation networks while the model for [14] is complex. Different from the above methods learning class boundary prediction, Xu et al. [19] explored an image filter using an image processing technique to enhance edges in the input images for building extraction. As the improved results still had blurry boundaries, they further applied a guided filter [9] which is edge-preserving to smooth the salt-and-pepper noise for the output. The guided filter relies on a window size parameter and a hard classification threshold which are problematic to set and selected by compromisation. It could not precisely deal with certain situations such as tree occlusion while missing some blurry irregular boundaries, which requires more accurate methods [19].

3   Method

Our proposed network consists of two parts: a semantic segmentation network and boundary enhancement structures for both encoder and decoder components. The semantic segmentation network predicts the probability of each pixel with respect to all semantic classes; the boundary enhancement structures predict the probability of each pixel being class boundary or not. Boundary prediction is generated from the encoder component and decoder component separately, by sharing features with the semantic segmentation network. With class boundary labels during training, boundary loss is then derived and added to semantic loss to jointly optimize the whole network for both semantic segmentation and edge detection task, similar as [11]. Each loss is a cross-entropy loss.

We use labels of class boundaries (boundaries between different class regions) to learn edge detection, and these labels are simply computed by the gradient from semantic segmentation ground truth (we use Canny edge detector to get class boundaries in binary values). The two tasks are closely related, and learning in one task would help to better align the features spatially, which benefits the other task as our final goal. Our network architecture is shown in Fig. 2 and explained below.

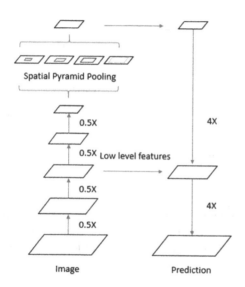

Fig. 1. The original DeepLabV3+ network.

3.1 Semantic Segmentation Network

We adapt the state-of-art DeepLab V3+ [6] model as the semantic segmentation network and ResNet-101 [10] pre-trained on ImageNet [8] as encoder component to gradually extract abstract features from the input image. Atrous convolution is used at the last few layers of the encoder component with different atrous rates for semantic information to avoid downsampling while having different fields-of-view, which is named Atrous Spatial Pyramid Pooling (ASPP). To recover fine spatial details for pixel level output, DeepLab V3+ applies a simple decoder module, which incorporates a branch of low level features from the encoder

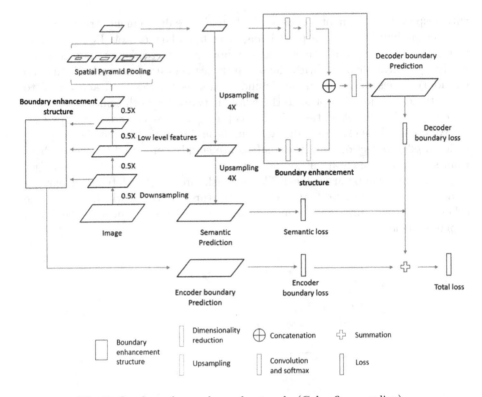

Fig. 2. Our boundary enhanced network. (Color figure online)

component by upsamping (default factor of 4) the semantic output from ASPP to the same resolution first and then performing concatenation. The features are then refined with a few convolutions (3×3) before another upsampling (factor of 4) to the input image resolution for final prediction. The original DeepLab V3+ network architecture is shown in Fig. 1. The cross-entropy loss for the semantic output is defined as

$$L_{semantic} = -\frac{1}{N} \sum_{i=1}^{N} \sum_{c=1}^{M} y_{i,c} \cdot log(p_{i,c}) \tag{1}$$

where i denotes each pixel i in the training images with total N pixels for total M classes, $p_{i,c}$ denotes the predicted probability of pixel i being class c and $y_{i,c}$ is a binary indicator of whether the ground truth label of pixel i is of class c (return 1 for true and 0 otherwise).

3.2   Boundary Enhancement Structure

However, the large factor for downsampling and upsampling stage in both components could lead to inaccurate localization of objects especially pixels near boundaries, and therefore degrade the final pixel-wise output. To mitigate this issue, we propose boundary enhancement structures (red blocks in Fig. 2) for the state-of-art semantic segmentation network of DeepLabV3+ to help the localization of objects. It builds upon the encoder component and decoder component separately to reinforce the boundary information to each of them, by explicitly forcing them to learn the boundary prediction. We select three levels of features generated from the first three levels of convolutional layers before downsampling in encoder component for more levels of information (compared to [7,11]), to perform dimensionality reduction (by 1×1 convolution to 32 channels) and upsampling to the original resolution first, then concatenate these level of features followed by convolution (3×3) and softmax classification, similar as [7]. We follow the same procedure for the decoder component, except that we select two levels of features: 1) the feature results after incorporating low-level features from the encoder component followed by convolution refinement; 2) the features from ASPP output. The ground truth of the class boundary map for each training image is just in binary values (indicating whether being class boundary or not), and calculated from the gradient of the semantic segmentation ground truth (we use Canny edge detector). With class boundary labels, the encoder boundary loss and decoder boundary loss can then be derived and added to semantic loss to form the total loss, which is used to optimize the whole network. The original cross-entropy loss for the boundary output from each of the encoder and decoder component is defined as

$$L_{boundary} = -\frac{1}{N} \sum_{i=1}^{N} y_i \cdot log(p_i) + (1 - y_i) \cdot log(1 - p_i) \qquad (2)$$

where i denotes each pixel i in the training images with total N pixels, p_i denotes the predicted probability of pixel i being class boundary and y_i is a binary indicator of whether the ground-truth label of pixel i is class boundary (return 1 for true and 0 otherwise). This is just a special case for the multi-class cross-entropy when class number equals to two. Then the total loss can be formulated as

$$L_{total} = L_{semantic} + \lambda \cdot L_{encoder\_boundary} + \lambda \cdot L_{decoder\_boundary} \qquad (3)$$

with λ equals to 2 to emphasize the boundary loss for both encoder and decoder components.

4   Results

4.1   Dataset and Experiment Setting

We evaluate our network for semantic segmentation of remote sensing imagery on the famous ISPRS 2D Semantic Labeling Vaihingen dataset[1] and Potsdam dataset[2]. The challenging Vaihingen dataset consists of 33 very high-resolution

---

[1] http://www2.isprs.org/commissions/comm3/wg4/2d-sem-label-vaihingen.html.
[2] http://www2.isprs.org/commissions/comm3/wg4/2d-sem-label-potsdam.html.

Infrared-Red-Green (IRRG) images from a small village of Vaihingen in Germany with many small buildings. Image size is 2500×2000 on average with a spatial resolution of 9 cm. Potsdam dataset consists of 38 very high-resolution IRRG images (extra RGB images are not used) from a typical historic city of Potsdam in Germany with large building blocks. Image size is 6000×6000 on average with a spatial resolution of 5 cm. Six classes are defined for both datasets as impervious surfaces, buildings, low vegetation, tree, car, and clutter/background. For the Vaihingen dataset, 16 images are made as combined training/validation data, leaving the rest as official testing data. For the Potsdam dataset, 24 images are made as combined training/validation data, leaving the rest for testing. We select images 5, 7, 23, 30 for validation, and the rest 12 images for training from the Vaihingen dataset following the method in [15]. We select image 2_11, 4_12, 6_7, 7_8 for validation and the rest 20 images for training from Potsdam dataset following [17]. Quantitative results are computed on the official testing data while qualitative visualization is made on validation data (quantitative results are computed using official eroded ground truth, which is obtained with a circular disc of 3-pixel radius to erode the ground truth boundaries, to ignore the uncertain border definitions).

We use an image patch size of 512×512 for training and testing as the whole image is too large to fit the GPU memory. We adopt the framework from [1] following almost the same setting but with a stride of 64 and 128 for the two datasets respectively to test overlapping patches, and average the overlapping prediction for the whole image to improve prediction near borders and uncertain areas. We use a large patch size to incorporate large context for classification and a small batch size of 8 to fit multi-GPU training. Experiment settings are as follows: momentum 0.9, weight decay 0.0005, initial learning rate 0.01 for our added edge components, and 0.005 for all the rest, all reduced by a factor of 10 at 25, 35, and 45 epoch (in total 50 epochs). We randomly crop 256 patches from every training image for one epoch. Data augmentation is random vertical and horizontal flipping. Training is done on 4 Tesla K80 GPU.

4.2   Evaluation and Discussion

We compare our network with state-of-the-art networks of DeepLabV3+ [6] and PSPNet [22], as well as FusionNet* (the close implementation of [7]) on Vaihingen and Potsdam testing data. For evaluation, we use F1, OA (overall accuracy), as well as IoU (Intersection over Union) and mean IoU (over all classes). F1 measures both precision and recall, while precision measures correctness, and recall measures completeness (TP denotes True Positive, TN denotes True Negative, FP denotes False Positive, FN denotes False Negative).

$$Precision = \frac{TP}{TP + FP}, \quad Recall = \frac{TP}{TP + FN}, \tag{4}$$

$$F1 = 2 \cdot \frac{Precision \cdot Recall}{Precision + Recall} \tag{5}$$

While overall accuracy only considers pixel correctness but not class spatial alignment, IoU (intersection over union) on the other hand calculates the overlapping ratio of prediction and ground truth with respect to the union of them for one class. It measures how close the prediction aligns with the ground truth spatially, which is very important to evaluate objects localization for semantic segmentation. Mean IoU calculates the average of IoU scores over all classes. To perform well, the IoU score for each class needs to be high, not just dominating classes.

$$IoU = \frac{Area\ of\ Overlap}{Area\ of\ Union}, \quad mean\ IoU = \frac{1}{N}\sum_{i=1}^{N}IoU_i\ (for\ N\ classes) \quad (6)$$

Quantitative results of F1, mean F1 score, OA (overall accuracy) as well as IoU and mean IoU score are shown Tables 1, 2, 3 and 4. Qualitative results are shown from Fig. 3 to Fig. 4. From left to right are the original satellite image, ground truth, and the prediction of each method respectively on validation image as well as the legend.

Table 1. F1 score on ISPRS Vaihingen official test dataset.

Model	Imp	Building	Low Veg	Tree	Car	Clutter	Mean	OA
FusionNet* [7]	86.16%	90.78%	77.66%	84.31%	67.83%	44.22%	75.16%	88.97%
PSPNet [22]	87.56%	91.98%	**78.84%**	84.98%	**75.19%**	58.01%	79.43%	90.31%
DeepLabV3+ [6]	88.07%	92.04%	78.65%	**85.15%**	73.07%	57.71%	79.11%	90.41%
Ours	**88.45%**	**92.33%**	78.73%	84.80%	73.62%	**63.49%**	**80.24%**	**90.60%**

Table 2. Intersection over Union (IoU) on ISPRS Vaihingen official test dataset.

Model	Imp	Building	Low Veg	Tree	Car	Clutter	Mean IoU
FusionNet* [7]	83.57%	88.46%	69.70%	79.51%	63.35%	28.76%	68.89%
PSPNet [22]	85.96%	90.67%	**71.64%**	80.66%	**74.96%**	42.51%	74.40%
DeepLabV3+ [6]	86.20%	90.95%	71.51%	**81.14%**	74.60%	43.23%	74.60%
Ours	**86.88%**	**91.36%**	71.53%	80.86%	74.45%	**49.47%**	**75.76%**

For quantitative results of the Vaihingen dataset, from Table 1 to Table 2 we can see that DeepLabV3+ outperforms FusionNet* in every aspect by a large margin, ranking top 1 for high overall accuracy and also top 1 for mean IoU score (without considering our method), indicating it is the state-of-the-art method with accurate localization of objects. And our method further outperforms DeepLabV3+ in almost every aspect (except for tree class and car IoU score with a very small difference). It makes more accurate pixel prediction, especially for impervious surfaces (from 88.07% to 88.45%), building (from 92.04% to 92.33%), and clutter/background (from 57.71% to 63.49%), with overall accuracy improved from 90.41% to 90.60%. Our method also makes closer alignment with ground truth, surpassing DeepLabV3+ in almost every IoU score, especially for impervious surfaces (from 86.20% to 86.88%), building (from 90.95% to 91.36%), and clutter/background (from 43.23% to 49.47%), with mean IoU improved from 74.60% to 75.76% by a large margin, indicating our boundary enhancement is effective. Our method also outperforms the state-of-the-art network of PSPNet in most aspects similarly.

From qualitative results in Fig. 3 we can see that all methods perform well in general for the majority of the buildings. FusionNet* could not handle well the large buildings on the top left corner, as well as being blurry or missing partially the large building in the middle left. DeepLabV3+ has large improvements for the top corner building as well as the buildings along the road. PSPNet could not fully recognize the building on the top corner and the building along the road in the middle, cutting it into half. Our method improves DeepLabV3+ for the top corner building significantly to complete recognition.

Table 3. F1 score on ISPRS Potsdam official test dataset.

Model	Imp	Building	Low Veg	Tree	Car	Clutter	Mean	OA
FusionNet* [7]	88.11%	92.66%	80.25%	83.44%	83.48%	43.10%	78.51%	88.43%
PSPNet [22]	89.81%	**94.50%**	**83.49%**	85.74%	84.30%	54.67%	82.09%	90.99%
DeepLabV3+ [6]	**90.10%**	94.35%	83.46%	85.45%	80.96%	57.43%	81.96%	90.98%
Ours	89.93%	94.47%	**83.49%**	**85.85%**	**84.34%**	**57.69%**	**82.63%**	**91.19%**

Table 4. Intersection over Union (IoU) on ISPRS Potsdam official test dataset.

Model	Imp	Building	Low Veg	Tree	Car	Clutter	Mean IoU
FusionNet* [7]	84.32%	90.10%	73.36%	75.62%	89.68%	28.87%	73.66%
PSPNet [22]	87.80%	93.30%	77.79%	80.12%	90.59%	39.96%	78.26%
DeepLabV3+ [6]	87.73%	93.16%	**77.95%**	79.93%	86.90%	**42.75%**	78.07%
Ours	**87.87%**	**93.44%**	77.87%	**80.34%**	**92.54%**	42.67%	**79.12%**

For quantitative results of the Potsdam dataset, from Table 3 to Table 4 we can see that DeepLabV3+ again outperforms FusionNet* in almost every aspect by a large margin, and ranking top 2 with a small difference from PSPNet (without considering our method), indicating it is a highly competitive method. Our method improves DeepLabV3+ in every aspect (except impervious surfaces with a small difference) at a high level, with overall accuracy improved from 90.98% to 91.19%. Our method also makes closer alignment with ground truth, surpassing DeepLabV3+ in almost every IoU score, especially for building (from 93.16% to 93.44%), tree (from 79.93% to 80.34%), and car class (from 86.90% to 92.54%), with mean IoU improved from 78.07% to 79.12% by a large margin, indicating our boundary enhancement is effective. Our method also outperforms the state-of-the-art network of PSPNet in every aspect.

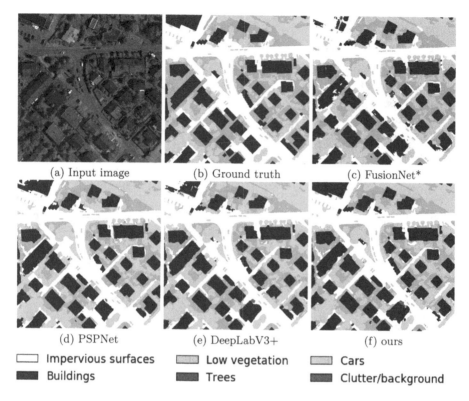

(a) Input image   (b) Ground truth   (c) FusionNet*

(d) PSPNet   (e) DeepLabV3+   (f) ours

☐ Impervious surfaces   ▨ Low vegetation   ▨ Cars

■ Buildings   ■ Trees   ■ Clutter/background

Fig. 3. Results of deep neural networks on Vaihingen validation image

From qualitative results in Fig. 4 we can see that all methods perform well in general for the majority of the scene. FusionNet* could not handle well the large background class in the middle, as well as the top and bottom buildings. PSPNet has even worse misclassification for the top buildings. DeepLabV3+ has improvements but the misclassification of the top buildings still exists. Our method improves DeepLabV3+ to generate perfect buildings while keeping the background well classified.

From both datasets, we observe consistent and obvious improvements for the classes with well-defined boundaries (e.g, man-made object classes), but not that consistent for vegetation classes since they have fuzzy boundaries, which is similarly indicated by [14].

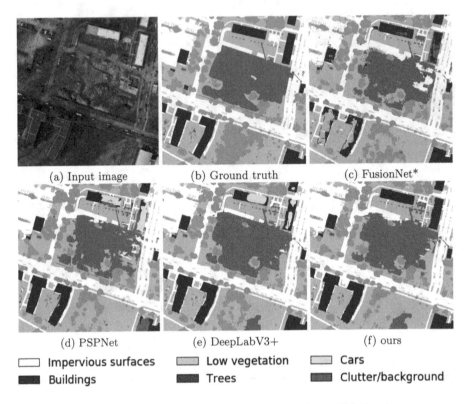

(a) Input image   (b) Ground truth   (c) FusionNet*

(d) PSPNet   (e) DeepLabV3+   (f) ours

☐ Impervious surfaces   ☐ Low vegetation   ☐ Cars

■ Buildings   ■ Trees   ■ Clutter/background

Fig. 4. Results of deep neural networks on Potsdam validation image

5 Conclusion

In this paper, we propose improved semantic segmentation with boundary enhancement based on DeepLabV3+, the state-of-art semantic segmentation network. We propose boundary enhancement structures for each of the encoder and decoder components. We reinforce the object class boundary information to different levels of features in both components, by jointly learning semantic segmentation and edge detection. By doing that, we force the features with better spatial alignment to mitigate the inaccurate localization caused by downsampling and upsampling in both encoder and decoder components. From both quantitative and qualitative results, we can see that the improvements of our method are consistent and obvious, and our method outperforms the rest with better prediction accuracy as well as spatial alignment with ground truth, indicating our method is effective for semantic segmentation of very high-resolution imagery in remote sensing application.

Future work may include more complex enhancement structure (e.g., incorporating more level of features, more skip connections), better ways of feature upsampling (e.g., object masks). Unsupervised and weakly supervised methods may also be incorporated to explore more data to make better boundary prediction and semantic classification.

References

1. Audebert, N., Le Saux, B., Lefèvre, S.: Beyond RGB: very high resolution urban remote sensing with multimodal deep networks. ISPRS J. Photogramm. Remote Sens. **140**, 20–32 (2018)
2. Badrinarayanan, V., Kendall, A., Cipolla, R.: SegNet: a deep convolutional encoder-decoder architecture for image segmentation. arXiv preprint arXiv:1511.00561 (2015)
3. Chen, L.C., Barron, J.T., Papandreou, G., Murphy, K., Yuille, A.L.: Semantic image segmentation with task-specific edge detection using CNNs and a discriminatively trained domain transform. In: Proceedings of the IEEE Conference on Computer Vision and Pattern Recognition, pp. 4545–4554 (2016)
4. Chen, L.C., Papandreou, G., Kokkinos, I., Murphy, K., Yuille, A.L.: Semantic image segmentation with deep convolutional nets and fully connected CRFs. In: International Conference on Learning Representations (ICLR) (2015)
5. Chen, L.C., Papandreou, G., Kokkinos, I., Murphy, K., Yuille, A.L.: DeepLab: semantic image segmentation with deep convolutional nets, atrous convolution, and fully connected CRFs. IEEE Trans. Pattern Anal. Mach. Intell. **40**(4), 834–848 (2018)
6. Chen, L.C., Zhu, Y., Papandreou, G., Schroff, F., Adam, H.: Encoder-decoder with atrous separable convolution for semantic image segmentation. In: Proceedings of the European Conference on Computer Vision (ECCV), pp. 801–818 (2018)
7. Cheng, D., Meng, G., Xiang, S., Pan, C.: FusionNet: edge aware deep convolutional networks for semantic segmentation of remote sensing harbor images. IEEE J. Sel. Top. Appl. Earth Observ. Remote Sens. **10**(12), 5769–5783 (2017)
8. Deng, J., Dong, W., Socher, R., Li, L.J., Li, K., Fei-Fei, L.: ImageNet: a large-scale hierarchical image database. In: 2009 IEEE Conference on Computer Vision and Pattern Recognition, pp. 248–255. IEEE (2009)
9. He, K., Sun, J., Tang, X.: Guided image filtering. IEEE Trans. Pattern Anal. Mach. Intell. **35**(6), 1397–1409 (2013)
10. He, K., Zhang, X., Ren, S., Sun, J.: Deep residual learning for image recognition. In: Proceedings of the IEEE Conference on Computer Vision and Pattern Recognition, pp. 770–778 (2016)
11. Liu, S., Ding, W., Liu, C., Liu, Y., Wang, Y., Li, H.: ERN: edge loss reinforced semantic segmentation network for remote sensing images. Remote Sens. **10**(9), 1339 (2018)
12. Liu, Y., Minh Nguyen, D., Deligiannis, N., Ding, W., Munteanu, A.: Hourglass-shape network based semantic segmentation for high resolution aerial imagery. Remote Sens. **9**(6), 522 (2017)
13. Long, J., Shelhamer, E., Darrell, T.: Fully convolutional networks for semantic segmentation. In: Proceedings of the IEEE Conference on Computer Vision and Pattern Recognition, pp. 3431–3440 (2015)
14. Marmanis, D., Schindler, K., Wegner, J.D., Galliani, S., Datcu, M., Stilla, U.: Classification with an edge: improving semantic image segmentation with boundary detection. ISPRS J. Photogramm. Remote Sens. **135**, 158–172 (2018)

15. Marmanis, D., Wegner, J.D., Galliani, S., Schindler, K., Datcu, M., Stilla, U.: Semantic segmentation of aerial images with an ensemble of CNSs. ISPRS Ann. Photogramm. Remote Sens. Spat. Inf. Sci. **2016**(3), 473–480 (2016)
16. Ronneberger, O., Fischer, P., Brox, T.: U-Net: convolutional networks for biomedical image segmentation. In: Navab, N., Hornegger, J., Wells, W.M., Frangi, A.F. (eds.) MICCAI 2015. LNCS, vol. 9351, pp. 234–241. Springer, Cham (2015). https://doi.org/10.1007/978-3-319-24574-4_28
17. Singh, S., et al.: Self-supervised feature learning for semantic segmentation of overhead imagery. In: BMVC, p. 102 (2018)
18. Xie, S., Tu, Z.: Holistically-nested edge detection. In: Proceedings of the IEEE International Conference on Computer Vision, pp. 1395–1403 (2015)
19. Xu, Y., Wu, L., Xie, Z., Chen, Z.: Building extraction in very high resolution remote sensing imagery using deep learning and guided filters. Remote Sens. **10**(1), 144 (2018)
20. Yuan, X., Zhang, J., Yuan, X., Buckles, B.P.: Multi-scale feature identification using evolution strategies. Image Vis. Comput. **23**(6), 555–563 (2005)
21. Zhang, Z., Liu, Q., Wang, Y.: Road extraction by deep residual U-Net. IEEE Geosci. Remote Sens. Lett. **15**, 749–753 (2018)
22. Zhao, H., Shi, J., Qi, X., Wang, X., Jia, J.: Pyramid scene parsing network. In: Proceedings of the IEEE Conference on Computer Vision and Pattern Recognition, pp. 2881–2890 (2017)

Recent Advances of Generic Object Detection with Deep Learning: A Review

Xin Li[1,2], Yingying Li[1,2(✉)], and Shushu Li[1,2]

[1] Anhui Agricultural University, Hefei, China
yyhgd@ahjzu.edu.cn
[2] School of Electronics and Information Engineering, Anhui Jianzhu University,
Hefei 230601, China

Abstract. Object detection is an important and challenging problem in computer vision. It has been widely applied in many vision tasks, such as object tracking, image segmentation, action recognition, etc. With the rapid development of deep learning, more state-of-the-art object detection methods based on deep learning with some modifications have effectively improved the detection performance. This paper comprehensively reviews object detection methods in the recent five years based on deep learning from object detection framework, including significant advances of the backbone network, multi-scale learning, data augmentation. Finally, we investigate the performance of typical object detection algorithms on popular datasets MS-COCO, PASCAL-VOC, and point out the existing problem for further research.

Keywords: Object detection · Deep learning · Backbone network · Multi-scale learning

1 Introduction

Object detection is one of the most fundamental tasks in computer vision. It plays an important role in many applications, such as object tracking [1], image segmentation [2], action recognition [3], etc. In recent years, object detection has been pushed forward by the success of deep learning techniques to a research highlight. Numerous research progresses on object detection have endlessly been achieved. It is necessary to provide researchers with timely reviews to guide future research on object detection.

Many reviews about object detection have been published. These reviews sum up all kinds of object detection methods from different research perspectives and under specific application scenarios. Wu [4] systematically reviews recent advances in object detection with deep learning, including detection components, learning strategies, applications, and benchmarks. Zhao [5] pays more attention to the typical generic architectures of object detection with progress and useful tricks. Their work also reviews several specific applications, such as salient object detection, face detection, and pedestrian detection. Li [6] provides

© Springer Nature Singapore Pte Ltd. 2020
X. Yuan et al. (Eds.): ICUIA 2020, CCIS 1319, pp. 185–193, 2020.
https://doi.org/10.1007/978-981-33-4601-7_19

a comprehensive review of generic object detection from 300 research contributions, from the aspects of detection frameworks, object proposal generation, feature representation, context modeling, etc. Jiao [7] provides an overview of the traditional and new applications and some new branches of object detection.

This paper focuses on the new advances of generic object detection in the recent five years, reviewing the research works of deep learning-based object detection. The paper aims to give a comprehensive review in various aspects of object detection, including object detection framework, significant advances of the backbone network, multi-scale learning, data augmentation. In addition to this, we investigate datasets and evaluation of classical object detection algorithms in recent years and we thoroughly analyze their performance.

The rest of the paper is organized as follows: The object detection framework is listed in Sect. 2. Then significant advances in various aspects of object detection are in Sect. 3. The evaluation method of object detection and the comparison of various performances are in Sect. 4. Finally, we conclude and discuss future directions in Sect. 5.

2   Object Detection Framework

Deep learning-based object detection frameworks usually can be divided into two categories: two-stage detectors and single-stage detectors. Two-stage detectors first generate a sparse set of proposals locations and then region classifiers as the next step. Single-stage detectors directly make a categorical prediction of objects at each location along with cascaded region classification as the same step.

2.1   Two-Stage Detector

The Two-stage detectors include the following two processes: one is to propose the candidate boxes, and the other is to make the decision of classifications using multiple feature maps at the top of the network. The most representative two-stage object detectors are the R-CNN [8] series, including fast R-CNN [9], faster R-CNN [10], and Libra R-CNN [11].

R-CNN applies CNNs to bottom-up region proposals in order to localize objects, generate a rich hierarchy of image features by supervised pre-training and domain-specific fine-tuning. Fast R-CNN employs a new training algorithm that fixes the disadvantages of R-CNN and SPPnet to improve training and testing speed while also increasing detection accuracy. Faster R-CNN presents Region Proposal Networks (RPNs) for more efficient and accurate region proposal generation, for RPNs can generate higher quality region proposals than Fast R-CNN for detection. Libra R-CNN integrates IoU-balanced sampling, balanced feature pyramid, and balanced L1 loss. Thanks to its overall balanced design, Libra R-CNN significantly improves the detection performance.

2.2 Single-Stage Detector

The single-stage target detection networks are integrating the two tasks of generating candidate boxes and providing the final classification of the input image as a whole process. The advantage of this framework is that it greatly improves the detection speed. The representative networks of single-stage are SSD [12] and YOLO [13], YOLO9000 [14], YOLOv3 [15], YOLOv4 [16].

SSD is a fast single-stage object detector for multiple categories, which discretizes the output space of bounding boxes into a set of default boxes over different aspect ratios and scales, and uses multiple feature maps at the top of the network to achieve improved performance. YOLO [13] takes object detection as a regression problem to predict bounding boxes and class probabilities directly from input images in one evaluation. YOLO pushes the application of object detection in real-time. But the first Yolo has poor position accuracy in small object detection. The later YOLO [14–16] make improvements on YOLO in positioning accuracy and detection speed, not only to general goals but also to small object detection. YOLOv4 [16] develops the previous object detection model and summarizes the influence of state-of-the-art Bag-of-Freebies and Bag-of-Specials methods of object detection during the detector training. So it is faster and more accurate than other detectors.

3 Review of Significant Advances

3.1 Backbone Networks

Deep learning networks bring a revolutionary breakthrough in object detection rather than just obvious improvements in performance on large databases. Their success results from training an effective backbone network on large labeled images. The most representative backbone networks used in object detection tasks are as follows.

VGG [17] modifies some parameters of the ConvNet architecture and increases the depth of the network by adding more convolutional layers with using very small (3 × 3) convolution filters in all layers. With the emergence of the convolutional neural network, image recognition has developed rapidly.

ResNet [18] uses a residual learning framework to lighten the training networks, which rebuilds the layers as learning residual functions with reference to the layer inputs, instead of learning unreferenced functions. These residual networks are easier to optimize and can gain accuracy from considerably increased depth. ResNet has lower complexity even if it has deeper layers, compared with VGG.

SpineNet [19] is the scale-permuted model instead of the scale decreased model, which provide two major improvements on backbone architecture: One is that SpineNet can retain spatial information as it grows deeper, the other, the connections between feature maps should be able to go across feature scales to facilitate multi-scale feature fusion. It is a good backbone architecture design for tasks requiring simultaneous recognition and localization.

EfficientNets [20] is a family of models with a new baseline, obtained by neural architecture search. This model firstly uses a simple and effective coefficient to quantify the relationship among all three dimensions of network width, depth, and resolution. Benefited from this balancing network depth, width, and resolution, EfficientNets achieve much better accuracy and efficiency than the previous backbone network.

CSPNet (Cross Stage Partial Network) [21] splits the gradient flow to make propagated gradient information through different network paths have a large correlation difference. CSPNet can greatly reduce the amount of computation, and improve inference speed as well as accuracy, so it can relieve the problem that previous networks require heavy computations, help people with cheap devices to enjoy the result of the backbone networks.

3.2   Multi-scale Learning

Neck refers to the fusion of features of the above different scales, with the purpose of generating multi-scale features with both high semantic information and accurate location information, and improving the ability of the model to detect targets of different scales.

FPN Network. The traditional method of extracting multi-layer features is the image pyramid, which is an effective but conceptually simple structure to interpret images with multi-resolution. By changing the scale of the image, the image layer by layer is compared to a pyramid. The higher the level, the smaller the image, and the lower the resolution. We can also extract features from the feature pyramid by using the convolutional network, but this will greatly increase the operation time and require more memory for operation. Therefore FPN in 2017 was put forward, the author through the bottom-up, namely network to process before, top-down, upsampling is used, the results of the sampling on the transverse connection is will and bottom-up generation feature of the same size of the map to merge, and the characteristics of different resolutions is a figure, FPN today is still used in many networks, such as Faster RCNN, Mask RCNN, DSSD [22], etc.

There are also some problems with the classical FPN network. For example, multi-scale characterization improves the detection effect of the deMulti-scale learning network, but at the same time makes it impossible for the multi-scale features to be fully utilized by the network. Therefore, AugFPN [23] is an improvement on the classical FPN structure. AugFPN innovation lies in three of the components, respectively is Consistent Supervision: narrow the features before fusion of different scale, the semantic gap between Residual Feature Augmentation: analysis on the characteristics of Residual enhance extraction rate constant of context information, reduce the information loss Feature map is on the highest pyramid level, Soft ROI Selection: adaptively learn better ROI. AugFPN's innovations make up for FPN's shortcomings. At present, a new feature pyramid structure called NAS-FPNnas [24] is proposed. The author makes full use of Neural architecture search with reinforcement learning and trains a controller to select the best model structure in a given search space through intensive learning.

SPP and ASPP Networks. The traditional neural network requires the input of a fixed size of the image, which requires the resize of the image before it is introduced into the network. As a result, the image information changes. To solve this problem, SPP [25] and ASPP [26] are proposed.

SPP extracts features from blocks of different sizes, respectively 4×4, 2×2, and 1×1. Put these three grids on the following feature map, and you can get 21 different Spatial bins. From these 21 blocks, each block extracts a feature, so as to extract the 21-dimensional feature vector. The entire process is completely independent of the size of the input, so you can handle candidate boxes of any size.

The ASPP parallel samples a given input by atrous convolution at different sampling rates. Compared to the conventional convolution operator, atrous convolution can obtain a larger size of the receiving field without increasing the number of kernel parameters. ASPP proposed to connect the feature maps generated by atrous convolution under different expansion rates in series, so that the neurons in the output feature map contain multiple accepting field sizes, encoding the multi-scale information, and finally improving the performance.

3.3 Data Augmentation

Training for a neural network often requires the support of thousands of pictures, and the more data, the better the experimental effect. However, this often does not occur in large data sets, which leads to a new field of data enhancement. MixUp [27] multiplies and superimposes two images at different coefficient ratios, and then adjusts the label using those superimposed ratios. With CutMix [28], it is to overlay the cropped image onto a rectangular area of other images and resize the label according to the size of the mixed area. The random erase [29] and CutOut [30] can randomly select rectangular areas in the image and populate them with a random or complementary value of zero. In addition, style transfer GAN [31] is often used for data enhancement, which can effectively reduce the texture deviation of CNN learning.

4 Evaluation and Databases

Average Precision (AP) is the common metric to evaluate the detection precision, defined as the average detection precision under different recalls, usually evaluated in one class. The mean Average Precision (mAP) refers to the average score of AP across all classes, which is used as an evaluation metric for many object detection datasets.

A number of well-known datasets for object detection have been provided in the past years [32] MS-COCO and PASCAL-VOC [32] are the most representative datasets for generic object detection. We investigate the performance of typical object detection algorithms with different backbone network on popular datasets MS-COCO, PASCAL-VOC. The results are shown Table 1 and Table 2.

Table 1. Detection results on the VOC 2007 test-dev dataset of some typical methods

Model	Backbone	mAP (%)	# of stage	Detection speed (fps)
RCNN [8]	VGG16	66	Two	0.5
Fast RCNN [9]	VGG16	70	Two	7
Faster RCNN [10]	VGG16	73.2	Two	7
Faster RCNN [10]	Resnet101	76.4	Two	5
YOLO [13]	Darcknet19	66.4	One	45
SSD [12]	VGG16	77.1	One	46
YOLOv2 [14]	Darcknet19	78.6	One	40
YOLOv3 [15]	Darcknet53	33	One	51
DSSD321 [22]	Resnet169	78.6	One	9.5
DSSD513 [22]	Resnet169	81.5	One	5.5
Soft Sampling [33]	VGG16	79.3	Two	–
R-FCN-3000 [34]	Resnet101	80.5	Two	30

Table 2. Detection results on the MS-COCO test-dev dataset of some typical methods

Model	Backbone	mAP (%)	# of stage	Detection speed (fps)
Mask RCNN [11]	Resnet101	33.1	Two	4.8
YOLO9000 [14]	Darcknet19	78.6	One	40
FPN [35]	Resnet50	35.8	Two	5.8
NAS-FPN [23]	Resnet50	44.2	Two	92.1
Cascade RCNN [23]	Resnet101	42.8	Two	–
D-RFCN + SNIP [36]	DPN-98	48.3	Two	2
TridentNet [37]	Resnet101	48.4	One	–

5 Conclusion

In recent years, deep learning-based object detection has developed rapidly. Detection accuracy and high precision in real-time systems are the ultimate goals of object detection. This paper provides a detailed review of object detection in recent five years, covering object detection framework, significant advances of the backbone network, multi-scale learning, activation function, data augmentation. Although significant advances in this domain have been achieved recently, there is still much room for further development. Finally, we propose several promising future directions, such as the interpretability of convolution, the combination of the actual mobile terminal, the balance of accuracy and speed.

Acknowledgements. This work was supported in part by the Natural Science Research Project of Educational Commission of Anhui Province of China under Grant (KJ2018A0521) and the Visiting Scholar Researcher Program through the Young Talents Foreign Visiting and Training Program of Educational Commission of Anhui Province of China under Grant (gxgwfx2018047).

References

1. Kang, H., et al.: T-CNN: tubelets with convolutional neural networks for object detection from videos. IEEE Trans. Circ. Syst. Video Tech. **28**(10), 2896–2907 (2018)
2. Wang, Y., Wang, L., Lu, H., et al.: Segmentation based rotated bounding boxes prediction and image synthesizing for object detection of high resolution aerial images. Neurocomputing (2020)
3. Herath, S., Harandi, M., Porikli, F.: Going deeper into action recognition: a survey. Image Vis. Comput. **60**, 4–21 (2017)
4. Wu, X., Sahoo, D., Hoi, S.C.H.: Recent advances in deep learning for object detection. Neurocomputing (2020)
5. Zhao, Z.Q., Zheng, P., Xu, S., et al.: Object detection with deep learning: a review. IEEE Trans. Neural Netw. Learn. Syst. **30**(11), 3212–3232 (2019)
6. Liu, L., Ouyang, W., Wang, X., et al.: Deep learning for generic object detection: a survey. Int. J. Comput. Vis. **128**(2), 261–318 (2020)
7. Jiao, L., Zhang, F., Liu, F., et al.: A survey of deep learning-based object detection. IEEE Access **7**, 128837–128868 (2019)
8. Girshick, R., Donahue, J., Darrell, T., et al.: Rich feature hierarchies for accurate object detection and semantic segmentation. In: Proceedings of the IEEE Conference on Computer Vision and Pattern Recognition, pp. 580–587 (2014)
9. Girshick, R.: Fast R-CNN. In: Proceedings of the IEEE International Conference on Computer Vision, pp. 1440–1448 (2015)
10. Ren, S., He, K., Girshick, R., et al.: Faster R-CNN: towards real-time object detection with region proposal networks. In: Advances in Neural Information Processing Systems, pp. 91–99 (2015)
11. Pang, J., et al.: Libra R-CNN: towards balanced learning for object detection. In: Proceedings of the IEEE Conference on Computer Vision and Pattern Recognition (2019)
12. Pang, J., Chen, K., Shi, J., et al.: Libra R-CNN: towards balanced learning for object detection. In: Proceedings of the IEEE Conference on Computer Vision and Pattern Recognition, pp. 821–830 (2019)
13. Redmon, J., Divvala, S., Girshick, R., et al.: You only look once: unified, real-time object detection. In: Proceedings of the IEEE Conference on Computer Vision and Pattern Recognition, pp. 779–788 (2016)

14. Redmon, J., Farhadi, A.: YOLO9000: better, faster, stronger. In: Proceedings of the IEEE Conference on Computer Vision and Pattern Recognition, pp. 7263–7271 (2017)
15. Redmon, J., Farhadi, A.: Yolov3: an incremental improvement, arXiv preprint arXiv:1804.02767 (2018)
16. Bochkovskiy, A., Wang, C.Y., Liao, H.Y.M.: YOLOv4: optimal speed and accuracy of object detection, arXiv preprint arXiv:2004.10934 (2020)
17. Simonyan, K., Zisserman, A.: Very deep convolutional networks for large-scale image recognition, arXiv preprint arXiv:1409.1556 (2014)
18. He, K., Zhang, X., Ren, S., et al.: Deep residual learning for image recognition. In: Proceedings of the IEEE Conference on Computer Vision and Pattern Recognition, pp. 770–778 (2016)
19. Du, X., Lin, T.Y., Jin, P., et al.: SpineNet: learning scale-permuted backbone for recognition and localization. In: Proceedings of the IEEE/CVF Conference on Computer Vision and Pattern Recognition, pp. 11592–11601 (2020)
20. Tan, M., Le, Q.V.: EfficientNet: rethinking model scaling for convolutional neural networks, arXiv preprint arXiv:1905.11946 (2019)
21. Wang, C.Y., Mark Liao, H.Y., Wu, Y.H., et al.: CSPNet: a new backbone that can enhance learning capability of CNN. In: Proceedings of the IEEE/CVF Conference on Computer Vision and Pattern Recognition Workshops, pp. 390–391 (2020)
22. Fu, C.Y., Liu, W., Ranga, A., et al.: DSSD: deconvolutional single shot detector, arXiv preprint arXiv:1701.06659 (2017)
23. Guo, C., Fan, B., Zhang, Q., et al.: AugFPN: improving multi-scale feature learning for object detection. In: Proceedings of the IEEE/CVF Conference on Computer Vision and Pattern Recognition, pp. 12595–12604 (2020)
24. Ghiasi, G., Lin, T.Y., Le, Q.V.: NAS-FPN: learning scalable feature pyramid architecture for object detection. In: Proceedings of the IEEE Conference on Computer Vision and Pattern Recognition, pp. 7036–7045 (2019)
25. He, K., Zhang, X., Ren, S., et al.: Spatial pyramid pooling in deep convolutional networks for visual recognition. IEEE Trans. Pattern Anal. Mach. Intell. **37**(9), 1904–1916 (2015)
26. Yang, M., Yu, K., Zhang, C., et al.: DenseASPP for semantic segmentation in street scenes. In: Proceedings of the IEEE Conference on Computer Vision and Pattern Recognition, pp. 3684–3692 (2018)
27. Misra, D.: Mish: a self regularized non-monotonic neural activation function, arXiv preprint arXiv:1908.08681 (2019)
28. Yun, S., Han, D., Oh, S.J., et al.: CutMix: regularization strategy to train strong classifiers with localizable features. In: Proceedings of the IEEE International Conference on Computer Vision, pp. 6023–6032 (2019)
29. Zhong, Z., Zheng, L., Kang, G., et al.: Random erasing data augmentation. In: AAAI, pp. 13001–13008 (2020)
30. DeVries, T., Taylor, G.W.: Improved regularization of convolutional neural networks with cutout, arXiv preprint arXiv:1708.04552 (2017)
31. Geirhos, R., Rubisch, P., Michaelis, C., et al.: ImageNet-trained CNNs are biased towards texture; increasing shape bias improves accuracy and robustness, arXiv preprint arXiv:1811.12231 (2018)
32. Everingham, M., Van Gool, L., Williams, C.K.I., et al.: The pascal visual object classes (VOC) challenge. Int. J. Comput. Vis. **88**(2), 303–338 (2010)
33. Wu, Z., Bodla, N., Singh, B., et al.: Soft sampling for robust object detection, arXiv preprint arXiv:1806.06986 (2018)

34. Singh, B., Li, H., Sharma, A., et al.: R-FCN-3000 at 30fps: decoupling detection and classification. In: Proceedings of the IEEE Conference on Computer Vision and Pattern Recognition, pp. 1081–1090 (2018)
35. Seferbekov, S.S., Iglovikov, V., Buslaev, A., et al.: Feature pyramid network for multi-class land segmentation. In: CVPR Workshops, pp. 272–275 (2018)
36. Singh, B., Davis, L.S.: An analysis of scale invariance in object detection SNIP. In: Proceedings of the IEEE Conference on Computer Vision and Pattern Recognition, pp. 3578–3587 (2018)
37. Li, Y., Chen, Y., Wang, N., et al.: Scale-aware trident networks for object detection. In: Proceedings of the IEEE International Conference on Computer Vision, pp. 6054–6063 (2019)

Security, Safety, and Emergency Management

Sentiment Analysis of Chinese Agricultural News Based on the JST Model

Chao Wang[1,2], Hui Wang[1,2], Caifeng Ye[1,2], Jiale Gao[1,2], Fei Li[1,2], and Lichuan Gu[1,2(✉)]

[1] Anhui Agricultural University, Hefei, China
{wangchao_ICLE,glc}@ahau.edu.cn, 1835435117@qq.com, 2294949851@qq.com, 1443302020@qq.com, 1906283312@qq.com
[2] Key Laboratory of Agricultural Electronic Commerce of the Ministry of Agriculture, Hefei, China

Abstract. Agricultural news usually describes objective facts, and its subjectivity is weak. Conventional sentiment analysis methods which can get high accuracy by definite sentiment trend are difficult to apply to the agricultural news filed. We propose a simple yet effective framework that allows us to accurately analyze the sentiment of Chinese Agricultural News. The basic idea is to create a dictionary of a positive and negative sentiment of agricultural news as prior knowledge and construct a sentiment classification model with a joint emotion-subject model (JST) and the dictionary. The practical merits of our approach are demonstrated in real-world datasets.

Keywords: Agricultural news · Sentiment classification · JST model

1 Introduction

Increasingly, people engage in information acquisition on the Internet by the online news, and understand the current situation through network news, express their opinions and emotions through comments. However, the large number and Continuous propagation of news, which makes it difficult to systemically extract and analyze valuable information to objectively evaluate the accuracy of news and make timely responses only by browsing and reading. Especially in the field of agriculture, the sentiment analysis of relevant news is more important. China is a largely agricultural country, the sentiment analysis and trend tracking of agricultural hot events have a great impact on agricultural development. Understanding the emotions in news content can help decision-makers to analyze public opinion tendency, and deal with public opinion emergencies in time. Meanwhile, the public can understand the development of relevant events in time and identify the authenticity of the information. Therefore, automatic recognition of positive and negative sentiment expressed in agricultural news has important theoretical and practical value.

© Springer Nature Singapore Pte Ltd. 2020
X. Yuan et al. (Eds.): ICUIA 2020, CCIS 1319, pp. 197–205, 2020.
https://doi.org/10.1007/978-981-33-4601-7_20

Sentiment analysis [12] is often called opinion mining [1] or tendentious-ness analysis, which is mainly a process of analysis, induction, and reasoning of sentiment in subjective texts. The core issue of text sentiment analysis is senti-ment classification. Generally, it can be divided into three categories according to the granularity of classification: binary classification (positive and negative), multi-classification (more fine-grained classification, which can reflect the differ-ent intensity of news sentiment). In this paper, we use a binary classification method to classify the sentiment of agricultural news, because of its weak sub-jectivity.

We propose an effective framework, which aims at classifying the sentiment of agricultural news via their prior knowledge. We aim to improve the accuracy of sentiment analysis of agricultural news, by combining a joint emotion-subject model with a sentiment dictionary that indicates the prior knowledge. Our exper-imental evaluation shows that our implementation can efficiently improve the accuracy of sentiment classification of agricultural news.

The rest of this paper is organized as follows: Sect. 2 reviews the related work on methods for risk assessment. Section 3 presents our proposed method in details. Section 4 discusses our experimental results. Section 5 cóncludes this paper with a summary.

2   Related Work

Sentiment analysis is an important part of natural language processing, which is a qualitative and quantitative computation process of the opinion, emotion, atti-tude of the entity in text [2,8]. It plays an important role in comment screening classification, opinion mining, user classification and clustering, public opinion prediction, and so on. From the surveying of recent related works, sentiment anal-ysis can be classified into two categories: supervised and unsupervised methods.

Supervised sentiment analysis methods are mainly constructing an appro-priate classification and prediction model of sentiment analysis, by using some machine learning methods to analyze and train the text with emotional mark-ers. Pang et al. [10] studied the sentiment classification accuracy of three machine learning methods, Naive Bayesian, maximum entropy, and support vec-tor machine, with a film review dataset, and shows that the accuracy of the support vector machine was the best and reached 80%. Chaffar and Inkpen [3] compares the sentiment classification effects of decision trees, naive Bayes, and support vector machines on document and sentence levels text, and proves that SVM is more accurate. Mullen and Collier [7] integrate the support vector machine method with various feature selection methods, shows that different features have a great influence on sentiment classification. Supervised sentiment analysis methods have to train classifiers with a large number of training samples, and the process of manually marking training samples is time-consuming and laborious, which limits the application of supervised sentiment analysis methods.

Unsupervised sentiment analysis methods are based on the discrimination of sentiment tendency at the level of words and phrases, then weight the sentiment polarity of each word or sentence to get the final sentiment tendency. Hu and Liu [4] judges sentiment of viewpoint sentences from the polarity of sentiment words. Firstly, establish the positive and negative sentiment word seeds manually, and then determine the sentiment polarity of new words by synonymy and near meaning. By calculating the mutual information between words and sentiment word seeds, Turney [11] gets the sentiment of words and then judges the sentiment of sentences according to the average semantic tendency of words. He et al. [5] designs a maximum entropy model based on the LMR template to recognize Chinese sentiment words, which assembles words, word position, and sentiment polarity into training features of the maximum entropy model to recognize the sentiment of all the words in the corpus. Unsupervised sentiment analysis methods lack in-depth analysis of the sentiment relationship of potential topics and related topics. However, assembling sentiment elements into topic models can better analyze the sentiment. Lin and He [6] assembles a sentiment layer into the LDA model and constructs the JST model, which becomes the main method of sentiment classification for news text.

But for the agricultural news, especially with the weak subjective sentiment, the accuracy of sentiment classification of the JST model needs to be improved. Therefore, this paper designs an algorithmic framework integrating JST and a sentiment dictionary to improve the accuracy of sentiment classification of agricultural news with insignificant subjective sentiment.

3   Proposal Method

3.1   JST Model

JST model is a probability modeling framework based on LDA [9]. It consists of four levels, which add the sentient level between the document and topic level of the LDA model, and can carry out sentiment analysis and topic extraction from document text. The framework diagram of the JST model is shown in Fig. 1.

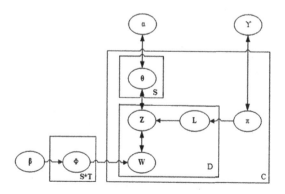

Fig. 1. Framework diagram of JST Model.

In a corpus C, there are N documents, i.e., $C = \{D_1, D_2, \ldots, D_N\}$, each of documents consists of n words, $D_i = \{W_{i1}, W_{i2}, \ldots, W_{in}\}$, the number of different topics is S, and the number of different sentiment is L. For each document D_i, select a distribution about documents, π_D, which is a polynomial distribution drawn from the Dirichlet distribution with a parameter of γ, $\pi_D \approx Dir(\gamma)$. For each sentiment label L_j under document D_i, select a distribution about topics, $\theta_{D,l}$, which also follows a polynomial distribution and is extracted from the Dirichlet distribution with a parameter of α, $\theta_{D,l} \approx Dir(\alpha)$. For each word in document D_i, select a sentiment tag and a topic, and select a word from the word distribution which is defined by the topic and sentiment tag. The classification performance of JST is close to the best performance of machine learning, but it saves a lot of annotation jobs. One way to improve the accuracy of sentiment classification is to introduce a sentiment dictionary as prior knowledge.

3.2   Sentiment Dictionary

In order to improve the accuracy of sentiment classification of agricultural news text, we introduce a positive and a negative dictionary as the prior knowledge of the JST model. The steps of making dictionaries are as follows:

1. Manually mark the positive and negative sentiment of agricultural news collected from Agricultural Information Network of China[1].
2. Divide the agricultural news that's labeled into two parts, one is positive, the other is negative news.
3. Respectively select 80% news from the two labeled news for training to obtain word frequency statistics, and then select Top-K as the positive and negative dictionary of agricultural news by further preprocessing.

There are 500 positive words and 400 negative words in the dictionary, as shown in Figs. 2.

priorpolarity=negative word1=橙色/	priorpolarity=positive word1=致富路/
priorpolarity=negative word1=火灾/	priorpolarity=positive word1=优质/
priorpolarity=negative word1=骤降/	priorpolarity=positive word1=高产/
priorpolarity=negative word1=袭击/	priorpolarity=positive word1=工艺/
priorpolarity=negative word1=污染/	priorpolarity=positive word1=防控/
priorpolarity=negative word1=过程/	priorpolarity=positive word1=监测/
priorpolarity=negative word1=遭遇/	priorpolarity=positive word1=创新/
priorpolarity=negative word1=幼虫/	priorpolarity=positive word1=推动/
priorpolarity=negative word1=干冷/	priorpolarity=positive word1=科技/
priorpolarity=negative word1=旱情/	priorpolarity=positive word1=创业/
priorpolarity=negative word1=洪灾/|	priorpolarity=positive word1=合作社/
priorpolarity=negative word1=洪涝/	priorpolarity=positive word1=减灾/
priorpolarity=negative word1=灾情/	priorpolarity=positive word1=助推/
priorpolarity=negative word1=飓风/	priorpolarity=positive word1=高质量/
	priorpolarity=positive word1=改革开放/|
	priorpolarity=positive word1=探索/
(a)	(b)

Fig. 2. Examples of the negative sentiment dictionary (a) and the positive sentiment dictionary (b) of agricultural news.

---

[1] http://www.agri.cn.

3.3   JST Model Combined with Prior Knowledge

The implementation of the algorithm is as follows:

1. Analyze and serialize the words in agricultural news text, and then fit them into a dictionary V.
2. Initialize three matrices: π_{dl} (document-sentiment), θ_{dlz} (document-sentiment-topic), and ϕ_{lzw} (sentiment-topic-words).
3. Iterate the following steps M times:

   (a) Select a word in the document, meanwhile compare the word with the positive and negative sentiment dictionary of agricultural news. If this word can correspond with the words in the sentiment dictionary of agricultural news, it will be assigned the corresponding sentiment label and a topic label; otherwise, it will be given a sentiment label and a topic label randomly.
   (b) Calculate the probability of word W_i according to the following equation when the topic label is k and the emotion label is j:

$$p(z_t = k, l_k = j|w, z_t, l_t, \alpha, \beta, \gamma) \propto \frac{(N_{wjk})_t + \beta(N_{jkd})_t + \alpha(N_{kd})_t + \gamma}{(N_{jk}) + v\beta(N_{dd})_k + \alpha(N_d)_t} \tag{1}$$

   (c) According to the probability, re-select a topic label and a sentiment label for the word.
   (d) Update the three matrixes π_{dl}, θ_{dlz}, and ϕ_{lzw}.
   (e) Repeat until all words in the document have been processed.

4   Experiments

4.1   Dataset and Experiment Settings

The dataset consists of 11055 agricultural news data from the Agricultural Information Network of China, as shown in Fig. 2. Figure 3 shows a part of preprocessed agricultural news data by word segmentation, removing stop words, deduplication, and other preprocessing operations.

Three evaluation metrics are introduced to quantitatively measure the accuracy of the JST model combined with prior knowledge, $P_a ccuracy$, $N_a ccuracy$, $W_a ccuracy$, which represent the accuracy of positive, negative, and entirety sentiment classification separately:

$$P_{accuracy} = \frac{N_p}{N_{np}} \tag{2}$$

$$N_{accuracy} = \frac{N_n}{N_{nn}} \tag{3}$$

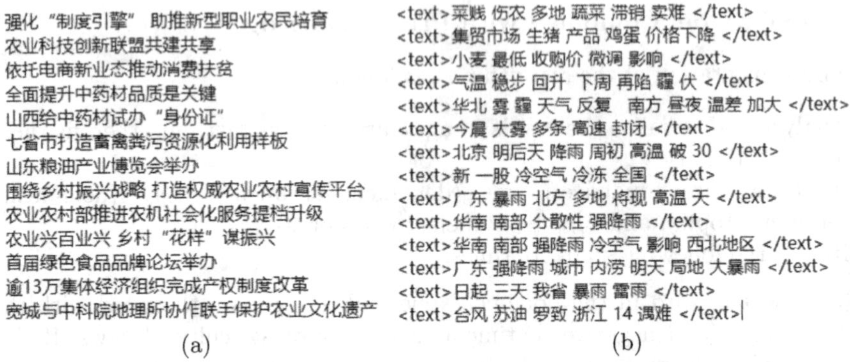

强化 "制度引擎" 助推新型职业农民培育
农业科技创新联盟共建共享
依托电商新业态推动消费扶贫
全面提升中药材品质是关键
山西给中药材试办 "身份证"
七省市打造畜禽粪污资源化利用样板
山东粮油产业博览会举办
围绕乡村振兴战略 打造权威农业农村宣传平台
农业农村部推进农机社会化服务提档升级
农业兴百业兴 乡村 "花样" 谋振兴
首届绿色食品品牌论坛举办
逾13万集体经济组织完成产权制度改革
宽城与中科院地理所协作联手保护农业文化遗产

(a)

<text>菜贱 伤农 多地 蔬菜 滞销 卖难 </text>
<text>集贸市场 生猪 产品 鸡蛋 价格下降 </text>
<text>小麦 最低 收购价 微调 影响 </text>
<text>气温 稳步 回升 下周 再陷 霾 伏 </text>
<text>华北 雾 霾 天气 反复 南方 昼夜 温差 加大 </text>
<text>今晨 大雾 多条 高速 封闭 </text>
<text>北京 明后天 降雨 周初 高温 破 30 </text>
<text>新 一股 冷空气 冷冻 全国 </text>
<text>广东 暴雨 北方 多地 将现 高温 天 </text>
<text>华南 南部 分散性 强降雨 </text>
<text>华南 南部 强降雨 冷空气 影响 西北地区 </text>
<text>广东 强降雨 城市 内涝 明天 局地 大暴雨 </text>
<text>日起 三天 我省 暴雨 雷雨 </text>
<text>台风 苏迪 罗致 浙江 14 遇难 </text>|

(b)

Fig. 3. (a) Raw data from agricultural news and (b) preprocessed data.

$$W_{accuracy} = \frac{N_a}{N_{na}} \tag{4}$$

In Eq. (2), $|N_p|$ represents the number of positive agricultural news with correct classification, $|N_{np}|$ represents the number of all positive agricultural news in the corpus. In Eq. (3), $|N_n|$ and $|N_{nn}|$ indicate the number of negative agricultural news with correct classification and the number of negative agricultural news in the corpus, respectively. $|N_a|$ and $|N_{na}|$ represents the number of agricultural news with correct classification and the total number of agricultural news in the corpus, respectively. A higher value of $P_{accuracy}$, $N_{accuracy}$, and $W_{accuracy}$ indicates the higher the accuracy of the model.

4.2   Knowledge Graph-Based Semantic Retrieval

The JST model has three parameters α, β, γ, and we set their values as follows:

$$\alpha = 50/\text{Num. of Topics}$$

$$\beta = 0.01$$

$$\gamma = 0.01$$

Since α is determined by the number of topics, the number of topics has a significant effect on the accuracy of the JST model. We show this effect through the following experiments.

Firstly, we set the number of topics to 1, 5, 10, 15, 20, 25, 30, and analyze the changes in the accuracy of three models:

Table 1. Accuracy of various JST model classifications (number of topics is five).

Method	$P_{accuracy}$	$N_{accuracy}$	$W_{accuracy}$
JST model without prior knowledge	56.69%	42.69%	49.69%
JST model with prior knowledge	57.39%	44.31%	50.85%
JST model with agricultural prior knowledge	**64.43%**	**51.72%**	**58.07%**

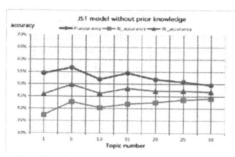

(a) JST model without prior knowledge

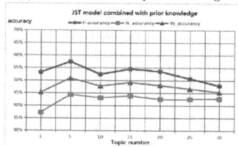

(b) JST model with prior knowledge

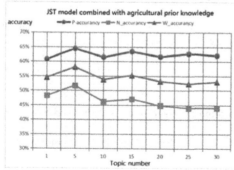

(c) JST model accuracy with agricultural prior knowledge

Fig. 4. Accuracy of JST models.

- JST model without prior knowledge, the original model is proposed by Lin and He [6].
- JST model combining a priori knowledge, which combines with general sentiment dictionary, such as 'HowNet'[2] and 'NTUSD'[3].
- JST model combining agricultural a priori knowledge, which introduces the positive and negative sentiment dictionaries about agricultural news created in Sect. 3.2.

It can be seen that the classification accuracy of the JST model combined with agricultural prior knowledge is higher than that of the other two models from Fig. 4. When the topic number is 5, the effect of sentiment classification of agricultural news is the best, as shown in Table 1.

5   Conclusion

In this paper, we construct a sentiment dictionary for Chinese agricultural news and improve the JST model by introducing this sentiment dictionary as prior knowledge. These improvements greatly increase the accuracy of the sentiment classification of Chinese agricultural news.

As the agricultural sentiment dictionary trained in this paper is limited in scope and depth, we will further expand this dictionary. At the same time, combining with other different sentiment classification methods, further improve the accuracy of sentiment classification of Chinese agricultural news.

Acknowledgements. This work is partially supported by the Natural Science Foundation of China under Grant (31771679, 31671589), the Anhui Foundation for Science and Technology Major Project, China, under Grants 18030901034, 201904e01020006, 201903a06020009, the Key Laboratory of Agricultural Electronic, Commerce, Ministry of Agriculture of China under Grant AEC2018003, AEC2018006, the 2019 Anhui University collaborative innovation project sn: GXXT-2019-013, the Hefei Major Research Project of Key Technology J2018G14.

References

1. Bing, L.: Opinion mining and sentiment analysis. Synth. Lect. Hum. Lang. Technol. **2**(2), 459–526 (2011)
2. Chen, L., Guan, Z., He, J.: Research progress of emotion classification. Comput. Res. Dev. **54**(6), 1150–1170 (2017)
3. Chaffar, S., Inkpen, D.: Using a heterogeneous dataset for emotion analysis in text. In: Butz, C., Lingras, P. (eds.) AI 2011. LNCS (LNAI), vol. 6657, pp. 62–67. Springer, Heidelberg (2011). https://doi.org/10.1007/978-3-642-21043-3_8
4. Hu, M., Liu, B.: Summarizing customer reviews. In: Proceedings of Knowledge Discovery and Data Mining, NY, USA, pp. 168–177 (2004)

---

[2] http://www.keenage.com.

[3] http://nlg.csie.ntu.edu.tw.

5. He, H., Li, S., Xiao, F.: A technical report on the analysis of Chinese emotional tendency. The first collection of Chinese tendency analysis and evaluation, pp. 46–55 (2008)

6. Lin, C., He, Y.: Joint sentiment/topic model for sentiment analysis. In: Proceedings of the 18th ACM Conference on Information and Knowledge Management, pp. 375–384. ACM (2009)

7. Mullen, T., Collier, N.: Sentiment analysis using support vector machines with diverse information sources. In: Proceedings of EMNLP-2004, Barcelona, Spain, pp. 412–418 (2004)

8. Nasukawa, T., Yi, J.: Sentiment analysis: capturing favorability using natural language processing. In: Proceedings of International Conference on Knowledge Capture, pp. 70–77 (2003)

9. Pan, Y.: Research on sentiment classification of news text based on JST model. Hebei University (2015)

10. Pang, B., Lee, L., Vaithyanathan, S.: Thumbs up? Sentiment classification using machine learning techniques. In: Proceedings of the Conference on Empirical Methods in Natural Language Processing, pp. 79–86. Association for Computational Linguistics (2002)

11. Turney, P.D.: Thumbs up or thumbs down? Semantic orientation applied to unsupervised classification of reviews. In: Proceedings of the 40th Annual Meeting on Association for Computational Linguistics, pp. 417–424. Association for Computational Linguistics (2002)

12. Zhao, Y., Qin, B., Liu, T.: Sentiment analysis. J. Softw. **21**(8), 1834–1848 (2010)

Target Track Recognition from Few-Labeled Radar Data with Outliers

Yuqi Fan[1(✉)], Guangming Shen[1], Xiaohui Yuan[2], and Juan Xu[1]

[1] School of Computer Science and Information Engineering,
Hefei University of Technology, Hefei 230601, Anhui, China
yuqi.fan@hfut.edu.cn, sgm@mail.hfut.edu.cn, xiaohui.yuan@unt.edu
[2] Department of Computer Science and Engineering,
University of North Texas, Denton, TX 76203, USA
xujuan@hfut.edu.cn

Abstract. The frequent occurrence of "black flying" and illegal invasion make it necessary to identify radar target tracks. Existing research on the radar flight target mainly focuses on the target identification. Existing research on the recognition of target track types ignores the impact of outliers in the track data and the small number of labeled data on the target track type recognition performance. In this paper, we propose a target Track Recognition algorithm based on a Semi-Supervised approach for few-labeled radar target track data with outliers (TRSS). We first remove the outliers and fill in the missing track points caused by the outlier removal. We then extract five basic flight features (BFFs) and an advanced flight feature (AFF) from the track data to obtain a strong recognition flight feature combination (SRFFC). Finally, a semi-supervised generative adversarial network (SSGAN) model is constructed to classify flight target tracks using SRFFC as the input. Simulation results show that the proposed algorithm TRSS can effectively improve the accuracy, precision, and recall performance of target track type recognition.

Keywords: Radar · Target track recognition · Generative Adversarial Network (GAN)

1 Introduction

The rapid development of aviation technology makes aircraft widely used. However, frequent "black flight" incidents and illegal invasion impose a great threat to personal privacy and facilities [2,7]. Radar can obtain the flying target information such as the distance, speed, and orientation of flying targets, which facilitates the detection and monitoring of flying targets [8].

This work was partly supported by the National Key Research And Development Plan under Grant 2018YFB2000505 and the National Natural Science Foundation of China under grant 61806067.

© Springer Nature Singapore Pte Ltd. 2020
X. Yuan et al. (Eds.): ICUIA 2020, CCIS 1319, pp. 206–214, 2020.
https://doi.org/10.1007/978-981-33-4601-7_21

There is extensive research on flying target recognition using radar data [3, 4,6,9,12,14,15]. In recent years, deep learning technology has been gradually applied to the field of radar target recognition. A model for high-resolution range profile (HRRP) target recognition was proposed to discover target regions through the recurrent neural network (RNN) and attention mechanism [13]. A method based on t-distribution random neighbor embedding and discriminating depth belief network (DDBN) was proposed for radar HRRP target recognition to solve the problem of imbalanced HRRP data [10].

The existing research on radar flight targets mainly uses spectrum information in radar echoes, polarization characteristics, and high-resolution range profiles to realize the recognition of target attributes and types. Note that the track of the target can reflect the intention and mission of the target. For example, when the radar detects that the target is in S-maneuver, the target may be avoiding the threat; when the radar detects that the target is circling, the target may be executing surveillance and detection tasks. The classification and recognition of the target track types can help us to understand the target intention and reduce the occurrence of "black flying" and illegal invasion.

There is little literature on radar target track recognition. An algorithm based on the convolutional neural network (CNN) was proposed in [1] to classify the radar target track data. However, the radar data are prone to kinds of noises such as recorder system errors, electromagnetic interference, and random interference during the acquisition of track data, which results in the existence of outliers in the radar target track data. These outliers hinder the in-depth processing and analysis of track data. The negative impact of outliers on the target track recognition is ignored [1]. Meanwhile, it is difficult to label a large amount of target track data, and hence how to use a small amount of labeled data is also a key to the correct target track recognition.

In this paper, we propose a target Track Recognition algorithm based on a Semi-Supervised approach for few-labeled radar target track data with outliers (TRSS). The main contributions of this paper are as follows.

We investigate the problem of flying target track recognition based on few-labeled radar target track data with outliers. We propose a target track recognition algorithm TRSS based on SSGAN. First, aiming at the outliers existing in the radar target track data, an outlier recognition method based on the improved Letts criterion is adopted to identify and eliminate outliers in the track; a missing data point filling method based on the improved linear interpolation is used to fill the missing data. We first remove the outliers and fill in the missing track points caused by the outlier removal. We then extract five basic flight features (BFFs) and an advanced flight feature (AFF) from the track data to obtain a strong recognition flight feature combination (SRFFC). Finally, a semi-supervised generative adversarial network (SSGAN) model is constructed to classify flight target tracks using SRFFC as the input. The simulation results show that algorithm TRSS can effectively improve the accuracy rate, precision, and recall performance of target track type recognition.

2   Problem Description

A radar target point reflects the flying target information at a certain time, including distance, azimuth, flight altitude and observation time, etc. A radar target track consists of a series of radar target points in a period of time. Since each point is detected at a specific time, the radar target track can be regarded as time-series data.

Each point in the original radar target track data contains 4 attributes: distance, azimuth, height, and time. Distance is the space distance from the point to the radar; azimuth denotes the angle that the x-axis rotates clockwise to the projection point of the target in the x-y plane with the radar being the coordinate origin, the true north direction being the y-axis, and the true east direction being the x-axis. The interval between adjacent points on the same track is 1 s.

We divide the radar target tracks into four types: line, arc, S-maneuver, and circle. We assign a label to each track type. Specifically, the label of line-type, arc-type, S-maneuver, and circle-type is 1, 2, 3, and 4, respectively. A track consisting of target points and the label of the track constitute a complete labeled radar target track data, which is as follows:

$$p1\left(\gamma_1, \theta_1, \varphi_1, t_1\right), p2\left(\gamma_2, \theta_2, \varphi_2, t_2\right) \cdots p_N\left(\gamma_N, \theta_N, \varphi_N, t_N\right), L \tag{1}$$

For the few-labeled radar target track data with outliers, we process the outliers in the target track, mine BFFs and AFF in the target track data, determine SRFFC, and then build an SSGAN model to conduct the target track recognition.

3   Algorithm

In this section, we propose a radar target track recognition algorithm based on SSGAN (TRSS) to recognize flying target track types on the basis of few-labeled radar target track data with outliers.

Algorithm TRSS consists of two modules: the outlier processing module and the target track recognition module. In the outlier processing module, the outliers are removed and the missing points are filled in. In the target track recognition module, we analyze the basic flight features and advanced flight features of the flight data, and we then extract a combination of strong recognition flight features, which are input to a constructed SSGAN to achieve the target track recognition.

3.1   Outlier Processing

The outlier processing module includes two stages: outlier recognition and missing point filling. In the outlier recognition stage, we use the outlier recognition method based on the improved Letts criterion to identify and remove outliers. In the missing point filling stage, the missing point filling method based on the improved linear interpolation is used to complete the filling of the missing points after removing the outliers.

Stage 1. *Outlier recognition based on the improved Letts criterion.*

According to Letts criterion, when the target data follows a normal distribution, the probability that the residuals between the target data and the mean fall within 3 times the standard deviation, i.e., $[-3\sigma, 3\sigma]$, is more than 99.7%. It can be considered that the target data that falls outside of the region is an outlier. In the original radar target track data, the probability of data residuals falling within $[-3\sigma, 3\sigma]$ is different. If the Letts criterion is used directly, the recognition effect will be confused. Therefore, we propose an outlier recognition algorithm based on the improved Letts criterion. We adjust the standard deviation times a factor k_σ, and we introduce a reference index to determine k_σ: Fluctuation constraint degree (FCD) which is the angle between the spatial straight lines between two points before and after the target point.

Assuming target track T includes N points $p_1(\gamma_1, \theta_1, \varphi_1, t_1)$, $p_2(\gamma_2, \theta_2, \varphi_2, t_2)$, $\cdots$, $p_n(\gamma_n, \theta_n, \varphi_n, t_n)$, the process of identifying and removing the outliers in the track data based on the improved Letts criterion is as follows:

Step 1: Convert each point $p_i \in T$ to the point in the space rectangular coordinate system. The track data obtained after the conversion is $p_1(x_1, y_1, z_1, t_1)$, $p_2(x_2, y_2, z_2, t_2)$, $\cdots$, $p_n(x_n, y_n, z_n, t_n)$.

Step 2: The least square method is used to fit $(x_1, x_2, \cdots, x_n)$, $(y_1, y_2, \cdots, y_n)$, and $(z_1, z_2, \cdots, z_N)$ to obtain the fitted datasets $(\widehat{x_1}, \widehat{x_2}, \cdots, \widehat{x_n})$, $(\widehat{y_1}, \widehat{y_2}, \cdots, \widehat{y_n})$, and $(\widehat{z_1}, \widehat{z_2}, \cdots, \widehat{z_n})$. Calculate the absolute value sets $dx_T = (dx_1, dx_2, \cdots, dx_n)$, $dy_T = (dy_1, dy_2, \cdots, dy_n)$, and $dz_T = (dz_1, dz_2, \cdots, dz_n)$ of the difference between the real data and the corresponding fitted data.

Step 3: The K-S test is used to test the normal distribution of dx_T, dy_T, and dz_T. If there is a set of data that do not meet the normal distribution, we perform a logarithmic operation on the data.

Step 4: Calculate the mean $\overline{dx_T}$, $\overline{dy_T}$, $\overline{dz_T}$, and the residual of the data in dx_T, dy_T, and dz_T. We then get the residual sets $rx_T = (rx_1, rx_2, \cdots, rx_n)$, $ry_T = (ry_1, ry_2, \cdots, ry_n)$, and $rz_T = (rz_1, rz_2, \cdots, rz_n)$.

Step 5: The data in rx_T, ry_T and rz_T are compared with $k_{\sigma i}(i = 1, 2, \cdots, n)$ times the standard deviation σ_{dx_T}, σ_{dy_T} and σ_{dz_T} of the corresponding sets dx_T, dy_T and dz_T. $k_{\sigma i}$ of the first two points and the last two points of each track are set as 3 by default. If $|rx_i| > k_{\sigma i} \cdot \sigma_{dx_T}$ or $|ry_i| > k_{\sigma i} \cdot \sigma_{dy_T}$ or $|rz_i| > k_{\sigma i} \cdot \sigma_{dz_T}(i = 1, 2, \cdots, n)$, the corresponding point is classified as an outlier and removed.

Stage 2. *Missing point filling based on the improved linear interpolation.*

After identifying and eliminating the outliers, the missing points will appear in the track data, so it is necessary to fill in the missing points. Linear interpolation is a common interpolation method used for data filling. However, when the point that needs to be interpolated is in the position where the direction of the track changes greatly, it is difficult to fit an accurate point using linear interpolation. Therefore, we propose a missing point filling algorithm based on the improved linear interpolation.

It can be known from the above analyses that the spatial position of the point is related to the fluctuation of the track segment where the point is located. Assuming that the spatial right-angle coordinate values of the forward and backward points of a missing point on the time sequence are $p_a(x_a, y_a, z_a, t_a)$ and $p_b(x_b, y_b, z_b, t_b)$, respectively, the process of filling in the missing point using the improved linear interpolation method is as follows:

Step 1: The predicted coordinates of the two interpolation points $p_{\hat{a}}$ and $p_{\hat{b}}$ are calculated by using p_a and p_b as reference points, respectively.

Step 2: The weighted average of $p_{\hat{a}}(x_{\hat{a}}, y_{\hat{a}}, z_{\hat{a}})$ and $p_{\hat{b}}(x_{\hat{b}}, y_{\hat{b}}, z_{\hat{b}})$ is used to obtain the interpolation point p_{ab}, where weights $w_{\hat{a}}$ and $w_{\hat{b}}$ of $p_{\hat{a}}$ and $p_{\hat{b}}$ are determined by the ratio of the time elapsed from p_a to p_i and p_i to p_b, respectively. The closer the time interval is, the greater the weight is.

Step 3: The interpolation point $p_{\widehat{ab}}(x_{\widehat{ab}}, y_{\widehat{ab}}, z_{\widehat{ab}})$ is calculated by the linear interpolation method, and $p_{ab}(x_{ab}, y_{ab}, z_{ab})$ is weighted and used as the padding value of p_i. Weights w_{ab} and $w_{\widehat{ab}}$ of p_{ab} and $p_{\widehat{ab}}$ are related to the FCD. As the point's FCD increases, $w_{\widehat{ab}}$ increases and w_{ab} decreases.

3.2   Target Track Recognition

In the target track recognition module, we extract five BFFs from the target track data. An SSGAN model is constructed to select the SRFF that contributes the most to the target track recognition among the BFF, and the AFF is extracted from the BFFs to improve the performance of the target track recognition. We then combine AFF and SRFF to get SRFFC as the input of the SSGAN model to achieve the target track recognition.

Stage 3. *Extraction of the BFFs.*

Multiple features appear during the target flight. When the target flies, its flight features change, and the difference of flight features under different track types may be significant. For example, when the track is a circle, the flight direction of the target is always changing, and the speed is usually maintained stable. Therefore, by analyzing the flight features which are calculated from the original radar target track, we can achieve more accurate recognition of the track types. We call these features as BFFs. Five BFFs are used in this paper, including distance (the Euclidean distance between two points), velocity, and acceleration, turning angle (the angle between the line connecting two points and the north direction), and direction.

Stage 4. *Selection of the SRFF.*

The accuracy of target track recognition using different BFFs is different. We use BFFs as the input of the SSGAN model and get the recognition results. We denote the BFF which obtains the highest recognition accuracy as SRFF and select the BFF with the highest track recognition accuracy, i.e. the turning angle, as the SRFF. The constructed SSGAN model will be introduced in Stage 7.

Stage 5. *Extraction of the AFF.*

We extract the AFF from the BFFs to further improve the performance of track recognition. Normally, the turning angle of the target during a straight flight will not change as frequently as that during circling, and the turning angle of each point is stable, so the fluctuation of the turning angle of adjacent points is small and close to 0. When the target is performing S-maneuver, the turning angle of adjacent points will show periodic fluctuations. Therefore, we extract the fluctuation value of the turning angle of adjacent points (TF) from the turning angles of the points in the target track and use TF as the AFF.

Stage 6. *Combination of the SRFFC.*

We combine SRFF and AFF to obtain a strong recognition flight feature combination (SRFFC) which is used as the input of the SSGAN model for target track recognition. Assuming that the SRFF vector is $A(a_1, a_2, \cdots, a_n)$ and the AFF vector is $B(b_1, b_2, \cdots, b_m)$, the SRFFC vector is $(a_1, a_2, \cdots, a_n, b_1, b_2, \cdots, b_m)$.

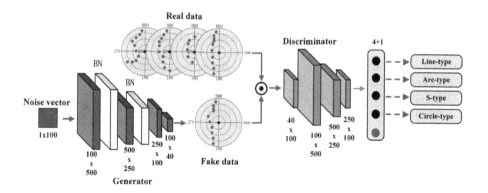

Fig. 1. The SSGAN model.

Stage 7. *Construction of the SSGAN model.*

We build an SSGAN [11] model to achieve accurate recognition of the target track with only a small amount of labeled data. The constructed SSGAN model is shown in Fig. 1.

4   Performance Evaluation

4.1   Simulation Setup

In this section, we simulate the original radar target track data set of multiple flying objects monitored by a single radar [5]. The data set contains the data of the four types mentioned above, and each type of track has 5000 data items. The number of labeled data for each type is 100. The monitoring period of each target track is $10s$, and the time interval between the points is $1s$; that is, each target track is composed of 10 consecutive points. Each track point includes 4 types of attributes: distance, azimuth, height, and time. Each track contains 1 to 3 random outliers. We use stratified sampling to choose 70% of the data to compose the training set, and the remaining 30% of the data are set as the test set.

Both discriminator and generator of the SSGAN model use Adam optimizer. The optimizer parameters β_1 and β_2 are set as 0.9 and 0.99, respectively. The learning rate is initialized as 0.001, and the batch size is set to 100. We use three performance metrics commonly used in deep learning classification tasks to evaluate the performance of the proposed algorithm TRSS: Accuracy, Precision, and Recall.

4.2   Model Validation

Experiment Results. We investigate the performance of flight track type recognition versus different feature combinations. The simulation results are shown in Table 1.

Table 1. Recognition performance of different flight features and feature combinations

Feature	Distance	Velocity	Acceleration	Turning angle	Direction	Distance+Tf
Accuracy	0.943	0.944	0.852	0.948	0.739	0.903
Precision	0.945	0.940	0.890	0.921	0.694	0.877
Recall	0.929	0.939	0.855	0.944	0.735	0.881

Feature	TF	Velocity+TF	Acceleration+TF	Turning angle+TF	Direction+TF
Accuracy	0.933	0.929	0.856	0.988	0.772
Precision	0.955	0.928	0.857	0.988	0.764
Recall	0.926	0.928	0.842	0.987	0.772

It can be seen that SRFFC achieves the best performance among all the feature combinations, showing that the SRFFC is effective in target track recognition. Compared with the use of turning angle or TF alone, SRFFC improves the results in terms of all the performance metrics, which demonstrates that the AFF and BFF can promote each other to improve the recognition performance and the AFF can effectively improve the track recognition performance.

Comparison to Benchmarks. We investigate the performance of the proposed algorithm TRSS against the CNN-based approach and RNN-based approach. The simulation results are shown in Table 2.

Table 2. Recognition performance of different algorithms

Algorithm	CNN	RNN	TRSS
Accuracy	0.826	0.972	0.988
Precision	0.792	0.973	0.988
Recall	0.818	0.973	0.988

We can observe that the performance of algorithm TRSS is significantly better than that of the two benchmark algorithms. When there is only a small amount of labeled data, TRSS greatly improves accuracy, precision, and recall performance. CNN extracts the features from the track data through convolution operation for recognition, and RNN considers the features of the track data in the time domain. However, the impact of outliers on recognition is ignored, so the performance of the two benchmark algorithms is worse than that of the proposed algorithm TRSS.

5   Conclusions

In this paper, we proposed a radar target track recognition algorithm (TRSS) based on SSGAN for few-labeled radar target track data with outliers. The algorithm consists of a outlier processing module and a target track recognition module. In the outlier processing module, we adopted the outlier recognition method based on the improved Letts criterion to identify and eliminate outliers in the track, and we used the missing point filling method based on the improved linear interpolation to realize the accurate filling of the missing points. In the target track recognition module, we introduced 5 BFFs and extracted an AFF from the BFFs. We then selected the SRFF from the BFFs and combined the SRFF with the AFF to obtain the SRFFC which is input into the constructed SSGAN model to achieve accurate target track recognition with a small amount of labeled data. The simulation results showed that the proposed algorithm TRSS could effectively improve the accuracy, precision, and recall performance of the target track recognition.

References

1. Fan, Y., Wen, P., Xu, X.: Research on radar target track recognition based on convolutional neural network. High Power Laser Particle Beams **31**(09), 93203-1 (2019)

2. Feng, D., Yuan, X.: Advancement of safety corridor and emergency management visualization in low altitude airspace. J. Electron. Meas. Instr. **30**(4), 485–495 (2016)
3. Guo, Y., Xiao, H., Fu, Q.: Least square support vector data description for HRRP-based radar target recognition. Appl. Intell. **46**(2), 365–372 (2016). https://doi.org/10.1007/s10489-016-0836-5
4. Lee, K.: Radar target recognition by frequency-diversity RCS together with kernel scatter difference discrimination. Progr. Electromagn. Res. **87**, 137–145 (2019)
5. Li, J.: Simulation and processing of radar raw echo data. Xi'an University of Electronic Technology (2014)
6. Li, L., Liu, Z.: Radar high resolution range profile recognition via dual-SVDD classifier. In: 2016 CIE International Conference on Radar (RADAR), Guangzhou, pp. 1–4 (2016)
7. Liu, Y., et al.: Unmanned aerial vehicle detection based on trajectory and pattern recognition. Comput. Eng. 1–11 (2019)
8. Liu, D.: Research on air target recognition algorithms based on video stream. Xi'an Technological University (2019)
9. Ma, J., Dong, Y., Li, Y., Li, L., Yang, J.: Multi-rotor UAV's micro-Doppler characteristic analysis and feature extraction. J. Univ. Chin. Acad. Sci. **36**(02), 235–243 (2019)
10. Pan, M., Jiang, J., Kong, Q.: Radar HRRP target recognition based on t-SNE segmentation and discriminant deep belief network. IEEE Geosci. Remote Sens. Lett. **14**(9), 1609–1613 (2017)
11. Salimans, T., Goodfellow, I., Zaremba, W.: Improved techniques for training GANs. In: Barcelona: Advances in Neural Information Processing Systems, pp. 2232–2242 (2016)
12. Xie, Q., Zhang, H.: Multi-level regularization enhancement of SAR images and its application in target recognition. J. Electron. Meas. Instr. **9**, 157–162 (2018)
13. Xu, B., Chen, B., Wan, J.: Target-aware recurrent attentional network for radar HRRP target recognition. Signal Process. **155**, 268–280 (2019)
14. Yuan, X., Kong, L., Feng, D., Wei, Z.: Automatic feature point detection and tracking of human actions in time-of-flight videos. IEEE/CAA J. Autom. Sinica **4**(4), 677–685 (2017)
15. Zhou, Y., Han, J., Yuan, X., Wei, Z., Hong, R.: Inverse sparse group lasso model for robust object tracking. IEEE Trans. Multimed. **19**(8), 1798–1810 (2017)

Time-Delay Rotor Control via Linear Quadratic Regulator

Juan Xu[1,3] , Yang Zhao[2], Zhanfeng Xu[2], and Benhong Zhang[1(✉)]

[1] School of Computer Science and Information Engineering,
Hefei University of Technology, Hefei 230009, China
`zhangbh@hfut.edu.cn`
[2] School of Mechanical Engineering, Hefei University of Technology,
Hefei 230009, China
[3] Anhui Fuhuang Technology Co., Ltd., Hefei 230088, China

Abstract. The active balancing control is important to suppress rotor vibration. However, there is an unavoidable delay in active balancing control of high-speed time-delay rotor system. Therefore, eliminating time delays is significant. In this paper, the integral transformation term is introduced to transform the dynamic model of time-delay rotor system into a dynamic model of rotor system without time delay. Based on the linear quadratic optimal control method, the influence of weight matrix Q and R is discussed. Moreover, the active balancing control law of time-delay rotor is designed. Then the simulation model of time-delay rotor control system is established in the Matlab. And we set up the experimental platform to carry out the experiment. The results show that the time-delay rotor online active balancing control method proposed in this paper can effectively suppress the vibration of the time-delay rotor system under different time-delay.

Keywords: Active balancing control · Linear quadratic optimal · Time-delay · Vibration control

1 Introduction

The vibration of the rotor system is the key to the stability of the rotating machinery [1,2]. The active balancing control can reduce the vibration of rotor system without stopping the rotor [3]. Active balancing control is an important method to suppress rotor vibration [4]. The traditional active balancing control method often ignores the time delay in the balancing process. In fact, the slight time delay will also lead to the reduction of the control efficiency during the automatic balancing process [5,6]. Seriously, the time-delay rotor system may be unstable and cause a major accident [7,8]. Therefore, it is of great significance to take the time-delay into account in the design of active balancing control of rotor system.

For online automatic balance delay control system, domestic and foreign scholars have conducted a lot of research. Zheng H et al. studied the active

© Springer Nature Singapore Pte Ltd. 2020
X. Yuan et al. (Eds.): ICUIA 2020, CCIS 1319, pp. 215–225, 2020.
https://doi.org/10.1007/978-981-33-4601-7_22

longitudinal vibration control, derived the frequency response function of the disturbance and control channels by using the quadruple parameter method, and analyzed the active control effect by numerical simulation [9]. Saeed et al. employed the nonlinear time-delay position-velocity feedback controller to control the system lateral vibrations, and showed how to harness the time-delays to reduce the oscillations of the system without affecting its stability [10]. Wang et al. accomplished the uncertainty quantification analysis under aleatory and epistemic uncertainties, and used a new hybrid time-variant reliability index to judge the safety levels for controlled structures [11]. Hu et al. designed a new rotor dynamic vibration absorber, and applied an on-off control method based on speed to reduce the vibration in time-delay rotor systems [12]. Zhang et al. proposed a robust predictive control model for positive delay systems with uncertainty and interval uncertainty [13].

However, the feedback control of time-delay systems is mainly applied in the structural vibration. It is very difficult to identify the stability characteristics of complex time-varying systems and achieve accurate solutions for nonlinear multi-degree-of-freedom systems with time-delay. In fact the time-delay problem in the rotor system cannot be ignored in the design of control law. Thus this paper proposed an active balancing control method for time-delay rotor based on LQR control, and the model is verified through a series of experiments.

2   Materials and Methods

2.1   System Dynamic Model

The rotor active balancing control system generally includes a rotating speed sensor, a vibration sensor, an active balance controller and an actuator, as shown in Fig. 1. The vibration sensor and the rotating speed sensor acquire the vibration signal caused by the rotor imbalance and the rotating speed signal of the rotor, and transmit the signal to the active balance controller [14]. The active balance controller analyses and processes the input signal to calculate the control output signal, which can drive the actuator to suppress the imbalance and the vibration.

The dynamic model of the time-delay rotor system consists of a rotating shaft, rigid discs and bearings that do not take into account mass. The mass of the rotor disc is m, the stiffness of the rotating shaft at the centre point is k, the damping coefficient of the time-delay rotor system is c, and the rotating angular velocity of the time-delay rotor system is ω. The rotating angle is α. Assuming that S point is the geometric centre of the disk, the axis of rotation passes through the geometric centre of the disk, and the centre of mass G of the rotor deviates from the geometric centre of the rotor, resulting in an eccentricity of S. The line connecting the AB lines is the z axis, and the disc is at O points. The centrifugal force of the disc caused by imbalance is F_r, the elastic restoring force of the elastic shaft is F_k, the damping force F_z is opposite to the moving direction of the rotor. The damping force is proportional to the absolute speed of the rotor. The space orthogonal coordinate system of the time-delay rotor system is established by taking the straight line of the initial position of F_c as the x-axis and the y-axis simultaneously perpendicular to the x-axis and the z-axis.

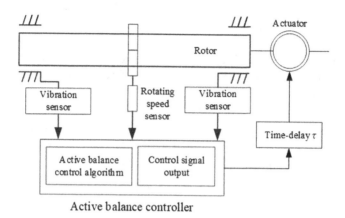

Fig. 1. The schematic of active balancing control system

When the time-delay rotor system rotates at an angular velocity ω, the dynamic equations of the rotor in both directions of x-axis and y-axis are as follows:

$$\begin{cases} m\ddot{x}_G + kx + c\dot{x} = 0 \\ m\ddot{y}_G + ky + c\dot{y} = 0 \end{cases} \tag{1}$$

where $m\ddot{x}_G$, $m\ddot{y}_G$ are the centrifugal force component generated on the x-axis and y-axis respectively in the process of rotor rotation. If the coordinate of G point is $G(x_G, y_G)$, the coordinates of S point is $S(x, y)$, and the coordinate relationship between the disc centroid G and the geometric centre S can be obtained:

$$\begin{cases} x_G = x + e\cos\alpha \\ y_G = y + e\sin\alpha \end{cases} \tag{2}$$

By taking the Eq. (2) into the Eq. (1), it can be written as:

$$\begin{cases} m\ddot{x} + c\dot{x} + kx = me(\dot{\alpha}^2 cos\alpha + \ddot{\alpha}\sin\alpha) \\ m\ddot{y} + c\dot{y} + ky = me(\dot{\alpha}^2 \sin\alpha - \ddot{\alpha}\cos\alpha) \end{cases} \tag{3}$$

When the rotor runs at a steady speed (i.e. the rotor rotates at a constant speed), $\ddot{\alpha} = 0, \dot{\alpha} = \omega$, and $\alpha = \omega t$, Eq. (3) can be simplified as:

$$\begin{cases} m\ddot{x} + c\dot{x} + kx = me\omega^2 \cos\omega t \\ m\ddot{y} + c\dot{y} + ky = me\omega^2 \sin\omega t \end{cases} \tag{4}$$

The above dynamics Eqs. (4) of time-delay rotor system can represented as matrix form:

$$M\ddot{X} + C\dot{X} + KX = F_r \tag{5}$$

Where mass matrix $M = \begin{pmatrix} m & 0 \\ 0 & m \end{pmatrix}$, damping matrix $C = \begin{pmatrix} c & 0 \\ 0 & c \end{pmatrix}$, stiffness matrix $K = \begin{pmatrix} k & 0 \\ 0 & k \end{pmatrix}$, centrifugal force vector $F_r = \begin{pmatrix} me\omega^2 \cos\omega t \\ me\omega^2 \sin\omega t \end{pmatrix}$, vibration of rotor $X = \begin{pmatrix} x \\ y \end{pmatrix}$.

During the active balancing control of the rotor, the controller drives the actuator to generate an active balancing control force F_c that acts on the time-delay rotor system.

$$M\ddot{X} + C\dot{X} + KX = F_r + F_c \tag{6}$$

Due to the inevitable time lag τ of the control signal transmitted to the actuator process, the active balance control force with time-delay is introduced into the dynamic equation of the time-delay rotor system:

$$M\ddot{X} + C\dot{X} + KX = F_r(t) + F_c(t - \tau) \tag{7}$$

Equation (7) is equivalent to Eq. (8):

$$\ddot{X} + M^{-1}C\dot{X} + M^{-1}KX = M^{-1}F_r(t) + M^{-1}F_c(t - \tau) \tag{8}$$

Convert Eq. (8) to state space, the state space equation can be expressed as:

$$\begin{cases} \dot{Z}(t) = AZ(t) + B_1 u(t - \tau) + B_p u_p(t) \\ Y(t) = DZ(t) \end{cases} \tag{9}$$

Where $Z(t) = \begin{pmatrix} X(t) \\ \dot{X}(t) \end{pmatrix} = \begin{pmatrix} x & y & \dot{x} & \dot{y} \end{pmatrix}^{\mathrm{T}}$, $A = \begin{pmatrix} 0 & I \\ -M^{-1}K & -M^{-1}C \end{pmatrix}$, $B_1 = B_p = \begin{pmatrix} 0 \\ M^{-1} \end{pmatrix}$, $u(t - \tau) = F_c(t - \tau)$, $u_p(t) = F_r(t)$, D is the output matrix, $Y(t)$ is the output.

2.2　Transformation of Dynamic Model of Time-Delay Rotor System

Since the state equation of the time-delay rotor system contains time-delay τ, in the rotor active balancing control process, the active balancing controller will input energy to the time-delay rotor system when the system does not need energy. That will reduce the efficiency of active balancing control and even lead to the instability of the rotor system [15,16]. Considering that it is relatively difficult to directly design the control law of the time-delay rotor system, in order to eliminate the influence of time-delay τ on the active balance control system, the following transformation is introduced [17]:

$$E(t) = Z(t) + \Gamma(t) \tag{10}$$

where $\Gamma(t)$ represents the integral term associated with τ,

$$\Gamma(t) = \int_{t-\tau}^{t} e^{-A(s-t)} e^{-A\tau} B_1 u(s) ds$$

By solving Eq. (10), we have

$$\dot{E}(t) = \dot{Z}(t) + \left[\int_{t-\tau}^{t} e^{-A(s-t)} e^{-A\tau} B_1 u(s) ds \right]'$$
$$= \dot{Z}(t) + A \int_{t-\tau}^{t} e^{-A(s-t)} e^{-A\tau} B_1 u(s) ds + e^{-A\tau} B_1 u(t) - B_1 u(t - \tau) \tag{11}$$

Combining the state space Eq. (9), we have

$$\dot{E}(t) = AE(t) + B_p u_p(t) + e^{-A\tau} B_1 u(t) \tag{12}$$

Finally, the state space equation of the time-delay rotor system without time-delay can be obtained as:

$$\begin{cases} \dot{E}(t) = AE(t) + Bu(t) + B_p u_p(t) \\ H(t) = DE(t) \end{cases} \tag{13}$$

where $E(t) = (\hat{x}, \hat{y}, \dot{\hat{x}}, \dot{\hat{y}})^T$ is the state variable of the transformed time-delay rotor system, $H(t)$ is the output vector of the time-delay rotor system, $A = \begin{pmatrix} 0 & I \\ -M^{-1}K & -M^{-1}C \end{pmatrix}$, $B = e^{-A\tau} B_1$, $B_p = \begin{pmatrix} 0 \\ M^{-1} \end{pmatrix}$, D is the output matrix of the control system.

2.3   Design of LQR Active Balancing Control Law

The optimal control algorithm is widely used in the field of active vibration control [18,19]. Linear quadratic control can obtain the optimal control law of state linear feedback, which is conducive to the realization of closed-loop optimal control. Furthermore, linear quadratic control can keep the error near zero with the minimum energy cost. Therefore, the linear quadratic optimal control theory is used to design the active balancing control law for time-delay rotors. According to the theory of optimal control method, the external excitation term of the time-delay rotor system can be ignored at first. When designing the optimal control law, we introduced a performance index of optimal control. The linear quadratic optimal performance index function of the system is given:

$$J = \frac{1}{2} \int_{t_0}^{t_1} [E^T(t)QE(t) + u^T(t)Ru(t)] \tag{14}$$

where Q and R are the positive definite gain matrix of the state variable and the semi-positive definite gain matrix of the input variable, t_0 and t_1 are the start time, the end time of active balancing control respectively. We set $t_0 = 0$, $t_1 = +\infty$.

The optimal control is to solve the optimal control law $u(t)$. The design of state feedback controller G is to minimize the performance index function J of the linear quadratic optimal control for the given system. The linear quadratic optimal control law is obtained as:

$$u(t) = -GE(t) \tag{15}$$

Among them, $G = R^{-1}B^T P(t)$, $p(t)$ is the solution of Riccati equation. Riccati equation is expressed as:

$$- PA - A^T P + PBR^{-1}B^T P - Q = 0 \tag{16}$$

The Riccati Eq. (16) is to obtain the feedback matrix G of the controller. Thereby the key of design the linear quadratic optimal control law is to select the appropriate weight matrix Q and R, and a linear quadratic optimal control law is designed by choosing appropriate weight matrices Q and R.

3   Results and Discussion

3.1   System Simulation Model

In order to verify the correctness and superiority of the online active balancing control method for time-delay rotor. The simulation experiments are carried out. The method proposed in this paper is mainly aimed at the medium-high speed rotor system. Thus in the experiment, the rotor speed is selected to be $3000r/min$, other parameters are taken from empirical values to more accurately simulate the actual working conditions. The relevant parameters of the rotor system are shown in Table 1.

According to the parameters of the above time-delay rotor system, take $\tau = 0.01s$ as an example, the parameter matrix in the state space equation of the time-time-delay rotor system can be obtained, as shown below:

$$A = \begin{pmatrix} 0 & 0 & 1 & 0 \\ 0 & 0 & 0 & 1 \\ -1333.333 & 0 & -0.1333 & 0 \\ 0 & -1333.333 & 0 & -0.1333 \end{pmatrix}, B = \begin{pmatrix} -0.0007 & 0 \\ 0 & -0.0007 \\ 0.6663 & 0 \\ 0 & 0.6663 \end{pmatrix},$$

$$B_p = \begin{pmatrix} 0 & 0 \\ 0 & 0 \\ 0.6667 & 0 \\ 0 & 0.6667 \end{pmatrix}, D = \begin{pmatrix} 1 & 0 & 0 & 0 \\ 0 & 1 & 0 & 0 \end{pmatrix}$$

Table 1. Related parameters of the time-delay rotor system

Disc quality	$m = 1.5\,\text{kg}$
Bending stiffness of the rotor	$k = 2000\,\text{N/m}$
Damping coefficient of the time-delay rotor system	$c = 0.2\,\text{Ns/m}$
Eccentricity of the rotor	$e = 0.002\,\text{m}$
Rotor speed	$n = 3000\,\text{r/min}$
Time-delay of the time-delay rotor system	$\tau = 0.001\,\text{s}$ or $\tau = 0.01\,\text{s}$

Based on the state space equation of the original time-delay rotor system, the integral transformation method is introduced to calculate the state space equation without time- delay. Since the vibration of the time-delay rotor system in the x-axis and y-axis direction is similar, we focus on the vibration in the x-axis direction, and the simulation model of the active balancing control of the time-delay rotor system is established.

3.2   Step Response Results and Discussion

Generally speaking, for the control system, step input is the most severe working state of the control system. If the control system can satisfy the control performance requirement under the action of step input, the control system can still satisfy the control performance requirement under the action of other signals. Thereby we select the step input as the input signal in the case of $\tau = 0.001s$ for the simulation experiment. In order to study the influence of weight matrix Q and R on the active balancing control system of time-delay rotor, we select different weight matrix Q and R, and calculate the state feedback matrix G, then the step response of the control system is obtained. The open-loop step response of the time-delay rotor system is shown in Fig. 2.

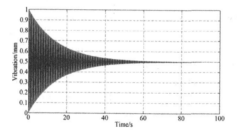

Fig. 2. Open-loop step response of time-delay rotor system

The weight matrix in this paper is selected separately,

$$Q = \alpha \begin{pmatrix} K & 0 \\ 0 & M \end{pmatrix} = \alpha \begin{pmatrix} 2000 & 0 & 0 & 0 \\ 0 & 2000 & 0 & 0 \\ 0 & 0 & 1.5 & 0 \\ 0 & 0 & 0 & 1.5 \end{pmatrix},$$

$$R = \beta \begin{pmatrix} 1 & 0 \\ 0 & 1 \end{pmatrix}$$

where α and β are undetermined coefficients. Assuming that the weight matrix R is invariant, the influence of the weight matrix Q of the rotor control system is discussed. Figure 3 shows the step response of the time-delay rotor system when α is 0.1,1,10 and 100 respectively.

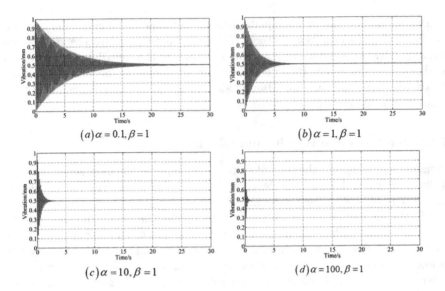

Fig. 3. Step response of time-delay rotor system with different α when time-delay $\tau = 0.001\,\mathrm{s}$

Assuming that the weight matrix Q is invariant, the influence of the weight matrix R of the rotor control system is discussed. Figure 4 shows the step response of the time-delay rotor system when β is 0.1,1,10 and 100 respectively.

From Fig. 3 and Fig. 4, it can be seen that when the weight matrix Q is larger, the time for the control system to reach stability decreases, but the steady-state error increases. When the weight matrix R is larger, the time for the time-delay rotor system to reach stability increases. Thus we combine the above simulation results about the weight matrix Q and R, and carry out several simulation experiments.

Further in order to simulate the actual situation of time-delay rotor system, we add the centrifugal force into the model. Combined with the simulation results of Q and R, the control feedback matrix is obtained by multiple simulation verification, then the appropriate weight matrix is selected. We set the rotational speed $n = 3000r/min$, when the model of the time-delay rotor system without active balancing control force, the time domain figure of the vibration in the x-axis direction of the rotor is shown in Fig. 5(a).

Firstly, assuming that the rotor system does not contain time-delay, the linear quadratic optimal control law is introduced to design the linear quadratic optimal control law of the rotor system, and the simulation results are shown in Fig. 5(b).

Then assuming that the rotor system are with some different time-delay, the linear quadratic optimal control laws of the time-delay rotor system are calculated respectively. The vibration control process of the time-delay rotor system are obtained when $\tau = 0.001\,\mathrm{s}$ and $\tau = 0.01\,\mathrm{s}$, as shown in Fig. 6. The different simulation results with different time-delay conditions are also compared in Table 2.

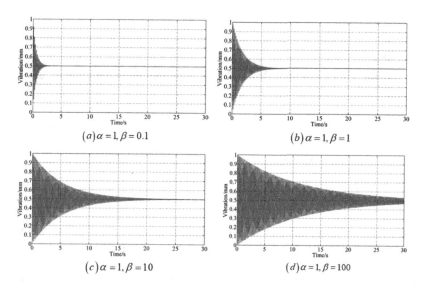

Fig. 4. Step response of time-delay rotor system with different β when time-delay $\tau = 0.001\,\text{s}$

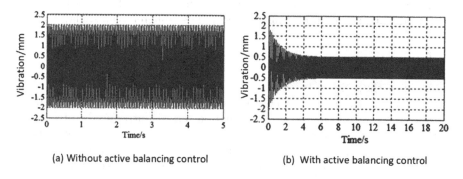

Fig. 5. Vibration time domain of rotor system

As can be seen from Fig. 6, the initial vibration of the time-delay rotor system is 2.03 mm, and the target balanced vibration is 0.5 mm. After active balancing control, when there is no time-delay in the active balancing control process, the time for the control system to reach the balance state is 5.2 s. When there is a

Table 2. Comparison of simulation results

Time-delay condition	Initial vibration	Balanced vibration	Balancing time
$\tau = 0\,\text{s}$	2.03 mm	0.5 mm	5.2 s
$\tau = 0.1\,\text{s}$	2.03 mm	0.5 mm	6.4 s
$\tau = 0.01\,\text{s}$	2.03 mm	0.5 mm	8.5 s

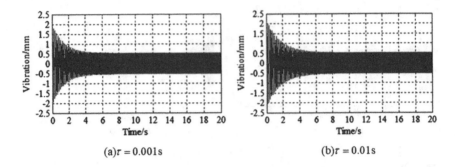

Fig. 6. Control process of the time-delay rotor system

time-delay $\tau = 0.001$ s in the active balancing control process, the time for the control system to reach the balance state is 6.4 s. While there is a time-delay $\tau = 0.01$ s in the rotor active balancing control process, the time is 8.5 s.

Therefore, the proposed active balancing control method can be applied not only to the case of small time delay, but also to the case of large time delay. The control effect is similar to that without time delay. That is to say the linear quadratic time-delay rotor active balancing control method in this paper can achieve satisfactory vibration control effects under different time-delay.

4   Conclusions

In this paper, the active balancing control method for the time-delay rotor system is proposed. The dynamic model of the time-delay rotor system with time-delay is established, and the integral transformation term is introduced to transform the time-delay rotor system dynamics model into a dynamic model without time-delay. Then, according to the linear quadratic optimal control theory, the active balancing control law of time-delay rotor is designed. Moreover, the influence of weight matrix Q and R on the design of control law is discussed. Finally, in order to verify the correctness of the proposed method, the simulation model of time-delay rotor control system is constructed in Matlab. Meanwhile, we set up the experimental platform to carry out the experiment. The results show that the method can effectively suppress the vibration of the time-delay rotor system under different time-delay.

Acknowledgments. This research was funded by the National Key Research and Development Plan of China (No. 2018Y FB2000505), Nation Nature Science Foundation of China (No. 61806067), and Nature Science Foundation of Anhui Province (No. 1908085M E132).

References

1. Shrivastava, A., Mohanty, A.R.: Identification of unbalance in a rotor system using a joint input-state estimation technique. J. Sound Vib. **442**(3), 414–427 (2019)

2. Ding, K., Wang, Z., Lu, X.: Vibration investigation of rotor system with unbalance and blade-casing rubbing coupling faults. J. VibroEng. **22**(2), 353–365 (2020)
3. Qiu, Z.C., Li, C., Zhang, X.M.: Experimental study on active vibration control for a kind of two-link flexible manipulator. Mech. Syst. Signal Process. **118**, 623–644 (2019)
4. Zhongbo, W., Chuan, M., Changsheng, Z.: Current compensation control of multiple frequency vibrations of the rotor in active magnetic bearing high speed motors. Proc. CSEE **38**(001), 275–284 (2018)
5. Xu, J., Sun, X.: A multi-directional vibration isolator based on Quasi-Zero-Stiffness structure and time-time-delay active control. Int. J. Mech. Sci. **100**, 126–135 (2015)
6. Raufmehr, F., Rezaei, M.: Fuzzy logic-based scalable video rate control algorithm for high-delay applications of scalable high-efficiency video coding. J. Electron. Imag. **27**(4), 043013.1–043013.11 (2018)
7. Heindel, S., Becker, F., Rinderknecht, S.: Unbalance and resonance elimination with active bearings on a Jeffcott Rotor. Mech. Syst. Signal Process. **85**, 339–353 (2017)
8. Mironchenko, A., Wirth, F.: Input-to-state stability of time-delay systems: criteria and open problems. In: 2017 IEEE 56th Annual Conference on Decision and Control (CDC), pp. 3719–3724, Melbourne (2017)
9. Zheng, H., Hu, F., Huang, Z.: Shaft longitudinal vibration active control based on the adaptive method. J. Vibr. Shock **37**(4), 203–207, 218 (2018)
10. Saeed, N.A., El-Ganaini, W.A.: Time-time-delay control to suppress the nonlinear vibrations of a horizontally suspended Jeffcott-time-delay rotor system. Appl. Math. Model. **44**, 523–539 (2017)
11. Wang, L., Xiong, C., Wang, X.: Hybrid time-variant reliability estimation for active control structures under aleatory and epistemic uncertainties. J. Sound Vib. **419**, 469–492 (2018)
12. Hu, H.L., He, L.D.: Control of critical speed vibrations of a single-span rotor by a rotor dynamic vibration absorber at different installation positions. J. Mech. Sci. Technol. **31**(5), 2075–2081 (2017)
13. Zhang, J., Yang, H., Li, M., Wang, Q.: Robust model predictive control for uncertain positive time-delay systems. Int. J. Control Autom. Syst. **17**(2), 307–318 (2019). https://doi.org/10.1007/s12555-017-0728-4
14. Li, H., Xu, G., Xu, G.: Mechanical vibration monitoring system based on wireless sensor network. Int. J. Online Eng. **14**(06), 126–137 (2018)
15. Wang, Z., Mak, C.M.: Application of a movable active vibration control system on a floating raft. J. Sound Vib. **414**, 233–244 (2018)
16. Hongxin, S., Jianqiang, L.I., Xiuyong, W.: Time delay compensation for the active cable vibration control using giant magnetostrictive actuators. J. Vib. Shock **36**(14), 208–215 (2017)
17. Kwon, W.H., Pearson, A.E.: Feedback stabilization of linear systems with time-delay control. IEEE Trans. Autom. Control **25**(2), 266–269 (1980)
18. Im, H., Yoo, H.H., Chung, J.: Dynamic analysis of a BLDC motor with mechanical and electromagnetic interaction due to air gap variation. J. Sound Vib. **330**(8), 1680–1691 (2011)
19. Brekhna, B., Mahmood, A., Zhou, Y.: Robustness analysis of superpixel algorithms to image blur, additive Gaussian noise, and impulse noise. J. Electron. Imag. **26**(6), 061604.1–061604.10 (2017)

Application Research of RFID Information in the Era of Internet of Things

WenHua Zhang[1], Lei Xu[2(✉)], and HongGang Liu[3]

[1] School of Control and Computer Engineering, North China Electric Power University, Baoding, China
zyc_hd@sina.com
[2] Jiangsu Power Information Technology Co., Ltd., Nanjing, Jiangsu Province, China
xulei2006@hotmail.com
[3] Information and Communication Branch of Chongqing Electric Power Company of State Power Grid, Chongqing, China
hg_liu621@163.com

Abstract. At present, with the further development of network technology, the Internet of things is gradually developing. The development of the Internet of things technology establishes the correlation between things promotes the sharing of object resources and information on a global scale, facilitates the adjustment and upgrading of industries, and promotes the further development of China and even the global economy. In order to promote the further development of the Internet of things, many researchers began to explore the integration of the Internet with other high-end technologies. In this case, RFID information began to gradually enter the field of the Internet of things. RFID technology, as a new non-contact radio technology, is an important foundation for the further development of the Internet of things. However, we must realize that there are still some problems in the application of RFID information in the era of the Internet of things, and further research is necessary. This paper first gives an overview of the concept and working principle of RFID information, and with the help of weight function algorithm, carries out experiments on RFID information security, analyzes the main security problems affecting the application of RFID information in the era of the Internet of things, and puts forward relevant Suggestions on this basis. Finally, it analyzes the specific application of RFID information in the era of Internet of things.

Keywords: RFID information · The Internet of Things · Weight function algorithm · Application research

1 Introduction

With the continuous progress of network technology, the world has changed greatly. Network technology not only promotes the independent development of the virtual world and the real world but also promotes the continuous integration between the two [1]. At present, with the emergence and maturity of 5G, artificial intelligence, VR, and other related network technologies, many researchers begin to study the Internet of everything,

© Springer Nature Singapore Pte Ltd. 2020
X. Yuan et al. (Eds.): ICUIA 2020, CCIS 1319, pp. 226–232, 2020.
https://doi.org/10.1007/978-981-33-4601-7_23

which is what we now call the Internet of things. The so-called Internet of things is based on things and realizes the organic connection between things with the help of network technology [2, 3]. At present, the application of the Internet of things has been gradually extended, and it has been applied in public security, environmental monitoring, logistics, and other aspects, and the era of the Internet of things has come [4]. The Internet of things can produce higher economic benefits than the traditional management method and continuously promote the upgrading and adjustment of industrial structure, which is the new point of China's future economic development. At the same time, we must also realize that the development of the Internet of things has also encountered many problems, among which the most significant is the problem of object recognition and data processing [5, 6]. After a lot of research, researchers found that RFID information can better solve this problem. This technology can automatically identify and manage a variety of objects and devices in different states. In particular, its label link can realize the uniqueness of object identification and fast analysis and processing of data, which is highly consistent with the establishment of standards for the Internet of things [7, 8]. However, there are still some problems in the application of RFID information in the Internet of things era, so it is particularly important to conduct in-depth research on the application of RFID information in the Internet of things era [9].

At present, RFID information has gradually become the most critical link in the development of the Internet of things. In order to make RFID information better applied in the Internet of things era, domestic and foreign experts and scholars have conducted in-depth research on RFID information, which mainly focuses on the security of RFID information, the applicable standards of RFID information, and the development trend of RFID information. On this basis, they have also proposed a series of theories to improve RFID information [10, 11]. However, through comparative analysis, it is found that these studies focus on RFID information itself, without considering its specific application environment. Therefore, these studies lack certain applicability. From this perspective, there are certain theoretical gaps in this study [12, 13].

In order to fill this theoretical gap, this paper first gives an overview of the concept and working principle of RFID information, carries out relevant RFID information security experiments with the help of a weight function algorithm, analyzes the main security problems affecting the application of RFID information in the era of the Internet of things, and puts forward relevant Suggestions on this basis [14, 15]. Finally, it analyzes the specific application of RFID information in the era of the Internet of things. On the one hand, it promotes the deep integration of the Internet of things and RFID information, and on the other hand, it provides a certain theoretical basis for future research on related aspects.

2 Method

2.1 Overview of RFID Information

The full name of PFID is radio frequency identification technology, which embodies the application of automatic identification technology in the development of radio technology. With the help of some high-level technology, this technology can automatically identify and manage a variety of objects and devices in different states. Radio frequency identification (rfid) technology is a non-contact two-way communication by means of radio frequency, so as to realize the identification of related things and the exchange of data. Rfid technology is mainly composed of two parts. The first part is an electronic tag, which is mainly used for data storage. The second part is a reader, whose main function is to read data. The time sequence of the coupler is used to realize the mutual communication between the reader and the electronic tag, which is not directly related to each other, mainly for the purpose of exchanging energy and data. At the current level of technology, RFID is mainly divided into three frequency bands: low frequency, high frequency, and UHF. Each frequency band is applied on different occasions. The principle of RFID is as follows: first, the radio frequency card enters a fixed magnetic field. By means of the antenna's transmitting signal reader, the corresponding induction current will be generated. When the energy concentration reaches a certain level, the radio frequency will be activated. In this case, the rf card can realize information transmission with the help of the embodiment in the card, and the central background information system can receive the sent information and process it to a certain extent with the help of logical operation. At present, with the gradual maturity of radio technology, RFID technology has been continuously developed.

2.2 Weight Function Algorithm

In RFID technology, in order to realize accurate object identification, relevant data security space must be established first. Data security space is a kind of security space established according to data protection in data transmission, which is the key to accurate object recognition. In the data security space of RFID information, the security weight between two adjacent vertices p and q can be expressed by f(p, q). The specific formula is as follows:

$$fi(p, q) = |Ii(p) - Ii(q)| \qquad (1)$$

Where, Ii(p) represents the security value of the space point p to be matched in the security space of I, while fi(p, q) represents the weight value of the other adjacent vertices p and q in the security space of I. The edge detection is realized by means of the representation of the object points with prominent changes and the edge structure data of the object is obtained. This kind of edge structure data is an important standard to detect the security of RFID information transmission and plays an important role in improving the data transmission effect. The weight function formula S(p, q) between two adjacent vertices p and q is as follows:

$$F(p, q) = \alpha \bullet \sqrt{f(p, q) \times g(p, q)} + f(p, q) \text{ and } S(p, q) = \exp\left(-\frac{F(p, q)}{\sigma}\right) \qquad (2)$$

Where, the main function is to adjust the proportion of data information and data edge information in the weight function, and represents the safety weight adjustment coefficient.

3 RFID Information Security Experiment

RFID system mainly consists of the following three parts, which are tags, readers, and data processing, each of which involves the security of information transmission. RFID information security involves all kinds of data and is closely related to the final identification result. Therefore, it is necessary to carry out relevant experiments on RFID information security to find out its specific security problems and ensure the security application of RFID information in the era of the Internet of things, so as to promote the further development of the era of the Internet of things.

This paper carries out simulation experiments on RFID information with the help of the Matlab 2012 system. The experimental objects mainly include tag, reader, and data processing, and test the probability of the occurrence of security problems in these three links, and calculate with the above algorithm. Three different application types in the Internet of things era were selected, and 10 experimental samples were selected for each type. After calculating the security probability of the three aspects of the system, the link with the highest weight of the security problem is found out, and then the security problem of the link is analyzed in detail, so as to obtain a relatively comprehensive data result. On this basis, the paper puts forward some suggestions to solve the problem of RFID information security.

4 Discuss

4.1 Security Problems and Counter Measures of RFID Information Application

Through the above RFID information security experiment, we can draw a conclusion: there are still many security problems in the application of RFID system information, which affect the further application of RFID information, and the main problems mainly appear in the tag part of the RFID system. The specific experimental data are shown in Table 1 and Fig. 1 below. The data in the figure is the result of the author's experimental arrangement.

From Fig. 1, we can find that in the three components of RFID information system, the RFID information application problem is most likely to occur in the tag, which is

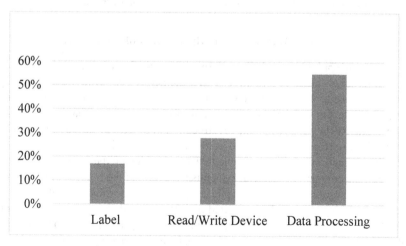

Fig. 1. RFID information application security analysis

Table 1. Label risk and safety data

	Risk categories	Risk index
Security risks	Data privacy	45.63%
	Location confidentiality	23.17%
	Data tamper risk	38.54%
Data risk problem	The data obtained	12.17%
	The data decoding	13.69%
	Data interference	27.38%

*Data came from the in-depth analysis of financial data in the experiment

mainly caused by the limitations of the tag itself. Because of the low cost of the label itself, it does not have sufficient capacity to deal with risks, so the label part is most prone to security problems. From the related data of label risk and security in Table 1, we can find that there are three major risk problems in labels, namely, the confidentiality of data and location and data tampering. Among them the most main security problem is the data security problem, because of the difficulty of data storage, often face to be cracked, interference and intercept, and other risks.

These security risks affect the application of RFID information in the era of the Internet of things, so relevant measures must be taken to reduce the risk. The countermeasures mainly include the following aspects: first, adopt a hierarchical protection strategy to protect label data; Second, it takes the form of killing tags so that the data can never be read again. Third, encrypt confidential data. As long as this can effectively ensure its security issues, continue to expand the scope of application of RFID information.

4.2 Application of RFID Information in the Internet of Things Era

(1) The specific application of RFID information on the Internet of things
    The Internet of things covers three layers: the perception layer, the network layer, and the application layer. These three layers contain a wide range of contents, the most important of which is the information collection content. It has been mentioned above that RFID is the automatic identification of objects in various states with the help of radio frequency signals, so as to achieve the acquisition of data. Therefore, RFID information is fully applicable to data collection on the Internet of things. At present, the country has gradually established a pilot of the Internet of things based on RFID information, and the application of RFID information in the era of the Internet of things has gradually shifted from the original closed-loop application to open-loop application, promoting the continuous integrity of the industrial chain of the Internet of things. At the same time, due to the outstanding technical advantages of RFID information itself, it can realize high efficiency and repeated reading and

writing of information, which makes the electronic tag information in the Internet of things unique, and "things" in the Internet of things become unique. Based on this, RFID information is more widely used in various areas of the Internet of things, including item tracking, real-time monitoring of items, smart furniture, and so on.

(2) Object to object interconnection mode based on RFID information

Based on the RFID information and correct interconnection model is with the aid of RFID and advanced intelligent sensing device to establish a connection between different objects, and then through the network transmission, transmit the information related to the background of the information processing center, so as to establish a connection between people and things, content, and content of the intelligent network, so as to achieve global information sharing items at any time. Only by means of RFID information can the complete establishment of the Internet of things be promoted, and the unique representation and personification of objects in the world can be realized, which has a profound impact on people's production and life.

5 Conclusion

In the era of the Internet of things, efforts are made to establish the interrelation between things and promote the real-time sharing of goods information around the world. The Internet of things (IoT) is a new subject generated under the development of economy and network technology. It is a highly intelligent network system developed by the comprehensive application of various high and new technologies. Among them, RFIP technology plays an irreplaceable role in the development of IoT and is also an important basis for the realization of IoT. Therefore, to strengthen the research on the application of RFIP information in the Internet of things and to find a scientific application approach to promote the sustainable development of the Internet of things, we must pay enough attention.

References

1. Alsinglawi, B., Elkhodr, M., Nguyen, Q.V.: RFID localisation for Internet of Things smart homes: a survey. Int. J. Comput. Netw. Commun. **9**(1), 81–99 (2017)
2. Ahmadi, H., Arji, G., Shahmoradi, L., Safdari, R., Nilashi, M., Alizadeh, M.: The application of Internet of Things in healthcare: a systematic literature review and classification. Univ. Access Inf. Soc. **18**(4), 837–869 (2018). https://doi.org/10.1007/s10209-018-0618-4
3. Wu, Z.-H.: Research on the application of Internet of Things technology to digital museum construction. Acta Geosci. Sin. **38**(2), 293–298 (2017)
4. Chen, C., Xu, X.: Design and application of traceability and supervision platform for broiler based on Internet of Things. Trans. Chin. Soc. Agric. Eng. **33**(5), 224–231 (2017)
5. Zhang, D., Yang, L.T., Chen, M.: Real-time locating systems using active RFID for Internet of Things. IEEE Syst. J. **10**(3), 1226–1235 (2017)
6. Yao, C.-Y., Hsia, W.-C.: An indoor positioning system based on the dual-channel passive RFID technology. IEEE Sens. J. **31**(99), 11–14 (2018)
7. Gope, P., Lee, J., Quek, T.Q.S.: Lightweight and practical anonymous authentication protocol for RFID systems using physically unclonable functions. IEEE Trans. Inf. Forensics Secur. **62**(99), 111–116 (2018)

8. Mala, H., Aghili, S.F., Ashouri-Talouki, M.: DoS, impersonation and de-synchronization attacks against an ultra-lightweight RFID mutual authentication protocol for IoT. J. Super-comput. **74**(12), 1–17 (2017)
9. Ciftler, B.S., Kadri, A., Guvenc, I.: IoT localization for bistatic passive UHF RFID systems with 3D radiation pattern. IEEE Internet Things J. **4**(4), 905–916 (2017)
10. Sun, C.: Application of RFID technology for logistics on Internet of Things. Aasri Proc. **1**(5), 106–111 (2017)
11. Sicari, S., Hailes, S., Turgut, D.: Security, privacy and trust management in the Internet of Things era – SePriT. Ad Hoc Netw. **11**(8), 2623–2624 (2017)
12. Zhao, C., Li, X.S., Chen, J.S.: Study on the application of Internet of Things in the logistics in forest industry. Appl. Mech. Mater. **15**(8), 664–668 (2017)
13. Shi, S., Yang, L.: Application of RFID in medical industry in the era of Internet of Things. China Med. Educ. Technol. **12**(17), 426–431 (2017)
14. Wang, H.: Analysis of the development of accounting informationization in the Internet of Things era. Acc. Finan. **18**(2), 141–147 (2017)
15. Pi, S., Yang, J., Wang, J.: Study on the application of the Internet of Things technologies in agricultural products logistics. Logist. Sci-Tech. **13**(7), 357–365 (2017)

Analysis of Investment Risk Assessment Model of Financial Institutions Under Economic Growth

Ke Zhao[✉]

Department of Economic Management,
Liaocheng Vocational and Technical College, Liaocheng 252000, Shandong, China
zhaoke66885@163.com

Abstract. As a result of the relaxation of restrictive policies and preferential fiscal and taxation policies, a large number of private capitals have entered the financial field, and local quasi-financial institutions have been greatly developed. Local financial institutions are a useful complement to formal finance, which plays an irreplaceable role in the market environment of structural financial mismatch in our country. However, the financial risk still exists because of its dissociation from financial supervision. With economic growth, the investment risk assessment model of financial institutions is constructed. The supervision of financial institutions and the main problems in investment risk assessment are analyzed. Through statistical regression analysis, the variable correlation analysis model of investment risk assessment of financial institutions is established. An expert database for the evaluation of investment risk data of financial institutions under economic growth is established. The recommended values of confidence of investors in financial institutions under economic growth are constructed. The information fusion processing is carried out based on the evolutionary method of adaptive global surplus regression analysis. The prediction and evaluation of the investment risk of financial institutions are realized. The empirical results show that the confidence level of investment risk assessment of financial institutions is higher and the accuracy of evaluation is better when the model is used to carry out the investment risk assessment of financial institutions under economic growth.

Keywords: Economic growth · Financial institutions · Investment risk assessment

1 Introduction

With the development of new Internet financial technology, third-party payment platforms such as P2P, Yu'e Bao, WeChat Pay have emerged, which accelerates the process of "financial disintermediation". This kind of light asset-heavy service relying on Internet technology has caused a serious impact on traditional financial business. Considering the loss of users and the pressure of market competition, traditional commercial banks began to strengthen the application of blockchain technology and enhance the layout of

© Springer Nature Singapore Pte Ltd. 2020
X. Yuan et al. (Eds.): ICUIA 2020, CCIS 1319, pp. 233–240, 2020.
https://doi.org/10.1007/978-981-33-4601-7_24

Internet finance [1]. In the transformation process from a planned economy to a market economy, financial control is carried out, which imposes different constraints on the state sector and the non-state sector. This kind of "financial dualism" leads to the mismatch between the supply of state-owned financial funds and the credit demand of private enterprises, which distorts the allocation of financial resources and produces structural financial mismatch. Financing difficulties Small and medium-sized enterprises are no way out of the dilemma. At the same time, it also creates a huge development space for private finance, especially the development of quasi-financial institutions [2].

According to the Circular on strengthening Shadow Banking, issued by the General Office of the State Council in early 2014, the definition of "a credit intermediary that does not hold a financial license and has insufficient supervision" is a quasi-financial institution in practice [3]. Generally, subjects such as microfinance companies, financing guarantee companies, pawnshops are included. They differ from the traditional financial institutions significantly in their modern finance, the particularity of the regulatory body, and folklore. Its business has the nature of finance, which reflects the financial innovation; its supervisory power lies in the local government, not the "one line and three meetings"; its capital source is mostly private capital. To a certain extent, quasi financial institutions have solved the problem of financing difficulties of private enterprises such as small and micro enterprises and self-employed enterprises, and have effectively made up for the shortcomings of traditional financial institutions and the market vacancies left behind. Although its scale is smaller, its stakeholders are narrower, and it is less likely to produce systemic financial risks, but due to the relevant legal norms, government supervision and industry self-discipline are lacking, and the barriers to entry of quasi-financial institutions are too low, and professional management is weakened [4–7].

As a useful supplement to formal finance, the local financial institution plays an irreplaceable role in the market environment of structural financial mismatch in our country. However, because of its dissociation from financial supervision, the financial risk still exists. The investment risk assessment model of financial institutions under economic growth is constructed. The variable correlation analysis model of investment risk assessment of financial institutions under economic growth is constructed based on statistical regression analysis and the sample regression analysis [8].

From the formal point of view, quasi-financial institutions and financial systems operate independently of each other, and the degree of direct correlation is not strong. However, there are many kinds of recessive connections between quasi-financial institutions and financial systems in actual operation, and potential risks are constantly accumulated and difficult to identify. In the absence of an effective coping mechanism, the risks of quasi-financial institutions are easily transmitted to the financial system. Moreover, with the further development of quasi-financial institutions, the connection with banks is bound to increase, and the channels of risk transmission will increase accordingly.

In the front end of the formation of private finance, we should strengthen management, introduce a variety of mechanisms, promote the standardized operation of private finance, and strictly examine and approve the quasi-financial institutions to be set up because they do not have a "financial license" but are engaged in the financial business. Not included in the scope of the national financial regulatory authority. Thus, although quasi-financial institutions have developed for many years, their regulatory problems have never been properly addressed.

2 Design and Implementation of Risk Assessment Model

2.1 Statistical Information Collection

To assess the investment risk of financial institutions under economic growth, the information processing algorithm is used to collect and analyze the prior data of the investment risk of financial institutions. The explanatory variable model and the control variable model for investment risk assessment of financial institutions are established, with the ratio of market value to book value, the ratio of assets to liabilities, the ratio of cash flow, and the mode of financing structure as the constraint parameters. Based on the regression analysis of investment risk statistics of financial institutions, the univariate economic sequence of investment risk of financial institutions is constructed by using a vector feature reconstruction method for $\{x_n\}$. A differential equation is used to express the investment risk of financial institutions, the information flow model is expressed as follows:

$$x_n = x(t_0 + n\Delta t) = h[z(t_0 + n\Delta t)] + \omega_n \tag{1}$$

Where, $h(.)$ and ω_n are the multivariate quantitative value function and the observation or measurement error of the economic sequence of investment risk of financial institutions, respectively [9].

Through correlation analysis of financing methods, the big data analysis model of investment risk assessment of financial institutions is established. In the context of asymmetric information, the evolution sequence of $x_n \to x_{n+1}$ in the investment risk classification space is obtained, which reflects the evaluation and evolution model of the economic sequence of investment risk of financial institutions. On the other hand, the descriptive statistical sequence $z_n \to z_{n+1}, z(t) \to z(t + 1)$ of the investment risk of financial institutions is obtained as well. The phase-space reconstruction trajectory of the series is expressed as follows:

$$X = [s_1, s_2, \ldots, s_K]_\mathbf{n} = (x_n, x_{n-\tau}, \cdots, x_{n-(m-1)\tau}) \tag{2}$$

Where, $K = N - (m - 1)\tau$, represents the orthogonal eigenvector of the economic sequence of investment risk of financial institutions, τ is the statistical characteristic sampling delay of investment risk of financial institutions, m is embedded dimension, and $s_i = (x_i, x_{i+\tau}, \ldots, x_{i+(m-1)\tau})^T$ is a set of scalar sampling sequences. Combining static tradeoff theory and financing priority theory, the paper evaluates the investment risk of financial institutions quantitatively. Assuming that the historical data of descriptive statistics of investment risk of financial institutions are expressed as $\{x_i\}_{i=1}^N$, the time and quantity of funds with the financing financial model is matched, the expression of the grey model of elastic financial analysis for investment risk assessment of financial institutions is expressed as Eq. (3):

$$\frac{dz(t)}{dt} = F(z) \tag{3}$$

In the comparison of financial elasticity values, if the embedded dimension is over 2 times the attraction dimension, the descriptive statistical analysis method is used to implement the dynamic early warning and venture capital assessment of the investment risk of financial institutions. The investment risks of financial institutions mainly refer to financial risks and operational risks. Internal control factors are the main factors inducing the investment risks of financial institutions. The supervision function of financial institutions is more dispersed, which is not conducive to coordinated management. The local government should concentrate on the management of financial institutions in a single department to establish a horizontal and vertical organizational structure of all-round financial supervision and establish reasonable management objectives and evaluation criteria [10]. Secondly, take the Financial Supervision Office as the core, construct the omni-directional supervision organization system to form the supervision joint force of the whole province. Establish local financial supervision centers at the local level and county level, joint various industry departments such as the Banking Regulatory Commission and the Insurance Regulatory Commission, t, and guide trade associations and other industry management institutions to strengthen self-restraint and establish a long-term communication and cooperation mechanism. Thirdly, gradually establish and improve the financial analysis and monitoring information system, the financial stability coordination mechanism, the financial risk coordination, and prevention mechanism, and the financial emergency handling mechanism.

2.2 Assessment and Prediction of Investment Risk of Financial Institutions

By using big data analysis method, set $I = \{i | s_i \geq s_j, \forall s_j \in S^1\}$, the characteristic distribution of total assets is obtained by $s_i = (x_1, x_2, \ldots, x_n)$, where $i \in I$. On this basis, the total asset turnover rate of financial institutions under-investment risk can be calculated by Eq. (4):

$$f(x_1) = f(x_2) = \ldots = f(x_n) = f^* \tag{4}$$

Using symbolic Overinv regression analysis and descriptive statistical analysis, the finance degree $s_i \in s^*$ of investment risk of a financial institution is obtained. Under constant cash holdings, the transfer probability of risk assessment of financial institutions can be expressed as $p_{ij}(k) = p\{A^j_{k+1}/A^i_k\} \geq 0$, then:

$$p_{ij}(k) = p\{A^j_{k+1}/A^i_k\} = \sum_{s_c \in S^2} p\{C^l_k/A^i_k\} p\{C^l_{k+1}/A^i_k C^l_k\} \tag{5}$$

When $i \in I, j \notin I$, from the investment risk assessment of financial institutions, the output is expressed as follows:

$$p\{A^j_{k+1}/A^i_k C^l_k\} = \sum_{s_c \in S^2} p\{C^l_k/A^i_k B^b_k\} p\{A^j_{k+1}/A^i_k B^b_k C^l_k\} \tag{6}$$

By using the sample regression analysis method of total sample statistical analysis, the expert database of investment risk data evaluation of financial institutions under economic growth is established, and the recommended value of confidence degree of financial institutions under economic growth is extracted [11]. And carry on the information fusion processing to extract the financial institution investment risk data association rule characteristic quantity is:

$$0 \leq p_{k+1} \leq p_k - \sum_{i \notin I} \sum_{j \in I} p_i(k) p_{ij}(k) \leq p_k \leq 1 \tag{7}$$

According to the quantitative regression analysis of the main factors involved in the financial market, the linear fitting formula for assessment of investment risk of financial institutions is expressed as Eq. (8):

$$p_{id}^{new} = \begin{cases} p_{id} + m()(X_{max} - p_{id}) & \text{if } m() > 0 \\ p_{id} + m()(p_{id} - X_{min}) & \text{if } m() \leq 0 \end{cases} \tag{8}$$

The economic game theory and regression analysis method are adopted to assess the investment risk of financial institutions, and the objective function of the optimization evaluation is obtained as Eq. (9):

$$\text{minimize} \quad \frac{1}{2}\|w\|^2 + C \sum_{i=1}^{n} (\xi_i + \xi_i^*)$$

$$\text{subject to} \quad y_i - (w' \Phi(x_i) + b) \leq \varepsilon - \xi_i$$

$$(w' \Phi(x_i) + b) - y_i \leq \varepsilon - \xi_i^*$$

$$\xi_i, \xi_i^* \geq 0, i = 1, 2, \cdots, n; C > 0 \tag{9}$$

Through the global optimization of the investment risk sequence of the financial institution, we obtained the global extremum $G_{best}^d(t)$ and individual extreme $G_{best}^d(t)$. Using the mean square error estimation method, the optimal output value of investment risk assessment of financial institutions is obtained:

$$\begin{cases} V_i^d(t+1) = W \cdot V_i^d(t) + C_1 \cdot R_1 \cdot (P_{best}^d(t) - P_i^d(t)) \\ \qquad\qquad + C_2 \cdot R_2 \cdot (G_{best}^d(t) - P_i^d(t)) \\ P_i^d(t+1) = P_i^d(t) + V_i^d(t+1) \end{cases} \tag{10}$$

Where, $V_i^d(t)$, $V_i^d(t+1)$ represent the capital structure, $P_i^d(t)$, $P_i^d(t+1)$ represent investment scale. The realization process of the model is shown in Fig. 1.

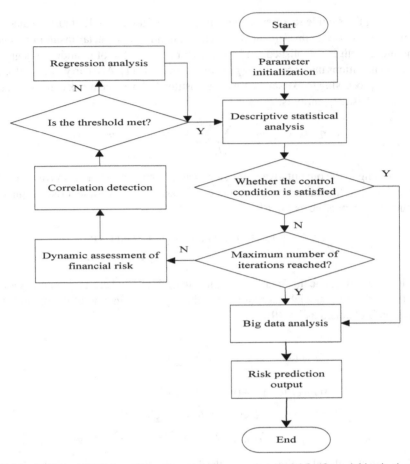

Fig. 1. Implementation flow of investment risk assessment model for financial institutions

3   Empirical Analysis and Testing

To verify the performance of this method in investment risk assessment of financial institution, the simulation experiment was carried out by using simulation software SPSS 14.0 and Matlab 7 with the data sources selected from 10, 000 enterprises' financial data. Of the 3072 sample observations used in this paper, the lowest leverage ratio was 0.71, and the proportion of enterprises with leverage not exceeding 20 percent was 6.45. In this paper, the residual error of an enterprise expected investment expenditure model constructed by Richardson is 1488 and 1584, accounting for 48.44% and 51.56% of the total, respectively. From the aspect of an inefficient investment, the mean value of the overinvestment group is 0. 049, which is higher than the total 0.047 and the underinvested 0. 046, indicating overinvestment was more serious than underinvestment. In terms of residual debt capacity and cash holdings, the average value of the over-investment group is higher than the overall average. According to the above empirical analysis model description, the investment risk prediction of financial structure is implemented, as shown in Table 1.

Table 1. Prediction evaluation model

Variable	Enterprise profit level	Risk index	Size	Financial elasticity group
SC	1	0.434***	0.541	0.232
PC	0.4334**	1	0.432	0.436
Size	0.323	0.433	1	0.743**
MB	0.654	0.322	−0.654	1
ALR	0.543**	0.343**	−0.353	−1.3443
Profitability	0.654	0.143	0.432***	0.322
Age	0.454*	1.344	0.232	0.156***

Table 1 shows that the average actual asset-liability ratio of underinvested enterprises is higher than that of target assets and liabilities, and there is excessive debt financing. The financial elasticity of over-investment enterprises is higher than that of underinvested enterprises, which indicates that firms with better flexibility tend to overinvest, while enterprises with low financial elasticity tend to underinvest. On this basis, the investment risk assessment is implemented, as shown in Fig. 2.

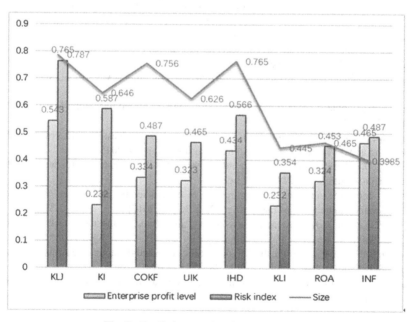

Fig. 2. Prediction results of risk assessment

As shown in Fig. 2, the proposed method increased the confidence level of investment risk assessment of financial institutions as well as the accuracy of evaluation.

4 Conclusions

The investment risk assessment model of financial institutions under economic growth is constructed. The supervision of financial institutions and the main problems in investment risk assessment are analyzed. The variable correlation analysis model of investment risk assessment of financial institutions under economic growth based on statistical regression analysis and the sample regression analysis. An expert database for the evaluation of investment risk data of financial institutions is established, the recommended values of confidence of investors in financial institutions under economic growth are constructed, the information fusion processing is carried out, based on the evolutionary method of adaptive global surplus regression analysis, the prediction, and evaluation of investment risk of financial institutions are realized. the proposed method increased the confidence level of investment risk assessment of financial institutions as well as the accuracy of evaluation. This method has good application value in investment risk prediction of financial institutions.

References

1. Yan, L., Jiang, A., Feng, Z.: Life cycle characteristics and financing matching analysis on the investment value of SME of technology type. Contemp. Econ. Sci. (03), 114–123 (2016)
2. Jin, Y., Jia, S.: Study on the influence of the introduction of leverage ratio on the asset structure of commercial banks. Int. Finan. Res. **350**(6), 52–60 (2016)
3. Bai, X., Sun, H., Wang, H.: M&A behaviors and market power an analysis based on Chinese A-share enterprises. Mod. Econ. Sci. **03**, 106–113 (2016)
4. Liu, H., Wan, Z., Zou, H.: The effects of monetary policy on the dynamic process of short-term market Interest rate an empirical research based on Shibor. Mod. Econ. Sci. **02**, 30–40 (2016)
5. Marcel, F.: Capital flows push versus pull factors and the global financial crisis. J. Int. Econ. **88**(2), 341–356 (2011)
6. Taguchi, H., Sahoo, P., Nataraj, G.: Capital flows and asset prices: empirical evidence from emerging and developing economies. Int. Econ. **141**(5), 1–14 (2015)
7. Dick, C.D., Menkhoff, L.: Exchange rate expectations of chartists and fundamentalists. J. Econ. Dyn. Control **37**(7), 1362–1383 (2013)
8. Pan, J.: Improvement of accounting method of large scientific research project based on evolutionary game theory. Manage. Eng. **22**(1), 36–40 (2017)
9. Qiao, Z.W., Sun, W.X.: Two improments to C4.5 algorithm. J. Jiangsu Polytech. Univ. **20**(4), 56–59 (2008)
10. Huang, S.C., Liu, Y.: Classification algorithm for noisy and dynamic data stream. J. Jiangsu Univ. Sci. Technol. (Nat. Sci. Ed.) **30**(3), 281–285 (2016)
11. Sun, B., Wang, J.D., Chen, H.Y., et al.: Diversity measures inensemble learning. Control Decis. **29**(3), 385–395 (2014)

Agricultural Products Risk Assessment Model Based on Enhanced RNN

Zihao Zhao[1,2], Jian Li[1,2], Xianzhang Shi[1,2], Aiwen Chen[1,2], Jiale Gao[1,2], Jun Jiao[1,2], Chao Wang[1,2], and Lichuan Gu[1,2(✉)]

[1] Anhui Agricultural University, Hefei, China
970241175@qq.com, glc@ahau.edu.cn
[2] Key Laboratory of agricultural electronic commerce of the Ministry of Agriculture, Hefei, China

Abstract. In recent years, with the improvement of the people's living conditions and the arousal of consumers' consciousness, the problem of Agricultural Product Quality Safety becomes a hot topic that more and more people pay attention to. This paper presents a safety risk assessment model for agricultural product quality and safety. The effectiveness and feasibility of applying neural network models to Risk Assessment are analyzed. Aiming at the problems of the disappearance of gradients in traditional recurrent neural networks when stretching the length of the network, an improved recurrent neural network algorithm is proposed. It can predict the risks better, and finally, achieve the purpose of providing a solid foundation for improving the agricultural product quality and risk early warning system in the future, thereby effectively reducing food safety risks.

Keywords: Risk assessment · Recurrent neural network · Adaptive Computation Time · Gated Recurrent Unit

1 Introduction

With the continuous improvement of living standards, people's requirement for food has changed from the "quantity" to "quality". However, because of the restriction of the level of productivity, management capability, and technology development as well as other factors, there are still many alarming issues in the food safety field. In recent years, the food safety incidents and the infant food nutrition and safety issues indicate that food safety has become worse and worse in China [1–3], which has drawn great attention and controversy from all walks of life and has accelerated the development of agricultural product quality and Safety Risk Assessment to some extent. Facing the increasingly serious crisis of agricultural product quality and safety, the government and people realize that post-event punishment is not as good as precautionary measures, quantitatively evaluate potential risk factors that endanger agricultural product quality

X. Yuan et al. (Eds.): ICUIA 2020, CCIS 1319, pp. 241–252, 2020.
https://doi.org/10.1007/978-981-33-4601-7_25

and safety, analyze the possibility of causing harm to human bodies, and prevent emergencies of agricultural product quality and safety to strengthen the comprehensive quality of handling emergencies has become a hot research topic.

Therefore, this paper explores the structure, feasibility, and effectiveness of the traditional recurrent neural network algorithm. Then, an Agricultural Products Risk Assessment Model Based on Enhanced RNN is put forward, using the improved neural network model to assess and predict the quality and safety risks of the agricultural products, to achieve the purpose of scientifically predicting the quality of agricultural products.

The rest of this paper is organized as follows: Sect. 2 reviews the related work on methods for risk assessment. Section 3 presents our proposed method in details. Section 4 discusses our experimental results. Section 5 concludes this paper with a summary.

2   Related Work

Agricultural product quality risk assessment needs to try all means to assess the possibility of adverse impacts on human health for risk sources. Compared with developed countries, there are more farmers in China, complex agricultural conditions, and weak awareness of agricultural product quality and safety, leading to hazard exposure evaluations. The related research is not comprehensive enough and lacks the key technologies and methods of independent innovation. In 2010, Zhang Dongling et al. [4] studied the extraction of latent variables of agricultural product Risk Assessment based on the evaluation data of vegetable export demonstration bases in Shandong Province and used factor analysis method as a research method to apply an ordered multi-class logistic regression model to risks. Bai et al. [5] and others used the exposure evaluation method to establish a risk study of aflatoxin on the quality and safety of agricultural products and established related risk indicators. Yang et al. [6] researched pesticide residues and carried out joint and domestic pesticide exposure Risk Assessment work. Ma [7] put forward suggestions to improve the agricultural product quality and safety Risk Assessment system based on the quality and safety status of agricultural products such as fruits in China and Shanxi. Tian et al. [8] conducted experiments using sample data of 721 producers in typical vegetable growing areas of facilities and built a naive Bayesian classification model to conduct Risk Assessments of the lack of comprehensive prevention and control of plant diseases and insect pests in vegetable growers. However, despite the promulgation of laws and regulations on the quality Risk Assessment of various agricultural products since the 21st century, standards for related technologies and a Risk Assessment system suitable for China's national and agricultural conditions have been continuously established, but they are not mature enough.

3   Risk Assessment Model Based on Enhanced RNN

3.1   RNN Network

The structure of the recurrent neural network (RNN) [9] is to imitate human brain neurons. There are many neurons in the entire network, and each neuron is connected. Because of this, it can be applied to the research of Risk Assessment. When there are many risk factors, each problem is affected by many factors, and there are still mutual influences between the risk factors, so we use a neural network to simulate the human brain and apply it to Risk Assessment. Traditional methods It is difficult to be efficient and accurate when conducting evaluations. Furthermore, considering that the production process of agricultural products is a continuous process, timing is mainline in the entire production process, and there is also an interaction between each state, but the traditional BP neural network [10,11]. The relationship between the time series states is not reflected in the training process of the model. During the training process, the correction of the weight values of the connections is only based on the current training state, which has more or fewer defects. RNN solves this problem well.

The biggest difference between RNN and traditional neural networks is the perceptron in the network, which introduces the concept of time. The output of the current time is affected by two factors, one is the input of the current time, and the other is the previous The time output is, in popular terms, that the entire network can well combine past information to affect the current output. The RNN model is shown in Fig. 1 and the right side of it is shown in Fig. 2.

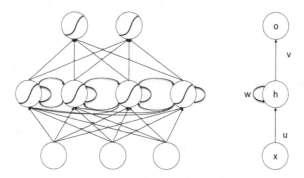

Fig. 1. Recurrent neural network.

The input unit of the RNN is recorded as $\{x_0, x_1, \ldots, x_t, x_{t+1}, \ldots\}$, and the output unit is recorded as $\{y_0, y_1, \ldots, y_t, y_{t+1}, \ldots\}$, and each RNN includes a layer or multi-layer hidden units. The hidden units are denoted as $\{s_0, s_1, \ldots, s_t, s_{t+1}, \ldots\}$. The hidden units of the RNN are the most important places in the entire network. The quality of a network depends mainly on the hidden layer. Figure 2 shows a recurrent neural network developed into a fully connected neural network. The training algorithm of the recurrent neural network is BPTT. Its algorithm principle is the same as the BP algorithm, and it is mainly divided into the following three steps:

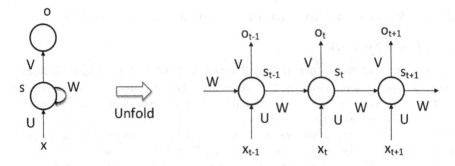

Fig. 2. Recurrent neural network timeline expansion.

1. Forward calculation of the output values of all neurons.
2. Calculate the value of the error term δ_j of each neuron inversely.
3. Calculate the gradient of each weight.
4. The gradient descent algorithm is used to update the weights.

3.2   Risk Assessment

There is a long-term dependence problem on RNN [12]. It is discussed from the characteristics of the RNN algorithm. As the number of hidden layers increases, the activation function of neurons is a tanh function and sigmoid function. After performing differentiating multiple times, after the above two activation functions are differentiated, a value of 0 is easy to appear, then the gradient of this layer will disappear, which is not meaningful for the training and learning of the neural network. So long short-term memory networks (LSTM) [13] solved this problem well. The LSTM model is a new neural network algorithm based on the recurrent neural network and improved by setting several gate units, which is good at solving long-term dependence problems.

Studies on the structure of deep neural networks in recent years have shown that as the depth of the network changes, the number of layers increases, the learning effect of the entire network will become better. If you look at the algorithmic characteristics of the recurrent neural network, when the number of layers increases, considering that the function value of the sigmoid function is close to 0 after multiple differentiation, the entire network may eventually have a very small gradient value [14]. The effect will decrease; using the tanh function as the activation function, when the hidden layer exceeds 5 layers, the computational cost of the entire network will increase. Therefore, it is proposed to use adaptive calculation times (ACT) [15, 16] to increase the depth, that is, in each learning process, by learning the same batch of data multiple times on the state S, the number of repeated learning is increased to increase the complexity of the neural network. The structure of the ACT-based recurrent neural network is shown in Fig. 3.

After the input signal is passed to the ACT-RNN, the difference from the previous RNN is that after the signal is passed to the hidden layer at time T,

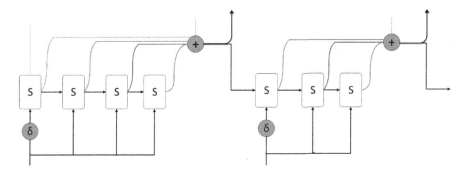

Fig. 3. The structures of ACT - RNN.

it will be divided into several signals and passed to the same state function. As shown in the figure above, it is divided into 4 signals. Passed to 4 identical state functions [17]. Assume that a threshold is set in advance, we set the total termination weight value to 1 and subtract the termination weight value of each step in turn and make a judgment until the remaining threshold value is less than ϵ and stop. The core of the algorithm is to calculate the sum that needs to be accumulated by stopping the probability sum of the neurons, as shown in Fig. 4:

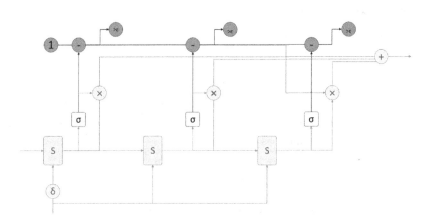

Fig. 4. ACT-RNN single step structure.

It can be seen from Fig. 5 that during the calculation of the RNN, the intermediate state S is shared in all steps, and the improved RNN is almost equivalent to the original RNN, except that each state and output calculation is extended to a variable number of intermediate updates. The arrow in contact with the box indicates the operation applied to all units in the box, and the arrow leaving the box indicates the sum of all units in the other box. In the rectangular box in the figure below, the model processes the input signal N times. After processing, the weighted summation is the final output, which virtually increases the computational complexity of the entire neural network [18]. The traditional recurrent neural network does not have a rectangular structure in the figure, but it and the two algorithms of adaptively calculating the number of RNN still process the data on the time series.

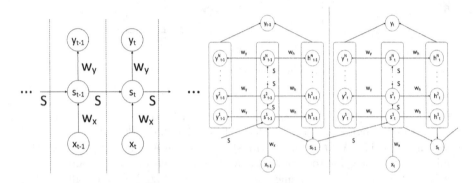

Fig. 5. RNN computation graph And RNN computation graph with adaptive computation time.

3.3   ACT-GRU Model

The general RNN calculation formula is:

$$\begin{cases} s_t = S(s_{t-1}, W_x x_t) \\ y_t = W_y s_t + b_y \end{cases} \tag{1}$$

In the ACT-RNN model, $N(t)$ represents the number of updates in step t, and defines the hidden state sequence $(St1, \ldots, S_t^{N(t)})$ and output sequence $(y_t^1, \ldots, y_t^{N(t)})$, the formula is as follows:

$$s_t^n = \begin{cases} S(s_{t-1}, x_t^1), & n = 1 \\ S(s_t^{n-1}, x_t^n), & otherwise \end{cases} \tag{2}$$

where $x_t^n = x_t + \delta_{n,1}$ is a binary mark increment at time t, which can identify repeated inputs or repeated calculations for the same input. In order to determine how many update calculations are to be performed on each input, we have

$$h_t^n = \sigma(W_h s_t^n + b_h), \tag{3}$$

where h is halting.

The activation value of the halting neuron is used to determine the halting probability. The calculation formula is as follows:

$$p_t^n = \begin{cases} R(t), & n = N(t) \\ h_t^n, & otherwise \end{cases} \tag{4}$$

If n is less than $N(t)$, then p is the probability of the current calculation method. If n is equal to $N(t)$, then p is the remaining probability value $R(t)$.

$$N(t) = \min(n' : \sum_{n=1}^{n'} h_t^n \geq 1 - \epsilon) \tag{5}$$

$$R(t) = 1 - \sum_{n=1}^{N(t)-1} h_t^n \tag{6}$$

where ϵ is a constant and, in our experiments, it is set to 0.01.

However, the multi-layer LSTM network model has a large amount of calculation, because there are more gate control units in the LSTM. Therefore, this article chooses a variant form of the LSTM GRU (Gated Recurrent Unit), which retains all the gates required by the LSTM. The characteristics of the RNN are retained to ensure that they will not be lost during long-term propagation. There is not much difference between GRU and standard LSTM. One of the purposes of using LSTM is to solve the accumulation of gradient errors in the deep network of the RNN. Zero or gradients soar to infinity [19]. However, the structure of the GRU is simpler. It has one less gate control unit than LSTM. From a calculation point of view, this reduces several matrix multiplication operations. GRU can save a lot of time when the training data is large, which is virtually reduced time complexity [20]. Therefore, this article uses the ACT-packaged GRU (ACT-GRU) as the training model for experiments. The flowchart of our method is shown in Fig. 6.

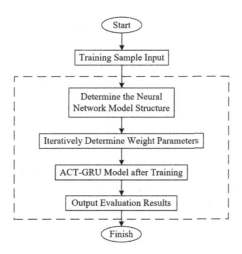

Fig. 6. ACT-GRU algorithm flowchart.

4   Experiments

This article divides the quality and safety of agricultural products into 4 levels, which are excellent, good, medium, and poor, which can be represented by 1-4. This paper uses the GRU neural network of multi-layer ACT as a model to train the LSTM neural network and conducts multiple experiments in LSTM, GRU, and ACT-GRU to analyze the experimental data of three different network models.

The data in this article comes from the base of the cooperative unit XX Network Technology Co., Ltd. The agricultural products in this article take the yellow peaches of Fuxiangyuan yellow peach cultivation base in Suzhou City, Anhui Province as the research object, and take the heavy metal indicators and pesticide indicators in the source risk as examples based on the collection of soil data in the test field and the pre-processing of later experimental data, taking heavy metals in the soil as an example, a comparison table of heavy metals and early warning risks and early warning levels is listed, as shown in Table 1.

Table 1. Heavy metal index and warning level.

Heavy metal type	Standard limit (mg/kg)	Heavy metal content C (mg/kg)	Warning level
Lead	≤0.1	$0 < C \leq 0.1$	a
		$0.1 < C \leq 0.2$	a+
		$0.2 < C \leq 0.3$	a++
		$C > 0.3$	a+++
Cadmium	≤0.05	$0 < C \leq 0.05$	a
		$0.05 < C \leq 0.1$	a+
		$0.1 < C \leq 0.15$	a++
		$C > 0.15$	a+++
Arsenic	≤0.05	$0 < C \leq 0.05$	a
		$0.05 < C \leq 0.1$	a+
		$0.1 < C \leq 0.15$	a++
		$C > 0.15$	a+++
Mercury	≤0.01	$0 < C \leq 0.1$	a
		$0.1 < C \leq 0.2$	a+
		$0.2 < C \leq 0.3$	a++
		$C > 0.3$	a+++

In Table 2, after pesticides are sprayed, the yellow peaches are tested for pesticide residues after a growth cycle, and the corresponding pesticide residue and risk warning level comparison table is listed.

This experiment applies the same test data to two neural networks, LSTM and GRU. Comparing the two algorithms, the experimental results are shown in Figs. 7 through 9.

From the above results, only a single LSTM neural network is used, and the accuracy and convergence rate of the prediction is slightly lower than the GRU neural network. In the actual measurement process, the running time of the GRU is shorter than the training time of the LSTM. This is precisely because the GRU

Table 2. Pesticide residue index and warning level.

Pesticide type	Standard limit (mg/kg)	Heavy metal content C (mg/kg)	Warning level
Metalaxyl	≤0.5	$0 < C \leq 0.5$	a
		$0.5 < C \leq 1$	a+
		$1 < C \leq 1.5$	a++
		$C > 1.5$	a+++
Rogor	≤1	$0 < C \leq 1$	a
		$1 < C \leq 2$	a+
		$2 < C \leq 3$	a++
		$C > 3$	a+++
Chlorothalonil	≤0.5	$0 < C \leq 0.5$	a
		$0.5 < C \leq 1$	a+
		$1 < C \leq 1.5$	a++
		$C > 1.5$	a+++
Chlorpyrifos	≤1	$0 < C \leq 1$	a
		$1 < C \leq 2$	a+
		$2 < C \leq 3$	a++
		$C > 3$	a+++
Mancozeb	≤5	$0 < C \leq 5$	a
		$5 < C \leq 10$	a+
		$10 < C \leq 15$	a++
		$C > 15$	a+++
Myclobutanil	≤0.5	$0 < C \leq 0.5$	a
		$0.5 < C \leq 1$	a+
		$1 < C \leq 1.5$	a++
		$C > 1.5$	a+++

reduces the number of gates and reduces training time. Combining the three, we found that the effect of using ACT-GRU is the best, both in terms of convergence rate and accuracy. It proves that in each round of training, increasing the number of calculations of the same batch of data can achieve better results.

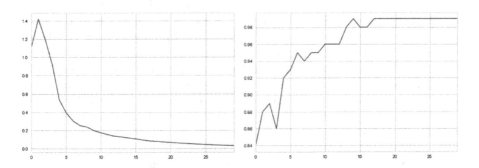

Fig. 7. LSTM loss function and accuracy curve.

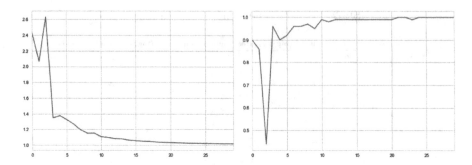

Fig. 8. GRU loss function and accuracy curve.

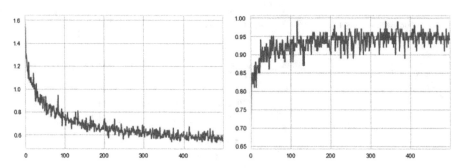

Fig. 9. ACT-GRU loss function and accuracy curve.

5 Conclusion

There is a problem that can not be ignored is strengthening the quality and safety management of agricultural products and improving people's food. Establishing an effective early warning mechanism for the quality and safety risks of the production of agricultural products at the source is especially important to promote the rapid popularization of high-quality agricultural products. Therefore, based on the above contents, this paper analyzes the current and domestic scholars' research on Risk Assessment methods and summarizes the advantages and disadvantages of Risk Assessment Methods. It proposes the application of neural network algorithms to agricultural product quality and safety Risk Assessment and analyzes the application of recurrent neural networks to risks evaluate the feasibility and effectiveness of the research work and applies the improved RNN to the Risk Assessment model. However, the disadvantage of the improved RNN is that the relative cost of calculation times and the number of prediction errors become very sensitive to the influence of the penalty factor. Therefore, an important direction of future work is to find a method to automatically determine and adjust the balance between accuracy and speed.

Acknowledgements. This work is partially supported by the Natural Science Foundation of China under Grant (31771679, 31671589), the Anhui Foundation for Science and Technology Major Project, China, under Grants 18030901034, 201904e01020006, 201903a06020009, the Key Laboratory of Agricultural Electronic, Commerce, Ministry of Agriculture of China under Grant AEC2018003, AEC2018006, the 2019 Anhui University collaborative innovation project sn: GXXT-2019-013, the Hefei Major Research Project of Key Technology J2018G14.

References

1. Zhihui, X., Xiaoyan, Z.: Investigation of Huangpu river dead pig incident. China News Weekly **9**, 40–42 (2013)
2. Shuqiu, Z., Shancang, Z., Zengmei, L., et al.: Study on the causes of agricultural product quality and safety emergency and countermeasures for emergency response - taking Shandong province as an example. Qual. Saf. Agricult. Prod. **5**, 16–19 (2013)
3. Guoyong, D.: Food safety: one vote rejection factor for food enterprises: a look at food safety ecology from the fuxi outdated meat incident. Time Econ. **9**, 28–29 (2014)
4. Dongling, Z., Qisheng, G., Zehui, Y.: Risk assessment and early warning model of agricultural product quality and safety: taking shandong vegetable export demonstration base as an example. Syst. Eng. Theory Pract. **30**(6), 1125–1131 (2010)
5. Yizhen, B., Xiaoxia, D., Peiwu, L., et al.: Application of exposure limit method to assess the risk of aflatoxin in peanut in China. Chin. J. Oil Crops **35**(2), 211 (2013)
6. Guiling, Y., Chen, C., Qiang, W., et al.: Construction of risk assessment program for multiple pesticide residues combined exposure. Qual. Saf. Agricult. Prod. **93**(3), 12–20 (2018)
7. Liping, M., Bianqing, H., Xiongwu, Q.: Risk assessment system and practice of agricultural product quality safety in China. Shanxi Agricult. Sci. **45**(4), 618–620 (2017)
8. Jiazhen, T.: Risk assessment of comprehensive prevention and control of pests and vegetables in protected vegetable farmers - an empirical analysis based on Bayesian statistical method. China Agricult. Resour. Reg. Planning **40**(2), 21–30 (2019)
9. Kolov, T., Karafiát, M., Burget, L., et al.: Recurrent neural network based language model. In: INTERSPEECH 2010, Conference of the International Speech Communication Association, Makuhari, Chiba, Japan, September. DBLP, pp. 1045–1048 (2010)
10. Li, Y.: Research, Analysis and Improvement of BP Neural Network. Anhui University of Science and Technology (2012)
11. Chen, Z., Ning, Z., Du, H., et al.: Prediction model of shale adsorption based on improved BP neural network. Fault Block Oil Gas Field **25**(02), 208–212 (2018)
12. Yi, Z., Feng, L., Li, Z., et al.: Human pose detection method based on long - and short-term memory networks. J. Comput. Appl. **38**(6), 1568–1574 (2018)
13. Hochreiter, S., Schmidhuber, J.: Long short-term memory. Neural Comput. **9**(8), 1735–1780 (1997)
14. Xia, Y., Wang, X., Gu, L., Gao, Q., Jiao, J., Wang, C.: A collective entity linking algorithm with parallel computing on large scale knowledge base. Supercomputing **76**, 948–963 (2020)

15. Graves, A.: Adaptive Computation Time for Recurrent Neural Networks (2017)
16. Figurnov, M., Collins, M.D., Zhu, Y., et al.: Spatially Adaptive Computation Time for Residual Networks (2016)
17. Yuan, X., Xie, L., Abouelenien, M.: A regularized ensemble framework of deep learning for cancer detection from multiclass, imbalanced training data. Pattern Recogn. **77**, 160–172 (2002)
18. Yuan, X., Buckles, B.P., Yuan, Z., Zhang, J.: Mining negative association rules. In: Proceedings ISCC 2002 Seventh International Symposium on Computers and Communications, pp 623–628 (2018)
19. Gu, L., Han, Y., Wang, C., Chen, W., Jiao, J., Yuan, X.: Module overlapping structure detection in PPI using an improved link similarity-based Markov clustering algorithm. Neural Comput. Appl. **31**(5), 1481–1490 (2018). https://doi.org/10.1007/s00521-018-3508-z
20. Rao, H.: et al.: Feature selection based on artificial bee colony and gradient boosting decision tree. Appl. Soft Computi. J. **74**(1), 634–642 (2019)

Environmental Monitoring of Communication Base Station Based on Zigbee

Jingliang Wang[1](✉) and Tiancheng Zhu[2]

[1] Jiangsu Maritime Institute, Nanjing 211100, China
Wangjingliang8803@126.com
[2] China United Network Communication Co., Ltd., Nanjing 210019, China

Abstract. Communication base stations are spread all over the country. Manually managed communication base stations are not only inefficient but also waste a lot of manpower and financial resources. To improve the management and maintenance level of communication base stations, according to the actual requirements of environmental monitoring of communication base stations, the monitoring system is determined to be composed of remote monitoring units, server end, and client end. The MQTT protocol is chosen as the backbone protocol of the system architecture, and the wireless network is used to realize data communication between each other. Using embedded technology, a remote monitoring unit including multiple ZigBee node modules are designed to detect the environmental temperature and humidity, smoke, UPS voltage, image, and other parameters of the base station. These data are transmitted to the gateway through the module and then transmitted to the server through the coordinator. Server database management program to achieve monitoring data records, historical data queries, user management, and other functions. Android Studio is used to design the client program, which provides real-time data viewing, control command sending, and other functions, meeting the requirements of client data input and output processing. The results show that the system is stable, reliable, and suitable for the environmental monitoring and management of communication base stations.

Keywords: Communication base station · Remote monitoring · MQTT protocol · Wireless network

1 Introduction

With the rapid development of communication technology, the number of communication base stations is also growing significantly. The operation environment of base stations will directly affect the stability of the equipment operation [1]. At present, manual inspection is still used in many small and medium-sized base stations to control the monitoring room environment, which is not only inefficient but also unable to find the potential danger in time [2]. Based on ZigBee technology, a real-time monitoring system for the base station environment is designed in this paper, which enables the operation and maintenance personnel to remotely view the working conditions, real-time images, and environmental parameters of each base station monitoring equipment anytime and

© Springer Nature Singapore Pte Ltd. 2020
X. Yuan et al. (Eds.): ICUIA 2020, CCIS 1319, pp. 253–261, 2020.
https://doi.org/10.1007/978-981-33-4601-7_26

anywhere through the mobile client. This system not only greatly reduces the work-load of base station maintenance personnel, but also improves the reliability of system operation and realizes the scientific management of the base station.

2 System Overview

2.1 Working Principle

ZigBee can be used as a communication medium in the system to transmit and receive field data [3]. The architecture of the communication system is shown in Fig. 1. Access control systems and monitoring systems are regarded as ZigBee nodes, and each node is connected to a ZigBee gateway. ZigBee gateway can be connected to a remote server through the network to realize information transmission [4]. The server is deployed in the cloud server to store and forward the received information. The mobile client obtains the required information and control through communication with the server. MQTT (Message Queuing Telemetry Transport) is a client-server based messaging publish/subscribe transport protocol [5]. This monitoring system uses this protocol to realize the mutual transmission of messages.

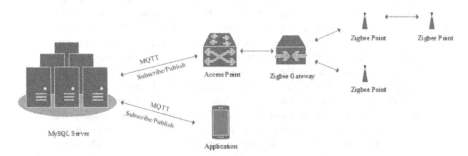

Fig. 1. System architecture

2.2 Main Functions of the System

This system mainly implements functions such as access control, environment monitoring, UPS power monitoring, and so on.

(1) Access control system: After reading the data, the program will call the remote transmission interface, verify the information, and then control the electromagnetic lock to open or close. When the machine room door is detected to be open, record the patrol personnel number and time, and upload the data to the service end. At the same time, start the timing subroutine. When the timing is over, the controller controls the electromagnetic lock to automatically close the door. When the electromagnetic lock is detected to be damaged, the alarm subroutine and camera control program are called to transmit the alarm information and image information to the mobile phone client through the remote transmission interface.

(2) Environmental monitoring system: it mainly realizes the functions of temperature and humidity collection, smoke concentration collection, air conditioning control, personnel intrusion monitoring, camera control, UPS power supply monitoring, and upload the collected parameters to the server.

(3) Mobile client: the mobile client mainly communicates with the server to realize the functions of temperature and humidity presentation, remote control of access control switch, video image presentation, UPS power and power display, remote control of air conditioning startup, and so on.

3 System Hardware Composition

CC2530 is selected as the main control chip in the environmental monitoring system of communication base station, which is connected with a temperature and humidity module, smoke detection module, a human body detection module, electricity detection module, air conditioning switch, access control switch, and RFID module [6, 7]. The hardware wiring of each environment parameter acquisition of the remote monitoring module is shown in Fig. 2.

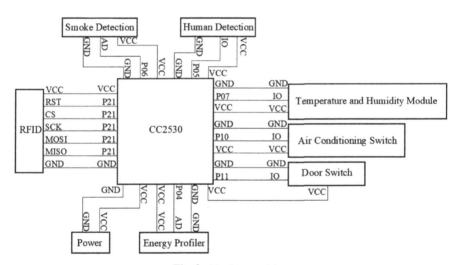

Fig. 2. Hardware wiring

Among them, the temperature and humidity module is used to detect the temperature and humidity inside the base station; the smoke module is used to detect whether there is a fire inside the machine room; the human body detection module is used to detect whether there is an illegal invasion in the machine room; the electricity quantity monitoring module is used to detect the power of UPS power supply to ensure the normal operation of the machine room; the air conditioner switch is used to turn on or off the air conditioner; the door switch is used to open the door of the machine room when the user swipes the card; RFID module detects whether someone swipes the card.

4 System Design

4.1 Coordinator Programming

The coordinator receives the data collected by each monitoring unit and uploads it to the server. Meanwhile, it sends the instructions from the client to realize the control of air conditioning and access control switch. According to the requirements of the operating environment of the base station, only when the temperature and humidity collection module and the air conditioner work together can the equipment in the computer room work in a suitable environment. The sensor uploads the regularly collected data to the coordinator, and the coordinator data processing module judges whether the current ambient temperature and humidity exceed the threshold value. If they exceed the threshold value, the corresponding equipment will be started to keep the environment in a stable range, and the data information will be uploaded to the client in real-time. The operation and maintenance personnel can view or conduct a manual intervention in real-time.

The software design adopts TI's ZigBee protocol stack, on which the secondary development is carried out [8, 9]. After the coordinator module is powered on, the ZigBee

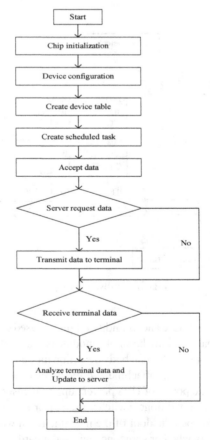

Fig. 3. The coordinator control flow

protocol stack initializes the CC2530 chip and configures it as coordinator mode. The flow of the coordinator control program is shown in Fig. 3.

4.2 Program Design of Monitoring Unit

After the coordinator module is powered on, the ZigBee protocol stack initializes the CC2530 chip and configures it as a terminal mode. Create the task that the terminal sends data to the coordinator regularly after initialization. The control flow of the monitoring unit is shown in Fig. 4.

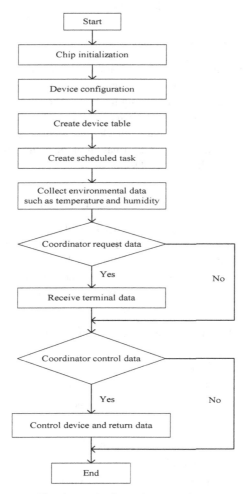

Fig. 4. Monitoring unit control flow

5 Design of Client

The system adopts C/S architecture [10], and uses Android studio to design client program [11], which is used to receive the data transmitted by the server and present the real-time data of the system. Users can adjust and monitor the running state of the system through client operation. The client starts from the user login verification, verifies the user's identity, and realizes the password memory function to avoid repeated login in a short time. After the successful login, the authority of the camera and the list of devices can be authenticated, and the parameters of each device can be viewed and the switches of the corresponding devices can be controlled. Configure the corresponding tools in the client and import the corresponding development package.

5.1 Implementation of Client Interface

The client data is transmitted through MQTT protocol, and the server provides an API interface for app calling, including user management interface, device module management interface, and historical data recording interface. The user management interface is responsible for user registration and login management. The equipment module management interface is used to add, delete, check, and modify equipment. The history record interface manages the historical information of the equipment, so as to facilitate the statistics and display of the historical status of the corresponding equipment.

5.2 Implementation of Client Real-Time Display Module

In order to realize the real-time display of environmental parameters on the client-side, it is necessary for each sensor to upload the collected data regularly. Where, the length of the environment parameter type stype is four bits, and the definition is shown in Table 1. Data is the content of data, the length is three bits, and it is not enough to fill with 0. According to the different types of stype, the sensor types can be distinguished.

Table 1. The definition of the environment parameter type

Stype	Message
Temperature	temp
Humidity	humi
Smokescope	smok
Human Proximity Switch	prox
Routing Inspection	rfid
UPS Power	upsd

After the sensor uploads the measured information to the server, the server distinguishes each device according to the type of uploaded message, analyzes the value of the environment parameter, and displays the result in the client. Hikvision camera is selected for monitoring. After the SDK is initialized, the device list can be obtained. The deviceSerial and CameraNo of the device can be found in the returned EZDeviceinfo array for real-time video monitoring. The environmental parameter values and video monitoring display interface of the base station are shown in Fig. 5.

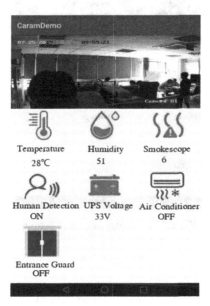

Fig. 5. The display of environmental parameters

5.3   Realization of Real-Time Control Module

The implementation of the control module is similar to the real-time display module. The ctype length is four bits. By defining the type of ctype, as shown in Table 2, you can determine the instruction type. Data: it is a control signal with three digits in length. If it's not enough, fill it with 0. On: 100, off: 000.

Table 2. The definition of the control parameter type

Ctype	Message
Entrance Guard	door
Air Conditioner	aric

Press the access control or air conditioning control button on the client to send out the corresponding message information, and the server receives the information to control the switch of the corresponding equipment. The software presentation is shown in Fig. 6.

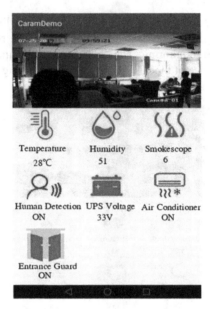

Fig. 6. The display of control buttons

6   Conclusion

A monitoring and management system of the base station is designed in this paper based on ZigBee technology and mobile client. According to different monitoring requirements, all the functions of the base station environment monitoring, equipment control, access control management, remote operation guidance can become true in this system. The application of a certain operator shows that the system not only meets the monitoring and management requirements of the base station but also improves the work efficiency of the base station management.

Acknowledgments. This research was supported by the enterprise practice training project of young teachers in Vocational Colleges of Jiangsu Province (Plan Number: 2019QYSJ057).

References

1. Liu, R.: Discussion on wireless mobile communication base station maintenance. China New Commun. **19**(14), 12 (2017)
2. Liu, H.: Discuss the maintenance and optimization measures of mobile communication base station. China New Commun. **12**, 5 (2019)
3. Wu, X., Mao, W.: Design and implementation of environmental detection system based on zigbee. In: Proceedings of the 3rd International Conference on Mechatronics Engineering and Information Technology (ICMEIT 2019) (2019)
4. Fang, R., Li, X., Gong, L., et al.: Design and implementation of multi-terminal internet of things gateway. Res. Explor. Lab. **37**(11), 133–136 (2018)

5. Xu, K., Ding, Q.: An internet of things communication gateway based on MQTT protocol. Instrum. Technol. (01), 1–4+43 (2019)
6. Bai, H.: Design of wireless sensor network node based on CC2530. Electron. Des. Eng. **27**(05), 147–150+155 (2019)
7. Chen, L., Guo, X., Tan, Y.: Design and implementation of remote monitoring system for intelligent agricultural greenhouse environment. J. Chin. Agric. Mech. **40**(06), 173–178 (2019)
8. Ma, J.: Design and implementation of ZigBee protocol stack in smart home system based on CC2530. Sci-tech Innov. Prod. (04), 76–78 (2017)
9. Yan, B.: Design and implementation of a test program oriented to protocol stack characteristic. J. Lanzhou Univ. Technol. **45**(03), 108–112 (2019)
10. Lin, W.: Comparative analysis of C/S and B/S architecture technology. Sci. Technol. Inf. **16**(13), 15–16 (2018)
11. Yu, Z., Qu, W., Ma, C.: Install the Android Studio development environment FAQ. Technol. Wind (18), 55 (2018)

Author Index

Printed in the United States
By Bookmasters